Legal Aspects
of the
Hotel and Catering
Industry

Legal Aspects
of the
Hotel and Catering
Industry

Margaret Richards, LL.B. (Wales), Barrister
Lecturer in Law

and

S. W. Stewart, LL.B. (London)
*Senior Lecturer in Law, University of Wales
Institute of Science and Technology*

Bell & Hyman
LONDON

Published by
BELL & HYMAN LIMITED
Denmark House
37–39 Queen Elizabeth Street
London SE1 2QB

First published in 1975 by
G. Bell & Sons Ltd
Second Edition (Published by Bell & Hyman) 1979
Reprinted with minor additions 1982 © M. Richards and S. W. Stewart

© M. Richards and S. W. Stewart 1975, 1979

Richards, Margaret
    Legal aspects of the hotel and catering industry.
    —2nd ed.
    1. Hotels, taverns, etc.—England—Law
    I. Title   II. Stewart, S. W.
    344.203'78   KD2517.H6

ISBN 0 7135 1176 1

Photoset and printed in Great Britain by
Redwood Burn Limited, Trowbridge, Wiltshire

Preface to First Edition

The hotel and catering trade is one of the fastest growing industries in the country today. The Government has long been aware of this fact. Indeed, the main purpose of the Development of Tourism Act 1969 was to promote the development of Tourism to and within Great Britain. The Act provided for the establishment of a British Tourist Authority and Tourist Boards in England, Wales and Scotland. These Boards, which have now been in operation for a few years, are making a valuable contribution to the growth of the tourist industry.

Those who choose the trade as a career are becoming increasingly aware of the need for and benefits to be derived from formal training. Thus educational establishments which offer courses ranging from college diplomas to university degrees are proving extremely popular and are expanding rapidly. Most of these courses state that the students should have a basic understanding of the legal aspects of their trade, and the purpose of this book is to fulfil such a need.

Although countless law books are available very few have been written with the hotel trade specifically in mind. As a result, students often encounter difficulty in their studies; they have to search for their information from many sources which may prove difficult, especially if library facilities are inadequate. It is hoped that this book will resolve such difficulty.

In some areas to which we make reference, e.g. those relating to industrial insurance and industrial injuries, we have not attempted to achieve detailed coverage because the relevant information can be found in numerous H.M.S.O. publications. It must be appreciated that law is constantly changing and as far as possible we have catered for this. The *Erroll Report's* recommendations with regard to the licensing aspect of the trade have also been discussed although the possibility of them being implemented in the near future is rather remote.

In addition, it is hoped that the book will be of interest and benefit to all those persons who earn their living by catering for guests whether they run public houses, private boarding houses, or just take in the occasional guest for 'bed and breakfast'.

We would like to record our appreciation of those who have given us considerable practical advice in the preparation of this book, especially to Mr O. W. Barnes, the Chief Inspector of Weights and Measures for the City of Cardiff, and Mr Tim McCausland, the secretary of the Cardiff and District Branch of the National Association of Licensed Hotel Managers.

Finally, it must be appreciated that any mistakes in the book are the responsibility of the authors.

M. E. R.
S. W. S.

Preface to Second Edition

The authors of this book welcome the opportunity to present its second edition. A text book, especially one dealing with legal topics, is usually in need of updating on the day of its publication, and over a period of years the changes in the law can become quite considerable. The legislature and the courts of law are ever active, especially in the field of social legislation and case decision. Thus we find that since the introduction of this book, the law of employment has been added to considerably, culminating in the Employment Protection (Consolidation) Act 1978 which has the effect of bringing into one statute provisions dealing with the formation of the contract of employment, termination of the contract by reason of redundancy, and extending provisions concerning unfair dismissals. This Act also restates the law, originally provided by the Employment Protection Act 1975, passed since this book was first published, relating to such matters as guarantee payments, payments whilst suspended from work on medical grounds, maternity payments, and certain circumstances in which an employee is to be allowed time off from work. Even since the 1978 Act became operative on 1st January 1979, Parliament has passed orders altering the limits of compensation to be awarded in redundancy and unfair dismissal cases, and in July 1979 it approved an order raising the qualifying period of continuous service which must be shown to exist before a complaint of unfair dismissal can be made from twenty-six weeks (which had operated since 16th March 1975) to fifty-two weeks (see page 125).

In the substantive law of contract as it applies to hoteliers, restaurateurs etc., the Food and Drugs (Control of Food Premises) Act 1976, the Race Relations Act 1976, and the

Unfair Contract Terms Act 1977, together with the Labelling of Food Regulations 1976 and the Tourism (Sleeping Accommodation Price Display) Order 1977, have introduced provisions which have to be observed by those offering the relevant services in favour of the customer.

The chapter on the Erroll Report's recommendations concerning alterations in the licensing laws has been retained despite the fact that these recommendations are still awaiting implementation since January 1973.

Finally, the authors again hold themselves responsible for any errors which have occurred and remain uncorrected.

M. E. R.
S. W. S.

Contents

work; References

Table of Cases

Table of Statutes

Table of Statutory Instruments

I

Fundamental Principles of Law

THE MEANING OF LAW

The intention of this book is to outline the law, present and future, which applies to persons who are engaged in the businesses of hotel management and catering of various kinds. The concepts of law involved in such a study are specialised and therefore, to provide for those who approach a study of law for the first time, it is necessary to give a brief and general outline of our law and its administration.

Law is essentially a collection of man-made rules to be observed by all human beings who reside within the sovereign territory to which those rules are intended to apply. The sovereign country can be the most sophisticated State or a newly developing nation. What matters is that it is recognised internationally as having an independent existence, that is, it is at least capable of determining its own internal issues. It is, however, necessary in any case that the rules have the authority of the supreme body in the State, whether that body be a monarch, a dictator or an organisation such as our Parliament, and also that the supreme body has the ability to enforce their observance and award punishment or redress through a court when a breach of the law occurs.

The reference above to law being made for the observance of human beings requires further explanation. The words 'human beings' are in fact too restrictive. Later, the formation of incorporated bodies or limited companies will be discussed (p. 18). Incorporation creates an additional entity which will be subject to the law in more or less the same way as the ordinary human being. Although the group applying for incorporation might comprise ten people, the result of incorporation is that eleven individuals, although one might be regarded as artificial, now become subject to the law; the people who comprise the incorporated body are regarded in law as being separate from it. The newly formed company can own property, enter into contracts and can sue and be sued as can any human being. With regard to the criminal law, its liability is not, however, completely extensive; it obviously cannot be found guilty of an offence for which imprisonment is a mandatory punishment and the only relevent offence of this nature is murder, but prosecution and punishment for all other offences ranging from (probably) manslaughter to the less serious regulatory offences has been facilitated by the Criminal Justice Act 1925, which allows an incorporated body to appear in a criminal court by way of representation e.g. by the company secretary, and the Criminal Justice Act 1948 which provides that a judge when sentencing following the establishment of guilt can, when the sentence applying to the offence is not mandatory, i.e. one necessarily of imprisonment, substitute a fine when he believes that the attendant circumstances warrant such a sentence. Of course an incorporated body cannot be found guilty of an offence which necessarily involves human volition, for example, bigamy and rape.

The law which operates and is recognised in a sovereign territory is called Municipal Law. Its success within the State is dependent upon the sanction that is behind it, that is, the ability of the State authority to enforce its observance and award punishment or redress through a court when a breach of the law occurs. Therefore moral rules or rules of etiquette which are generally observed because society considers that they are synonymous with proper behaviour are not necessarily a part of the legal rules of the State because in many cases a breach of these rules cannot be redressed by the State in any way. Adultery is an example. This behaviour is not a breach of any law of the United Kingdom.

MUNICIPAL LAW

The Municipal Law of the United Kingdom can be conveniently classified into public law and private law.

Public law

Public law concerns itself with those branches of law which

involve the State. For the purposes of understanding the subject-matter of this book it is necessary to briefly explain the meanings of the following branches of public law, i.e. (1) constitutional law, (2) administrative law and (3) criminal law.

Constitutional law. This branch of law controls the constitution and the structure of the organs of central and local government. It deals, therefore, with such matters as would be included in the distribution and exercise of the functions of government and the relationship of government to the ordinary individual in his civic capacity. Constitutional law, therefore, comprises the law which relates to such topics as the method of electing the Sovereign and defines his or her powers and prerogatives; the forms of the legislative or law-making body and its powers, the status of ministers and their relationship with the civil service through which they act; the relationship between central and local government, especially where subordinate legislative or executive powers are delegated to the latter; and the constitution of the courts of justice.

Although constitutional law is to be found in Acts of Parliament and court decisions, the greater part of its substance consists of conventions founded on custom, tradition and precedent: for example, before a Bill which has passed both Houses of Parliament can become law it must receive the Royal Assent.

Administrative law. There is no firm line between constitutional law and administrative law. The latter comprises the rules which govern the exercise of executive functions by authorities and officers to whom such functions have been entrusted by the constitution. It is particularly important in the context of the subject matter of this book with respect to the powers of local authorities, etc., in the exercise of their duties of granting liquor licences and the powers of supervision granted to them under the Offices, Shops and Railway Premises Act 1963 and the Fire Precautions Act 1971, etc.

Criminal law. The State has recognised from very early times that certain types of human behaviour which cause injury or loss to individuals are detrimental to the community as well as to the individual concerned. The purpose of the criminal law is to *deter*, by means of an appropriate punishment, the commission of criminal offences.

An acknowledged definition of a criminal offence is that it is 'a wrong whose sanction is punitive, and in no way remissible by a private individual but remissible by the Crown alone if remissible at all'.

This definition, besides including the idea of punishment, illustrates the essential characteristic of State control in that a criminal proceeding can only be abandoned by the Crown if at all. A civil action can always be settled out of court even after proceedings have commenced.

The original idea of a criminal offence was that the relevant behaviour involved an extreme breach of a moral rule. However, the increasing complexity of our society has made it necessary that certain standards of citizen behaviour should be observed to safeguard individual interests and the efficient flow of activities which make up present-day community life. These standards have been established by Parliament in numerous statutes such as the Factories Acts; Offices, Shops and Railway Premises Act, Health and Safety at Work Act, Licensing Acts, Food and Drugs Act, etc. Breaches of the provisions contained in such statutes, although involving only a minor breach of a moral rule, if any at all, are punishable as criminal offences after a trial by a criminal court, normally a Magistrates' Court.

Private law

Private law, in its numerous branches, exists to enable private, as opposed to State, redress to be taken against individuals who cause personal injury, damage to property or in any other way infringe upon the public rights of other persons. The redress obtainable through the courts is usually in the form of damages to compensate the injured party for the loss he has suffered, although in appropriate cases the court can award an equitable remedy which can have the effect of ordering action by the offending party to restore the original position between the parties.

The branches of private law which relate to the practices of a hotelier or a caterer are (1) tort and (2) contract.

Tort. That an individual living within a community has a duty to be careful with regard to the person, property and rights of his fellow citizens has been recognised since the earliest forms of society emerged. The law of tort is therefore the earliest form of law and it is the root from which criminal law and the law of contract eventually emerged. Most crimes are also torts and many breaches of contract can be redressed by an action in tort.

Professor Winfield has defined tortious liability as 'arising from a duty primarily fixed by law: this duty is towards persons generally and its breach is redressable by an action for unliquidated damages'.

Tort is a product of Common Law (see p. 6), and most duties will be seen to have been established by that source of law. The reference to *unliquidated* damages is important. It means that the damages awarded are determined by the court as opposed to an action for a breach of contract when 'liquidated damages' are assessed by the parties when the agreement is made.

It is obvious that the law of tort is important in respect of a hotelier's duty towards his customers and also towards his employees.

Contract. A contract comes into existence when two or more parties enter into an agreement through which each will gain or expect to gain an advantage from the others, and the agreement is intended to have legal consequences, so, if a breach occurs, an unsatisfied party can take action in the appropriate court. Sometimes this possibility is eliminated by a qualification in the agreement that 'it will be binding in honour only' or 'it will be a gentleman's agreement'.

Again it is obvious that this branch of law governs agreements made between a hotelier and his customers and also a hotelier and his employees.

SOURCES OF LAW

English law differs from most other systems of law in that it is not dependent upon a formally enacted code. This does not mean that our law contains no element of codification, on the contrary, during the past one hundred years or so legislation has become extremely important. On the other hand, since the Norman Conquest, English law has grown imperceptibly day by day, first of all by the unification of recognised local customs into rules common to the whole country, and then, at a later date, by the decisions of judges sitting in the more important law courts.

The main sources of English law are:
1. the Common Law;
2. Equity;
3. Legislation.

Common Law

The Common Law has its origins in the customs which existed and operated in the localities of Britain before and for some time after the Conquest.

The creation of a system of central government and centralised royal courts caused the fragmented existing law to be moulded into a uniform structure which now applies to all parts of the country. It is called the Common Law because it does not originate from any formally enacted edict but rather from the decisions of judges based upon what had been accepted by the courts in the past. It is possible, even at this time, for a custom, hitherto confined to a small locality or connected with a particular trade usage, to be recognised by a court and so become a part of the Common Law. However, the daily growth of the Common Law now results from the decisions of the appellate courts when they are confronted with cases based upon novel circumstances, or when interpretations have to be given of ambiguous phrases in statutes relevant to the cases being reviewed.

Equity

One opinion is that Equity is a part of the Common Law. In so far as the principles which are called equitable principles are the decisions of courts, this is true, but, if the Common Law had been perfect Equity would never have emerged as a separate stream of justice.

The only remedy provided by the Common Law was that of compensation or damages and in the thirteenth century it ceased to provide remedies to redress wrongs resulting from circumstances which had not hitherto been decided by the courts.

The need for development gave rise to the Chancery Court which was prepared to redress wrongs not recognised by the Common Law courts and also to provide remedies which, instead of relying upon the granting of compensation, compelled the wrongdoer, if it were possible, to restore the injured party to his former position, that is he, the defendant, was compelled to do, or refrain from doing, the act which had caused or was causing the alleged damage.

The equitable remedies which are relevant to the discussions which follow are:

1. *Specific Performance*—an order to do what has been promised will be done;

2. *Injunction*—an order to refrain from doing what has agreed shall not be done;
3. *Rescission*—an order that the parties concerned shall be restored as far as is possible to their original state.

Until 1873 the two streams of law, Common Law and Equity, were administered in separate courts. Since the Judicature Acts 1873–5, Common Law and Equity can be administered in any court, although their principles remain separate.

Legislation

The final stage in any legal system is that of legislation, that is, provisions of law formally enacted by the supreme governmental body of the State. In the United Kingdom legislation in general takes the form of a statute which has been passed by the House of Commons and the House of Lords and which has received the assent of the Sovereign.

There are several advantages in legislation:

1. The law can be altered quickly when necessary.
2. A complicated area of Common Law or Equity can be classified in the form of a code or, several related statutes can be consolidated.
3. The statute can provide legislation which can deal with situations arising in the future.

Frequently a statute will contain an *enabling section* which confers power upon the Secretary of State to make appropriate regulations, or *statutory instruments* which have the effect of operating as if contained in the statute. This is called *delegated legislation*. An example is the power of the Secretary of State to publish regulations relating to the payment of wages in different areas of employment under the Wages Councils Act 1959.

Local authorities are also empowered to make laws and this form of delegated legislation appears in the form of bye-laws.

THE COURTS

The present structure of the supreme courts in England and Wales springs from the provisions of the Judicature Acts 1873–5, the Appellate Jurisdiction Act 1876, the Criminal Appeal Act 1966 and the Courts Act 1971.

The Supreme Court of Judicature established a two-tier system of supreme courts: (1) a Court of Appeal and (2) a High Court. The Judicature Acts abolished the then existing appellate jurisdiction of the House of Lords, but this was restored by the Appellate Jurisdiction Act in 1876, although by an oversight it was not made part of the Supreme Court.

The courts are divided into two streams; (*a*) those administering civil justice and (*b*) those administering criminal justice. The hierarchy of each stream can be summarised in the following diagrams:

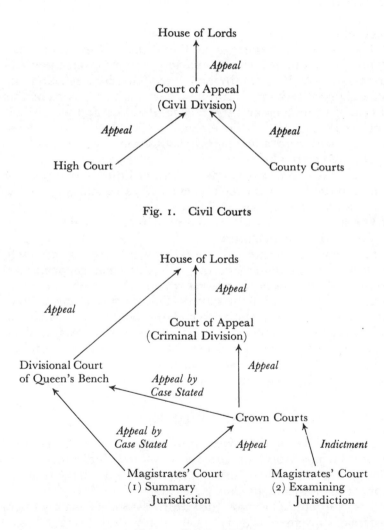

Fig. 1.   Civil Courts

Fig. 2.   Criminal Courts

The House of Lords

The House of Lords functioning as an appellate court comprises the Lord Chancellor, nine specially appointed Lords of Appeal in Ordinary and peers who hold or have held high judicial office.

The court hears appeals from both divisions of the Court of Appeal, and, since the Administration of Justice Act 1960, from the Divisional Court of the Queen's Bench Division, mainly in criminal cases.

An appeal to the House of Lords requires a certificate from the lower court qualifying the case as an appropriate one for examination by the House of Lords, that is, concerning a point of law of general public importance.

Court of Appeal

Until 1966 the Court of Appeal considered appeals from courts of civil jurisdiction only. The Criminal Appeal Act 1966, merged the Court of Criminal Appeal into the Court of Appeal forming two divisions in that court, the Civil Division and the Criminal Division.

Judges who are entitled to sit in both divisions of the court are the Lord Chancellor, the Lord Chief Justice, the Master of the Rolls, and the Lords of Appeal in Ordinary, but the Master of the Rolls is head of the court and he sits habitually. The permanent judges of the court are the Lords Justices of Appeal in Ordinary. Since the incorporation of the Criminal Appeal Division the Lord Chief Justice sits in that division with Lords of Appeal in Ordinary and selected judges of the High Court.

Appeals are heard from the High Court and the County Courts in the Civil Division and from the Crown Courts in the Criminal Division.

The High Court

The High Court is divided into three divisions, the Queen's Bench Division dealing with Common Law litigation such as breaches of contract and actions in tort, the Chancery Division with responsibility for those matters formerly dealt with in courts of Equity, for example, partnership, mortgages, trusts, companies and some revenue and bankruptcy matters, and the Family Division which deals with important family matters such as matrimonial disputes and the care, adoption or guardianship of children. The Judicature Act 1873 provided that all courts can administer Common Law and equitable remedies irrespective of their jurisdiction.

Of these, for the purposes of this book, the Queen's Bench Division is the most important. This division has the greatest number of judges and is presided over by the Lord Chief Justice.

Each of the divisions has a separate divisional court. That of the Queen's Bench has an important function in that it can hear appeals on points of law from the Magistrates' Courts and Crown Courts, when acting as appeal courts, by way of case stated. In appeal by case stated, the complete written statements of evidence are submitted to the Divisional Court so that the judges can decide upon the point of law about which the lower courts are uncertain. This appellate jurisdiction can be exercised by two judges without a jury.

The Crown Courts

The Courts Act 1971 established as from the 1 January 1972 a centrally administered Crown Court, a part of the Supreme Court, to replace the circuit courts of assize and the local courts of quarter sessions.

The Crown Court has the power to act anywhere in England and Wales and is in continuous session within six circuits which give complete coverage of the whole territory concerned.

The Act provides that each circuit shall have, besides the High Court judges allocated to it, circuit judges who are assisted by part-time judges called Recorders.

Each circuit has within it a number of courts whose jurisdiction is classified into three tiers. First-tier courts deal with both civil and criminal cases and are served by High Court and circuit judges or Recorders. Second-tier courts, whilst supervised by High Court and circuit judges, can hear criminal cases only. The jurisdiction of third-tier courts is limited to less grave criminal cases and are served by circuit judges or Recorders.

The Crown Court has jurisdiction to deal with all trials on indictment and has taken over the jurisdiction of courts of quarter sessions to hear appeals from the Magistrates' Courts following convictions by summary process and also appeals arising out of licensing adjudications. It is mandatory for magistrates to sit with a judge as members of a Crown Court hearing appeals unless the Lord Chancellor directs otherwise.

The County Courts

The County Courts Act 1846 created the County Courts to hear minor civil disputes and relieve pressure in the Common Law courts. There are about 400 County Courts in England and Wales divided amongst sixty-three circuits, each with its own judge. The jurisdiction of these courts in Common Law and Equity is contained in the County Courts Act 1959 (as amended) and has an upper limit of £1000 in most actions.

Appeals from the County Court lie to the Court of Appeal (Civil Division).

The Magistrates' Courts

The Magistrates' Courts Act 1952 defines a Magistrates' Court as any justice or justices of the peace acting under any enactment or by virtue of his or their commission or under Common Law.

Most magistrates or justices of the peace are appointed by the Lord Chancellor and on the recommendation of the local authority within whose boundaries they will serve, from lay members of the community. Larger local authorities have in addition legally qualified magistrates called *stipendiary magistrates*.

Magistrates' Courts, although they have numerous administrative functions and jurisdiction in civil disputes, deal mainly with the trial of criminal offenders. The functions of each court in this respect are twofold:

1. It can try summary offences or indictable offences which can be tried summarily, and can impose sentences of imprisonment of up to six months. For such trials the court must comprise one stipendiary magistrate or at least two lay magistrates. Appeal lies to the Crown Courts at the instance of the convicted person or by way of 'case stated' to the Divisional Court of the Queen's Bench by either the prosecutor or the defence.
2. It acts as an examining court in connection with the more serious cases, i.e. those which have to be tried on indictment before a Crown Court. This means that all the evidence in connection with the case must be presented to the magistrates who must decide whether or not there is a *prima facie* case against the accused person. If they decide that there is a *prima facie* case, the accused is indicted to stand trial at the Crown Court; if not, the accused must be discharged.

One of the main administrative functions of magistrates is to control the licensing of hotels and other catering establishments, through a specially appointed committee (see Chapter 15).

The Industrial Tribunals

Besides the hierarchy of courts outlined above, there have existed for many years bodies called tribunals created under various Acts of Parliament, which administer justice in the social sectors for which vast areas of law have been enacted. Tribunal justice now plays an increasingly important role in the determination of disputes within their jurisdiction, and they successfully supplement the established courts in that they are organised to deal more adequately with the increasingly complex welfare law which has been created, both with regard to speed and specialisation.

s. 128 of the Employment Protection (Consolidation) Act 1978, reenacting the provisions of Acts which it has replaced, allows the Secretary of State to issue regulations for the establishment of industrial tribunals, and Schedule 9 of the same Act lays down rules to be followed respecting the proceedings which apply to cases coming before them.

Industrial tribunals are comprised of lay experts under the supervision of a legally qualified chairman. The law members are chosen to give equal representation to employers and employees.

s. 135 of the 1978 Act confirms the existence of the Employment Appeal Tribunal created by the Employment Protection Act 1975, which consists of High Court and Court of Appeal judges, at least one judge of the Court of Session (the Scottish court of Appeal), and lay members qualified by knowledge and experience in industrial relations, chosen to give equal representation between employers and employees. Its purpose is to hear appeals on questions of law from the industrial tribunals in matters relating to disputes under the provisions of the Equal Pay Act 1970, the Sex Discrimination Act 1975, the Race Relations Act 1976 and the Employment Protection (Consolidation) Act 1978, and it may sit in divisions anywhere in Great Britain.

Further appeal from the Appeal Tribunal lies, with the consent of that tribunal or the Court of Appeal or the Court of Sessions, to the two last named courts, depending upon whether the original proceedings were in England and Wales or Scotland.

REFERENCES TO CASES AND STATUTES

Cases

The names of cases are determined by the following:
1. The type of court, i.e. criminal or civil in which they are tried and
2. The status of that court.

Criminal cases are generally called *R. v.* the name of the accused or convicted person. *R.* signifies the monarch, either Regina or Rex, according to whether the monarch is a queen or a king; *v.* is short for *versus* (against).

In many summary trials the *R.* in a case may be replaced by the name of the prosecutor. This is especially so in liquor-licensing cases. Thus in the case of *Vane v. Yianappoulas* which is mentioned later in this book, the name Vane was that of the police officer who initiated the prosecution against Yianappoulas; and was maintained even when the case was examined in the House of Lords.

When an appeal is taken to the House of Lords from the Court of Appeal (Criminal Division), the Director of Public Prosecutions presents the Crown's case and the name of the case will show his intervention, e.g. the name will be altered from *R. v. Jenkins* to *D.P.P. v. Jenkins* (the appellant).

In civil cases the names of the litigants are cited, thus, *Jones* (the plaintiff) *v. Smith* (the defendant). If the Crown is a party in the litigation the names *The Queen* or *The King*, as appropriate, will signify that fact.

The order 'plaintiff' *v.* 'defendant' is maintained in both the High Court and the Court of Appeal, but if the appeal reaches the House of Lords the name will signify 'appellant' *v.* 'respondent'. If therefore, in *Jones v. Smith*, it is the latter who appeals in the House of Lords, the name is changed to *Smith v. Jones*.

The most important cases decided by the superior courts are made the subject of law reports and the source of the report is indicated by letters and figures shown after the date of the decision. The letters refer to one of the various series of law reports which are being or have been published, whilst the figures indicate the volume during the relevant year and the page of that volume on which the report of the case begins. *Vane*

v. Yianappoulas (1964) 3 All E.R. 820, therefore indicates that the
report of the House of Lords examination of this case can be
found on page 820 of the third volume of the 1964 series of the *All
England Law Reports*. The same case was also reported in the
Weekly Law Reports and its source in that series is shown as
(1964) 2 W.L.R. 1335.

The present series of semi-official law reports relevant to this
book are those dealing with Appeal Cases (A.C.), and Queen's
(or King's) Bench Division cases (Q.B. or K.B.). Therefore
Vane v. Yianappoulas (1965) A.C. 486 indicates that the House of
Lords examination of this case can be found on page 486 of the
1965 volume of Appeal Cases.

Statutes

Statutes are referred to by their short titles and the year in
which they received the Royal Assent, for example, the Licensing Act 1964. The provisions which form the statute are numbered as 'sections', 'subsections' and even paragraphs of
subsections. Therefore *s*.8 (1) (*a*), Licensing Act 1964 refers to
paragraph *a* of subsection 1 of section 8 of that Act and deals
with the transfer of a justices' licence upon the death of the
holder.

Reference has already been made to the frequent use of en-
abling sections in statutes which give power to the appropriate
Secretary of State to make regulations which will have effect as
if enacted in the statute. These regulations are known as
Statutory Instruments and are numbered in the year in which
they are made. Statutory Instruments 1972, No. 1485, refers to
regulations made under the enabling section 11 of the Wages
Councils Act 1959, and is called the Wages Regulations
(Licensed Non-Residential Establishment) (Managers and
Club Stewards) (Amendment) Order 1972, and relates specifically to an amendment of a previous order which laid down
the standard of payment for accrued holiday remuneration on
termination of employment in respect of managers and club
stewards.

2

Running a Business

Before embarking upon his business, however large or small, a hotelier must determine the character of the legal organisation upon which he will base his venture. There are three main choices open to him. Whether he wants a small guest house or a chain of hotels, he must decide if they will be in the form of a one-man business, a partnership or a company. All have advantages and disadvantages, needing careful thought.

ONE MAN BUSINESS OR SOLE TRADER

The man who sets up in business on his own (a sole trader) bears a personal risk when entering upon the venture. If it is profitable, then he is entitled to reap the profits for himself, but should it fail then he must bear all the losses himself. A creditor is entitled to claim not only against the business property, but also against any personal property the sole trader may own, such as his home or his car. Thus, the sole trader's liability for his debts is unlimited: should he be unable to meet them, he must resort to the bankruptcy court.

One legal formality which must be complied with before setting up in business as a sole trader (or in a partnership or as a company) is that if the businessman intends using a name for his firm other than his real name he must register the firm under the Registration of Business Names Act 1916. The purpose of this Act is to prevent known rogues setting up in business under assumed names and defrauding the public. It also ensures that two persons with a similar trade do not set up in separate businesses in the same area, carrying the same fictitious name. Application must be made within fourteen days of commencing business (forms are obtainable from the Registrar of Business Names, Pembroke House, 40–56 City Road, London). Failure to register or a false statement made on registration carry penalties of a continuing daily fine or imprisonment or both: it may also render unenforceable any contract entered into by the trader. Upon receipt of the Certificate of Registration, he must display it in a position within the main business premises. All businesses which trade under fictitious names must diplay the true surnames on all stationery.

Most businessmen have occasion to borrow money to finance their business venture. Various ways exist of raising loans privately, e.g. credit may be obtained from a building society or local authority when land is given as a security. In future, the majority of loans will be caught by the Consumer Credit Act 1974 when that Act is fully implemented (circa 1980). In general, people who lend money will have to be licensed. If the loan is over £30 but under £5,000 then the strict formalities set out in the Act must be complied with: all pertinent details of the transaction must be stated in writing. The creditor who fails to comply with these rules will have difficulty in enforcing the agreement.

If the interest charged by the creditor in any personal credit bargain agreement (even above £5,000) is found to be extortionate, then the courts will have power to re-open that agreement so that justice may be done between the parties. Account will be taken of all the circumstances, e.g. the age and business capacity of the debtor or the interest rates charged.

PARTNERSHIPS

The law concerning partnership is controlled by the Partnership Act 1890 which defines partnership as the relation subsisting between persons carrying on a business in common with a view to profit. Generally a partnership consists of not more than twenty persons. It is customary for a partner to contribute financially to the business or to make available his professional or trade skill in the forming of the venture.

No special formalities need be complied with in order to form a partnership, although it is advisable to draw up the agreement in writing, with the help of a solicitor.

If the name of the firm does not consist of the true names of all the partners the firm must be registered under the Registration of Business Names Act 1916 (see page 15 above). When issuing a catalogue or business letter the true names and nationalities of the partners must be shown therein.

The rules contained within the Partnership Act (outlined below) apply to a partnership, unless the parties agree otherwise.

Partners have an equal share in the profits of the business. They also share equally any losses. So, the success of the venture depends very much upon the mutual trust between them. They work as a team, each having the right to participate in the management and to transact business on behalf of the firm. Each partner is, in effect, an agent, so every contract made by him which is within the normal business of the firm will bind it unless the other contracting party knows that that partner is exceeding his authority.

A partner may be sued by a creditor of the firm for any unpaid debt: he is fully liable for that debt to the limit of his financial resources. In turn, he may claim from the other partners equal proportions of that debt as losses are shared equally. No new member can be admitted without the consent of the other partners. All property and stock used in the business is partnership property. A debt acquired against a partner may be pursued after his death against his estate.

A retired partner is liable for debts incurred by the firm during the time that he was a partner unless the other partners release him and the firm's creditors agree. He will not be liable for debts incurred after he ceases to be a partner, unless the creditor was misled into believing he was still a partner. A new partner does not inherit past debts. He is only liable for debts which arise after he joins.

A partnership may be formed:

1. For a set period of time, e.g. five years;
2. For the carrying out of a special venture, e.g. to run a catering establishment for the duration of a festival. The partnership ceases when the venture ceases;
3. For an indefinite time, known as a partnership 'at will', in which case it ceases to exist when one or more of the partners so request.

Limited partnerships

A limited partnership is a special form of partnership. Again, not more than twenty persons can make up such a firm. The purpose is to have one or more partners who contribute financially in the setting up of the firm but whose liability for its debts is then limited to the amount they put into the business. In return for this limitation of liability, the limited partner must leave his financial contribution within the firm and must take no part in the management, although he is allowed to inspect the books. Should he break the rule and take part during such time he then becomes liable for debts incurred during that time. At least one partner must be a general partner, whose liability for debts is unlimited.

A limited partnership must be registered with the Registrar of Joint Stock Companies, otherwise every limited partner will be liable as a general partner. The Register, open to members of the public for inspection, shows the amount of capital contributed by a limited partner.

COMPANIES

We have seen that with both the one-man business and the partnership, although the property of the firm and the assets belong to the owner and the partners respectively, nevertheless the outstanding disadvantage of both is the unlimited liability they each have for debts. Therefore the possibility of forming a company must also be considered because the assets and liabilities then belong to the company and not the members.

Formation

Some companies, such as the B.B.C., come into existence following the grant of a Royal Charter, whilst others, such as the National Coal Board, are formed following a special Act of Parliament. The majority of companies, however, are limited companies and are incorporated and registered under the Companies Act 1948. A registered company may be public, in which case its shares, quoted on the Stock Exchange, can be bought by members of the public, or it may be private, in which case the shares are not offered for sale publicly.

Although public companies, such as Trust Houses Forte, are well known and deal in vast sums of money, the greater number of companies are private. In 1971–2 97 per cent of companies were private, comprising a total of 480 000.

A registered company may be:

1. Limited by shares, in which case the liability of a member to contribute to the company's assets is limited to the cost of the

shares. However, although a member's liability is limited to the amount, if any, unpaid on his shares, the company's liability for its own debts is not limited. The majority of companies fall into this category.

2. Limited by guarantee (normally, non-profit making groups) when the member's liability is limited to the amount he guarantees to contribute to the firm's debts.

3. Unlimited, in which case the liability of a member is unlimited.

The purpose of forming a company is to acquire or to continue with an existing business. The money, called the *capital*, which is needed to run the business is obtained:

(a) by the issuing of shares to people wishing to purchase them who then become members with voting rights;

(b) by granting debentures to people who lend money to the company. Debenture holders, who receive interest upon their loans, are not members of the company and therefore cannot vote at general meetings.

The essence of a registered company is that it is regarded as a legal person, separate from those members who comprise it. The company can have its own banking account, its own property, incur debts and be a creditor of other people. But it must transact its business through human beings who act as its agents, and its policies are controlled by directors. A public company must have at least seven members and two directors whilst a private company need have only two members and a sole director. (See p. 71 for the ability of directors or employees to make contracts on behalf of the company.)

It is usual for directors to be paid a salary. Profits can be used to issue dividends to shareholders or can be ploughed back into the business in order to improve it. In most private companies the directors and the shareholders are usually the same persons.

Registration of a company

In order to register a company, certain documents and stamp duties have to be delivered to the Registrar of Companies. Of these the most important are as follows:

1. A *memorandum of association*, which states the purpose for which the company is formed. It is the company's charter, giving details of its capital and informing not only shareholders but also outsiders of its permitted range of enterprises.

The company's name is stated in the memorandum. A limited company must have the word 'Limited' in its name to inform the public of its status. The company's name must receive official approval: it must not mislead or be too like that of another company: Registration of Business Names Act 1916 (see page 15.)

2. The *articles of association*, which regulate a company's internal affairs. The articles deal with such matters as the holding of general meetings, directors' powers of management and dividends.

3. The names of directors.

4. A statement of the nominal share capital.

Upon registration a certificate of incorporation is granted by the Registrar.

Meetings

A public company must hold a meeting of its members not earlier than three months from the time when it is first entitled to commence business. This is known as the statutory meeting. An annual general meeting must be held by every company at least once in every calendar year with no greater gap between each meeting than fifteen months. It is also possible to call an extraordinary meeting if shareholders representing not less than one-tenth of the total paid-up share capital so request.

At such meetings decisions are reached by passing resolutions. An ordinary resolution is passed by a majority of the members present and voting at the meeting. An extraordinary resolution requires advance warning to the shareholders and then the resolution must be passed by a three-quarters majority of those present who are entitled to vote. A special resolution requires twenty-one days' advance warning to shareholders followed by a vote passed by a three-quarters majority of those present who are entitled to vote.

Winding-up

Whenever a company decides to finish in business or whenever it becomes insolvent, it is wound up. The company goes into liquidation with a liquidator being appointed to wind up its affairs. His job is to sell off any property and other assets belonging to the company in order to meet outstanding debts. Should there be any surplus, this is then distributed amongst the members.

Private companies

The main principles of company law apply to private companies, but there are both advantages and disadvantages in being a private company.

A private company is restricted in its right to transfer its shares, its numbers are limited to fifty and it is prohibited from inviting any members of the public to subscribe for shares or debentures. A private company need have only two members and one director, and need not hold a statutory meeting. The private company is permitted to commence business, including the making of contracts, as soon as it is incorporated, whereas a public company, which must comply with further requirements dealing with shares, cannot commence business until it receives a trading certificate.

It is always possible for a business which starts life as a one-man business to be turned into a partnership or a limited company. In fact, it is quite customary for thriving expanding businesses to be put on to a firmer footing in this way.

Notes on proposed changes in company law

A Bill promoting changes in Company Law was published in 1978. Its principal features are as follows:-
1. To introduce new rules dealing with the formation of public companies. (These rules emanate from the European Economic Community and now that Great Britain is a member of the Community our laws are being amended accordingly.) The main feature is the introduction of a new definition of 'public companies'. A public company will be a company limited by shares or limited by guarantee with a share capital whose memorandum states that it is to be a public company and which has been registered or re-registered as a public company under the Bill. Private companies will be those companies which are not public companies. Public companies will have the designation of 'Public Limited Company' or P.L.C. (or an equivalent in Welsh) in place of 'Ltd.', thus enabling an outsider to see at a glance that a company is a public company and to make it distinct from other types of company. Existing public companies must re-register in this new form or become private companies. The minimum number of persons who may form a public company shall be two

instead of seven. The memorandum is to be in a new pre-scribed form.

2. To introduce rules dealing with the share capital of public, and, in some cases, private companies. The Bill sets out requirements dealing with the subscription, the maintenance and the reduction of share-capital. There is also to be a revision of the rules governing the distribution of profits as dividend by the companies.

3. Following the publication of a White Paper entitled 'The Conduct of Company Directors' provisions are to be introduced dealing with the duties and conduct of company directors, and in particular, transactions which give rise to a conflict of their interests in their private and official capacity, especially loans to directors. The Bill sets out the degree of care, diligence and skill to be expected of directors.

FINANCIAL AID FOR THE BUSINESS

As well as raising money privately by the methods outlined on page 16, a hotelier can explore a number of public schemes which exist to aid the development of a business. The schemes are so numerous that it is not possible to go into each of them in detail. In general, the restaurant-owner or shopkeeper is advised to consult the Council for Small Industries which will advise him, whilst the hotelier should go to his regional Tourist Board.

Of particular interest to the hotelier is the Development of Tourism Act 1969 which enables the Tourist Board to grant or lend money for the development of tourism.

As an example, two schemes currently being administered by the Wales Tourist Board under *s*.4 of the Act are the Special Tourism Projects Scheme and the Small Establishments Loans Fund, the latter covering guest houses, holiday chalets and the like. These schemes have a dual purpose, to provide full-time employment opportunities and to improve the tourist amenities within an area. Funds are available for a range of activities from building or improving accommodation, to purchasing furniture and other equipment. The project must be sited in a 'Development Area'. All loans under these Schemes are at the discretion of the Tourist Board and no one loan shall exceed £50,000. Projects when completed must be available to the public in general and increase spending by the visitor throughout the year.

REGISTRATION OF HOTELS AND OTHER TOURIST ACCOMMODATION

Part III of the Development of Tourism Act 1969 enables provision to be made by Order in Council for compulsory registration of hotels and for their classification and grading (s.17). The Order would affect all hotels and establishments in Great Britain at which sleeping accommodation is provided by way of trade or business. The Order may give the power to inspect premises, issue certificates of registration, charge registration fees, require proprietors to furnish information and impose penalties for refusing to comply with the Order.

This compulsory registration scheme is not yet in force. However, the Tourist Boards do run a voluntary registration scheme which enables hoteliers to have details of their establishments included in a book published for tourists.

ACQUISITION OF PROPERTY

Purchasing land and property for the purposes of a business venture and building or converting property for such use are complicated technical procedures. In a book of this size it is impossible to set out such rules with sufficient accuracy. Professional help should be sought both to complete a property deal and to ensure that the necessary planning permissions and building regulations have been complied with. For fire regulations see page 173.

INSURANCE

Insurance plays an important role in our everyday lives. Sooner or later we need to insure our homes, our property and our lives against a variety of risks. In fact, insurance covers such a wide field that it is possible to take out policies against most risks whether it be rain spoiling a cricket match or the smashing of a plate-glass window. Sometimes it is compulsory to take out insurance policies, e.g. third-party cover for car-drivers (Road Traffic Act 1972) or policies on behalf of employees. At other times it is a matter of personal choice as with a life insurance policy.

Although many categories of insurance exist, the two most important for the business man are the following:
1. Property insurance, covering buildings and personal possessions against all risks.
2. Liability insurance covering injuries caused to other persons.

An insurance policy is a contract between a person (the insured) and the insurance company (the insurer). The purpose of the contract is to cover a risk. In return for a premium paid by the insured, the company will provide financial compensation if the event insured against occurs, or will indemnify the insurer against the loss he suffers.

Formation of the contract

On page 61 the basic principles concerning the formation of a contract are set out. Those principles also apply to insurance contracts. In addition, the following points relate specifically to insurance policies.

Policy

Insurance contracts are set out in a written document called a policy. The insured must first complete a proposal form which becomes the basis of the policy. Once accepted, the policy comes into existence at the agreed time. It is quite common for the insurance company to provide a temporary cover (cover note) pending the issuing of the policy which provides cover to the insured but allows either side to back out before the policy is issued. This is a separate contract.

A contract of the utmost good faith

An insurance contract comes into a special category of contract known as contracts 'of the utmost good faith' which place a special burden upon the insured.

When seeking a policy the insured is under a duty of the utmost good faith to disclose to the insurance company all the material facts which are likely to influence its judgment when evaluating the risk to be insured. He cannot remain silent as he would be able to do in ordinary contract. Some examples of material facts are as follows:
1. On a fire policy, it would be material to disclose information concerning any previous fires on the premises.
2. On a theft policy, it would be material to disclose the facts that an employee had a conviction for smuggling. In *Roselodge*

v. Castle (1966) a burglary policy was held to be voidable when no disclosure was made that the sales manager had been convicted of smuggling diamonds many years ago.

Insurance contracts are weighted heavily in favour of the insurance companies. Every condition, however small, must be complied with, otherwise the company may refuse to meet the claim. In particular, if the insured misrepresents material facts either deliberately or in all innocence the insurance company may avoid liability.

In the main, the statements made in the proposal form (known as *warranties*) which induce the company to issue the policy are incorporated into the insurance contract itself and then become the terms of the contract. It is quite usual to see this clause in a policy:

'I declare that the particular statements made by me above are true and I agree that they shall be the basis of the contract between me and the company.'

This can be especially harsh in life policies. A question commonly asked is: 'Are you suffering from any physical defect or disease?' The insured answers 'No.' A post-mortem examination after his death then reveals that he has been suffering from a disease for many years. If the insured knew or ought to have known this fact the company has the right to withhold payment. It may even have the right to withhold payments if the insured's death was due to some cause other than the disease, e.g. as a victim of a bank-raid. So the insured should always read the policy carefully before signing and compare policies from different companies.

Most insurance policies contain a long list of exceptions showing the situations when the insurance company will not be liable, e.g. tornadoes, earthquakes and terrorist activities.

Insurable interest

The insurer must have an interest that he wishes to protect. In the case of life assurance a person may take out a policy on his own life and on the life of his spouse. Also, an employer can insure against loss caused to him by his employee's sickness or death—the 'key-man' insurance policy.

With regard to property, a person must establish that he has some legal rights in or over that property. So the owner of a business can insure the property and its contents. He can even insure against loss of profits if, for example, the business premises are put out of action by fire, but usually this is a separate policy: merely insuring the business premises does not, by itself, cover profits.

Notice clause

Most policies require the insured to notify the insurance company of a loss or a claim within a specified time-limit. Care must be taken to see that this is complied with otherwise the claim may lapse.

Risks covered by policies

It is not always easy to determine the extent of the risks covered by the contract, but usually the negligent actions of the insured are covered, e.g. *Harris v. Poland* (1941) (see below).

However, a policy does not usually cover the wilful acts of the insured, e.g. under a fire policy, the deliberate setting fire to the building by the insured.

The burden of proof that the loss comes within the risk covered is on the insured. So, if property is insured against fire and burglary the insured must prove that the burglary or fire did in fact take place.

Before succeeding in a claim under an insurance policy the insured must prove:

1. That there has been a loss;
2. That the loss was caused by the risk insured against.

The loss may arise from a number of causes, but the insured will only recover from the insurance company if the most important cause (the proximate cause) of the loss was covered by the policy. For example: fire breaks out in a hotel bedroom. Water used to extinguish the fire seeps through to the lounge downstairs and damages valuable paintings. The proximate cause is the fire, so if the risk insured against is fire then a claim will succeed.

Premium

Details of the method and the time for payment of the premium are set out in the contract. Premiums should be paid promptly. Although most policies allow a few days grace for payment, the insured may run the risk that his property is not covered during these days, so late payment is not a good habit to acquire.

Indemnity

One vital question the insured must ask himself when negotiating the terms of a policy is this: 'If I have to make a claim under my policy, how much money will I receive?'

In policies such as life assurance or accident policies the actual amount is specified in the agreement, for example, a policy taken out by a man in favour of his wife, on his own life, for £10 000 means that the company will pay his widow £10 000 on his death.

The majority of other insurance contracts are classified as contracts of indemnity, and the purpose of such a contract is to reimburse the insured against the actual loss he has suffered rather than give him a profit out of the disaster. The parties fix the maximum figure up to which the insurance is to operate and the premium payable is assessed in relation to this figure. Remember the insurance company will never pay more than the figure agreed but they may pay less as they only aim to cover the *loss* actually suffered. Let us examine this principle in relation to total or partial loss of goods.

Total loss

A house may be insured for £10 000 as that is its value at the time the policy commences, but, through lack of care, has reduced in value over the years. If, at the time it burns down it is worth only £8000, that is the total amount which the insurance company will pay out.

Sometimes people try to over-insure. For example, a house may be worth £10 000 but it is insured for £12 000. The insurer will receive only £10 000 in the way of compensation as this is the value of the property at the time of the disaster. So there is nothing to be gained in over-insuring property. However, in this era of inflation, over-insurance tends to be the exception rather than the rule. It is more likely that the property is under-insured.

To help house-holders keep up with the true increase in the value of their property, many insurance companies now offer 'index-linked' policies, whereby policies are automatically adjusted to the annual rate of inflation.

The same principles apply to goods. Cars tend to decrease in value but often owners forget to reduce the amounts for which they are insured. Items such as diamonds or silver generally increase. The owner may not recover the full value if they are stolen and have been under-insured as the company contracts to pay the cost of re-instatement or the sum insured, whichever is *the less*. Single items of value may need separate policies, e.g. jewelry, silver or plate-glass.

Partial loss

In situations where the property is only partially damaged, the insurance company's liability is essentially based on the cost of repairs or the sum insured, whichever is the less.

If the insurance policy contains a 'subject to average' clause (as do most policies) and the property is under-insured the insured will never recover the full cost of repairs from the company.

The following example illustrates this: fire damages furniture in a hotel lounge. The true value of the furniture amounts to £2000. The furniture is insured up to £1000. The contract contains a 'subject to average' clause. The fire causes £1000 worth of damage to the furniture, i.e. damage estimated at half of the value of the furniture. The company will pay half the value insured against, which means that the hotelier will receive £500.

Fire insurance

Until now we have been considering insurance policies in general. The rules already mentioned apply, of course, to fire policies as well. However, there are some features which relate specifically to fire insurance.

The word 'fire' is interpreted in its popular sense. As a rule, damage caused by an explosion is not covered by a fire policy unless the explosion is caused by the fire. However, if the explosion caused the fire, the insurance company will be liable for the damage unless the policy expressly excludes damages from explosion.

As an exception to what has been said, many fire policies do cover explosions which occur from gas appliances used for domestic lighting and heating and domestic boilers.

In the majority of cases fires commence accidentally, but the term 'fire' is not confined to those situations. It also covers loss caused through accidentally putting articles into the grate. In *Harris v. Poland* (1941) a woman hid her jewelry in a grate to protect it against theft. Later the same day she lit a fire in the grate, having forgotten about the jewels, which were then damaged. It was held that the damage so caused came within the terms of the policy, so the insurance company was liable.

Liability insurance

The purpose of such insurances is to give cover to the insured if he becomes legally liable in respect of damage done to third parties, for example, the guest who is injured through the hotelier's negligence or the employee who is ill after eating bad food. Most policies make it a condition that they will fight the claim on behalf of the insured and insist that the insured shall not make any admission of liability to the injured party.

Coupled with this type of insurance there now exists the Employer's Liability (Compulsory Insurance) Act 1969, which compels employers to insure against liability for bodily injury or disease sustained by his employees and arising in the course of their employment (see p. 152).

3
Hotels and other Catering Establishments

Many years ago Dr Samuel Johnson expressed the opinion that a characteristic of an English inn was the welcome it accorded to its guests—the more noise they made, the more trouble they gave and the more good things they called for, the more welcome they were. Although some of these sentiments would not be true today, the modern luxury hotel being far removed from the wayside taverns and coaching inns of centuries past, nevertheless the laws applicable to inns in those days have survived.

In particular an inn-keeper, or, as he is more commonly referred to these days, a hotel proprietor, still owes the same obligations towards his guests which were established centuries ago by the custom of the realm, with the support of decided cases. They were formed in the days when travelling was a hazardous occupation. To ensure that inns were a safe haven of rest, not only was the inn-keeper under a duty to receive all guests but a further liability was imposed upon him whereby he was responsible for the safety of his guest's property: he was thus discouraged from acting in collusion with the bad characters who infested the roads. He became, in effect, an insurer of the property of his guests. Even today, the hotel proprietor cannot escape from these duties and liabilities, although he may limit some of the liabilities by complying with the rules set out in the Hotel Proprietors Act 1956.

DEFINITION OF 'HOTEL'

Before examining the laws governing hotels we need to know the precise meaning of the word 'hotel'. (Establishments not coming within the definition of a hotel, e.g. a guest house, a private hotel, or a farm taking in paying guests are excluded from these special liabilities.)

It was not until this century that Parliament first defined the word 'hotel'. By s.1(3) of the Hotel Proprietors Act 1956 the expression 'hotel' means:

> 'an establishment held out by the proprietor as offering food, drink, and if so required, sleeping accommodation, without special contract, to any traveller presenting himself who appears able and willing to pay a reasonable sum for the services and facilities provided and who is in a fit state to be received'.

Whether or not a place constitutes a hotel depends upon all these requirements being satisfied; it is essentially a question of fact in each case. The distinction between a hotel and other establishments is not an easy one to draw. The following points explain some of the difficulties:

1. The fact that the word 'inn' or 'hotel' appears in the name is not a conclusive test. Neither, presumably, is the use of the word 'motel', but it is probable that the very purpose of a motel, namely, to attract the passing motorist, means that motels are generally within the definition.
2. A hotel is not obliged by law to display a sign outside the premises, indicating that it is a 'hotel'.
3. Sometimes a notice stating 'No coaches' is displayed outside premises. Whether or not such a notice removes the premises from within the definition has not yet been decided by the courts. But it is submitted that such a notice does not necessarily remove the status of a hotel from an establishment. As the hotel proprietor has the right to refuse food and drink if he has insufficient quantities the notice could be interpreted as an indication that he cannot cope with large numbers.
4. The holding of a licence for the sale of intoxicating liquor is not a conclusive test; the word 'drink' in the definition does not necessarily refer to alcoholic drink: thus, a temperance hotel may come within the Act if it satisfies the requirements.
5. The general assumption is that public houses are not hotels: the majority of them do not supply sleeping accommodation. But of course, a public house which also provides food and sleeping accommodation could come within the definition.
6. Boarding houses, 'private' hotels and residential hotels are generally excluded. Admittedly, many of them do have some

characteristics of a hotel, e.g. they may hold a licence for liquor and they must keep a register, but they cannot serve drinks to casual callers.

7. A restaurant is not a 'hotel' as it does not provide sleeping accommodation, but a restaurant forming part of the hotel, not having a separate entrance, is part of the hotel. In *Orchard v. Bush* (1898) the plaintiff called into the defendant's hotel for a meal. He was not intending to stay overnight. After he had eaten, he discovered that his coat, which he had hung up in the restaurant, was missing. The plea by the defendant that the restaurant did not form part of the hotel and therefore the defendant was not liable for the coat, failed.

8. An off-licence which is situated under the same roof as a hotel, but having a separate entrance, is not within the definition.

9. The keeping of a hotel register is not a conclusive test as occupiers of any premises where lodging or sleeping accommodation is provided for must keep a hotel register (see p. 84).

10. The display of a notice under the Hotel Proprietors Act 1956 restricting liability of a hotel proprietor for lost or damaged property belonging to a guest is not a conclusive test because at the end of such a notice it states that the display of such a notice is not an admission that the establishment is a hotel.

To sum up, it can be seen that even though an establishment may have some characteristics of a hotel, unless the proprietor holds himself out as prepared to receive, feed and, if necessary, accommodate all travellers or casual visitors, then the place in question is not a hotel.

Prior to the passing of the 1956 Hotel Proprietors Act, the Law Reform Committee which was formed to consider changes in the law relating to hotels discussed the possibility of abolishing the distinction between hotels and other establishments but eventually decided to retain the distinction.

DUTIES OF HOTEL PROPRIETOR

Having identified a hotel it is now possible to examine the duties of the proprietor. The hotel proprietor—in the case of a company-owned hotel run by a manager the company is the proprietor—must accept as guests all people who are travellers and entertain them at a reasonable price without any special or previous contract, unless he has some special grounds for refusal.

Let us examine the rule in more detail.

Traveller

A traveller is a person who uses the hotel temporarily or for a more permanent stay 'in order to take what the inn can give'. He may stay an hour, a night, a week or even a few months. At one time the term 'traveller' merely referred to people who stayed at an inn, during the course of their journey, for food and lodging, but nowadays the meaning is extended and can include local residents who call in just for a meal. In *Orchard v. Bush* (1898) a business man on his way home from a business trip, who called into a hotel for a meal, was classified as a 'traveller'. This case was followed in *Williams v. Linnitt* (1951), where a farmer, who resided within one mile of the defendant's inn and who frequently called in for a drink, was held to be a traveller and, as such, entitled to the protection given by the Common Law to a guest.

Although a person may be a 'traveller' when he first arrives at a hotel, he may cease to be one at a later stage. He then takes on the character of a lodger or a boarder. There is no rule of law which explains when this happens. It is all a question of fact depending upon the circumstances: the length of his stay in the hotel, although not conclusive, is bound to be one of the factors taken into account. Once the guest becomes a lodger then the Common Law duty of the proprietor to entertain him ceases: the relationship is then based upon the law of contract and the lodger can be evicted after being given reasonable notice to leave. If the rule were otherwise then a guest would have the right, provided he paid his bills and conformed to the hotel regulations, to stay in the hotel for ever, yet leave when he so wished, while the hotel proprietor would be bound to provide him with board and lodging without any right to give him notice to quit. In *Lamond v. Richmond* (1897) a lady of good character was given notice to quit the hotel where she had been staying for seven months. She had paid her bills regularly but was disturbing the other visitors as she was under a delusion that enemies were seeking to injure her.

She claimed that she had a right to remain in the hotel. It was admitted that there were vacant rooms in the hotel and that her own room was not required for anybody else. It was held that on the facts submitted to the court, she had ceased to be a traveller and that the notice to quit was valid.

Must entertain all travellers

All travellers are entitled to be entertained irrespective of sex, creed or colour. It is submitted that if a proprietor refuses to accept children then he is in breach of his duty. The proprietor may not pick and choose his guests: he holds himself out as being willing to receive all comers. In *Constantine v. Imperial Hotels* (1944) Mr Learie Constantine, the West Indian Cricketer (later knighted and appointed diplomat), was awarded damages by the court after being refused a hotel room without any just cause; the fact that he was able to book into another hotel belonging to the same company was said to be no excuse for its behaviour.

This common law rule is now strengenthened both by the Sex Discrimination Act, 1975 (see page 55) and by *s*.3 of the Race Relations Act, 1976, which makes it unlawful for a person to discriminate on the grounds of colour, race, nationality or ethnic or national origins, in the provision of accommodation in a hotel, boarding house or other similar establishment and in the provision of facilities for refreshment (see page 53).

Without special contract

A traveller is entitled to walk into a hotel and make use of the amenities offered without having come to an arrangement with the proprietor beforehand. The proprietor only discharges his liability if he has reasonable grounds for refusal. Failure to book in advance is not sufficient justification to refuse service to the traveller. This is one of the distinguishing features of a hotel: private and residential hotels differ in that they enter into a contract with their guests to accommodate them, the conditions under which the guest stays at such a hotel being governed by the terms of the contract (see p. 56).

At a reasonable price

The duty of the proprietor is to charge his guest reasonable prices. Little if any guidance can be gained from old case law on what is reasonable. In any case, this common law rule has virtually been overtaken by the Tourism (Sleeping Accommodation Price Display) Order 1977—for full details see page 52.

It must not be thought that the Common Law rules were devised solely for the benefit of the traveller. The inn-keeper was given protection against the dishonest traveller. Whilst he was obliged to accommodate all travellers (unless justified in refusing) he did not have to trust them and was entitled to demand a reasonable sum, in advance, as payment: this, undoubtedly, was the forerunner of the present-day deposit. In fact, some hotels now go so far as to ask their guests to pay the accommodation bill, in full, in advance. Furthermore, Common Law remedies were and still are available to the inn-keeper against the guest who refuses to pay his bill.

Duty to provide refreshment

The duty to provide refreshment to travellers is one which the proprietor must fulfil unless he has a reasonable excuse. There is no definition of the term 'refreshment' so presumably the offer of a simple meal such as sandwiches and a drink is sufficient especially where the request is outside normal meal times. The proprietor has a reasonable excuse if all the tables have been booked by other guests but it could be argued that a proprietor who fills the tables with local bookings so that he is unable to supply a genuine traveller is acting unreasonably. He also has a reasonable excuse if he needs the food for the next meal, or if he has no more food in the hotel (*R. v. Higgins* (1947)). A proprietor is liable to a fine should he unreasonably refuse to provide refreshment.

It seems therefore, a fairly simple matter for a proprietor to evade this responsibility. Perhaps it would be more sensible to make the duty stricter but to confine it to those persons who have booked accommodation at the hotel.

In addition to the excuses already mentioned a hotel proprietor may justifiably refuse to serve a customer who is drunk, or is under the influence of drugs, or is behaving improperly and is not in a fit condition to be received. What is meant by the term 'fit condition'? Can it include the state of a traveller's dress and even lack of it? It has been agreed that a chimney sweep appearing in his working clothes can be refused refreshment at an inn (*Pidgeon v. Legge* (1857)). In *R. v. Sprague* (1899) the proprietor was found not guilty for failing to serve a lady dressed in 'rationale' cycling costume as she refused to sit in the bar to which he had directed her. An Irish decision in 1959, although only persuasive and not binding upon an English court, helps to illustrate the point. There, a traveller who failed to obtain a meal in two hotels because he refused to take off his overcoat, was awarded damages against one of the hotel proprietors. Evidence produced indicated that the coat was in good condition, the weather was bitterly cold, and, because of a recent illness, the doctor had advised him to wear a top coat on long journeys. The judge stated that the refusal to serve him was unreasonable.

So here the rule revolves around acting reasonably. Undoubtedly the class of hotel in question must be a factor to be taken into account. Although public opinion may guide his feelings surely the proprietor is entitled to maintain the standards of dress he desires within his property?

Any guest who insists on bringing into the room a dog which is likely to be dangerous or unclean can be refused refreshments. In *R. v. Rymer* (1877) the owner of two large dogs, one of them so dangerous that it wore a muzzle, repeatedly brought them into a bar. When the customers eventually complained the proprietor refused to serve him. The court regarded the proprietor justified in his refusal because of the annoyance caused to others, as well as the fact that the dogs were unclean. The wording of the rule is wide enough to allow any proprietor to exclude all dogs if he so chooses; he does not need to wait for proof that the dog is dangerous or unclean. It is sufficient if, in his opinion, he feels that the animal is likely to be dangerous or unclean. (See also Food Hygiene Regulations 1970, Chap. 14.)

Duty to provide accommodation

A traveller who is offered accommodation is entitled to be provided with such reasonable and proper accommodation as the proprietor in fact possesses; the standard must be that which it would be reasonable to expect in that particular establishment. A traveller arriving at a small village inn cannot complain that he is not supplied with all the amenities to be found in large modern hotels. The proprietor merely undertakes that the accommodation which he offers is reasonably fit for the purpose, but he does not warrant that it is the best that can be devised, not does he promise that such accommodation shall protect the guest or his goods from every form of danger. However, the locality and pretentiousness of an establishment should have no bearing upon its cleanliness so a guest who finds his room dirty or the bed linen soiled is justified in bringing an action against the proprietor for failing in his duty to provide reasonable and suitable accommodation.

The guest is not entitled to insist upon a particular room; the proprietor's duty is completed once he supplies a reasonable room. However, if, when booking accommodation in advance, the proprietor expressly agrees to provide a particular room, it is submitted that it would be a breach of contract, entitling the guest to damages, if the proprietor fails to carry out that promise.

Luggage and goods

Along with the duty to accept guests lies the duty to receive and take in all the luggage and goods with which a person usually travels, even those goods which do not belong to him personally. In *Robins v. Gray* (1895) a commercial traveller staying at a hotel was sent some samples of sewing machines which belonged to his employers. Lord Esher, commenting that the duty of the inn-keeper regarding luggage was based upon the custom of the realm, said that the inn-keeper was bound to take in the machines; he could not accept the guest and refuse the luggage.

At first sight it may seem that such a rule is harsh, especially if a guest brings into the hotel goods which do not belong to him. However, the rule is not so one-sided as if may appear to be at first sight. As we shall see later, a proprietor has a right to seize goods belonging to his guest should the guest fail to pay his bill and this right (a lien) can be enforced not only against the person who brings in the goods, but also against the true owner.

Moreover, the hotel proprietor can refuse to accept goods which are of an exceptional nature and character. In the opinion of Lord Esher a packet of dynamite or a tiger could certainly be refused!

Causing more difficulty perhaps is the problem of the pet dog. A guest may be justified in bringing a dog into the hotel but only if the dog appears harmless and the hotel proprietor refuses to house it in an outhouse or does not have outside accommodation. It seems then that the dog must be kept in the guest's bedroom or other private room and can be refused admission into any public room; '. . . in my opinion, a guest cannot, under any circumstances, insist on bringing a dog into any room or place in an inn where other guests are' (*per* Manisty, J., in *R. v. Rymer* (1877)). The rule is flexible enough to allow the proprietor the right to refuse admission to dogs whom he considers to be dangerous yet make it lawful for animals such as guide dogs to enter the premises.

The proprietor is not obliged to take in a person's luggage if he seeks neither refreshment nor accommodation. However, should the parties come to an arrangement for the luggage to be left in the hotel then the proprietor acts as a bailee of the goods, which means that he will be liable for their loss or damage only if he acts negligently.

Car-parking accommodation

Here, too, the inn-keeper is bound to supply only such garage accommodation for his guest's car as he in fact possesses, and the test of reasonableness is again applied. Although the traveller arriving at a small hotel cannot complain that his motor car is not placed in a garage of the quality to be found in the most modern and luxurious establishment or even that he is not provided with any accommodation at all for his motor car, nevertheless, if garage accommodation is offered, then it must be reasonable. Presumably a garage, or even a car-parking area, which is pitted with large holes could constitute a danger and may incur the proprietor's liability. In *Winkworth v. Raven* (1931) no fault was found on the part of the proprietor for damage caused to a guest's car. The guest had put his car into the inn garage which was open on one side; as a result of an unusually severe frost, water in the engine froze and thereby damaged the car. To suggest that the inn-keeper owed a duty to provide a place in which the guest could put his car, so built or so equipped with heating apparatus that the car could not be damaged by frost, was said to be putting the proprietor's duty much too high.

GROUNDS FOR REFUSING ACCOMMODATION

By its very nature a hotel opens its doors to all callers. The proprietor may only refuse to entertain or receive a guest if he has reasonable grounds for so doing. But what constitutes a reasonable ground?

Hotel full

The very fact that the hotel is full is obviously a good ground for refusing to accommodate a guest for the night. A hotel is full if all its bedrooms are occupied. In olden days a bed shared by several persons (presumably of the same sex) was considered to be a normal and reasonable practice, but nowadays this would not be tolerated. In *Browne v. Brandt* (1902) a guest, when told that all the bedrooms were full, asked if he could sleep downstairs in the lounge. The court agreed that the proprietor was justified in refusing this request. So, it follows that the duty is merely to fill existing bedrooms. To allow guests to sleep in the public rooms would lead to overcrowding, which, in turn, would constitute health and fire hazards.

The late arrival of a guest is no justification for refusing to accommodate him. As was pointed out in *R. v. Ivens* (1835) the later a traveller arrives the more need he has for refreshment and accommodation.

Drunkenness and improper behaviour

Also a ground for refusing accommodation is drunkenness or other improper behaviour by a traveller. If a guest behaves in an immoral manner, e.g. using the hotel for the purposes of prostitution or homosexuality, thereby bringing the hotel into disrepute, or if he is drunk, or if he annoys other guests by being noisy in his room the proprietor has the right to ask him to leave; should he refuse the proprietor may use such force as is necessary to evict him.

In addition, a proprietor who holds a justices' licence may refuse admittance to and may eject from his premises any person who is drunk, violent, quarrelsome or disorderly or any person whose presence would subject him to a penalty under the Licensing Act 1964.

Identity of traveller

Under the Common Law a hotel proprietor must accommodate a guest even if he refuses to reveal his identity and address. However, this rule has been superseded by the statutory duty of a hotel proprietor to keep a register. All guests must disclose their name and nationality whilst aliens must furnish additional details (see p. 84). Statements in the register must be preserved for twelve months. It follows, therefore, that a proprietor is justified in refusing accommodation to a person who fails to provide these particulars.

Sickness

The traveller who is unwell has more need of accommodation

than the healthy traveller and therefore, the proprietor is only entitled to refuse him accommodation if reasonable in the circumstances.

When a guest is taken ill during his stay, then, if he is suffering from a disease which is notifiable under the Public Health Act 1936, *or* if he is suffering from food poisoning, a duty is placed on the doctor attending him to inform the proper officer. Any guest who exposes others to a risk of infection by his conduct is liable to a fine. Any hotelier who has an infected room must treat the room before re-letting and obtain a certificate from the Community Physician of the Area Health Authority or any registered practitioner that the work has been done to his satisfaction: failure to do so will render the proprietor liable to a fine.

The duties discussed in this chapter relate specifically to hotels within the meaning of the Hotel Proprietors Act 1956. The rules relating to the booking of accommocation are common to all catering establishments and are discussed in a later chapter.

4
Liability of Hotel Proprietor for Loss of or Damage to Guests' Property

HISTORICAL BACKGROUND

An inn-keeper has been held responsible for the safe-keeping of his guests' property for many centuries. Probably his liability for loss of or damage to property arose as a safeguard to the guest against the dishonest inn-keeper. As this rule of law was formed well before the laws of contract came into existence any attempt by the inn-keeper to exclude his liability by inserting such a term into an agreement with his guest was of no effect.

Three exceptional situations existed when the inn-keeper could escape liability. Thus, he was not liable if the loss of the goods was due to:

1. Act of God.
2. Action by the King's enemies.
3. The guests' own negligence.

Not only was the inn-keeper responsible for all property brought into the inn by his guests, but the full value of the lost articles had to be repaid to the guest which meant that, if e.g. valuable jewelry were stolen, the inn-keeper could find himself paying out large sums of money.

Parliament realised that this was placing too heavy a burden upon the inn-keeper so in 1863 the Innkeepers' Liability Act was passed. This limited to £30 the liability of an inn-keeper for the loss of or damage to his guests' property, provided he exhibited a copy of s.1, of the Act in a conspicuous part of the hall or entrance of the inn. However, the Act was found to be of limited

benefit to the inn-keeper:
1. He was still liable for the full value of the goods if they were lost or damaged
   (a) through the wilful act, default or neglect of himself or his employees, or
   (b) after they had been deposited expressly for safe custody with him by the guest.
2. The hotel proprietor was liable for the loss of goods brought in by all travellers, even if they were only staying for a short time, perhaps, for example, to enjoy a meal.
3. Most important of all was the fact that the protection of the Act did not extend to horses, carriages, or at a later stage, motor cars. As a result, inn-keepers could find themselves liable to reimburse a guest who had his car stolen from the hotel car park. Attempting to escape liability by displaying a notice in the car park, purporting to exempt the proprietor from liability, was of no avail. Neither was the defence that a car park was not 'within the inn' (*Williams v. Linnitt* (1951)) where the court emphasised that proprietors could not exempt themselves from their Common Law liabilities.

As a result of this and similar decisions, discontent became rife amongst hoteliers and eventually led to the setting up of a Law Reform Committee in 1952 to consider whether or not changes were desirable in the law. The Committee received evidence from the Law Society and various organisations connected with the hotel trade who suggested an amendment to the Common Law liability of the inn-keeper as an insurer of his guests' goods. Surely the traveller did not need to be protected these days against highway robbers acting in league with the inn-keeper? The idea was put forward that the time had come to eliminate the distinction between hotels and other establishments and make liability for lost or damaged goods dependent upon one ground only, namely, the negligence of the inn-keeper. In spite of these strong pleas, however, the Committee recommended retention of the Common Law liability, but in a modified form. They were influenced in this decision by two factors. Firstly, apart from motor car cases, the evidence produced to the Committee showed few cases of hardship because most hoteliers insured against their liabilities; for them insurance was a simple and comparatively cheap process. Secondly, in the ordinary course of events a guest would have difficulty in proving negligence against the hotelier.

HOTEL PROPRIETORS ACT 1956

The modifications recommended by the Law Reform Committee were incorporated into s.2 of the Hotel Proprietors Act 1956, which superseded the Innkeepers' Liability Act of 1863. The position now is as follows: a hotel proprietor is strictly liable with certain exceptions to make good or to account to a guest for any property which has been lost, stolen or damaged, but can limit his liability by displaying an appropriate notice.

The following points should be noted.

A personal liability confined to inn-keepers

This is a special rule of law relating only to hotel proprietors. It does not extend to owners of private hotels, restaurants or similar establishments, whose liability for loss or damage rests upon negligence.

It is the hotel proprietor who is personally liable for any such loss or damage, no matter whether the goods are stolen by a burglar, by the hotel servants, by other guests or even if the loss is unexplained. It is in this way that the proprietor acts as an insurer of the goods against loss or damage. No liability arises, however, if the goods are lost or damaged through the fault of the guest himself (see later).

The liability is strict

This is a legal term meaning that the proprietor is liable for goods lost within the hotel even though he or his servants have not been negligent. Furthermore, his illness or insanity does not relieve him of responsibility. Neither is it of any effect for him to warn guests that there may be people of dubious character staying in the hotel.

He cannot contract out of his strict liability by making a special agreement. In *Williams v. Linnitt* (1951) a guest claimed compensation against the inn-keeper for the loss of his car which had been stolen from the hotel car park. The inn-keeper pleaded that he had exempted himself from liability by displaying a notice to that effect in the car park. The court held that the inn-keeper could not evade his liability in this way. (*Note:* since 1956 cars are exempt from the strict liability rule but a similar notice displayed elsewhere in the hotel and referring to other goods is still ineffective.)

Premises covered by the liability

The goods must be lost or damaged 'within the hospitium of the inn'. This includes not only the inn itself but also any outbuildings such as outhouses, garages, or stables, which are regarded as forming part of the hotel precincts. Although a guest normally keeps his property (e.g. luggage, clothing, sporting equipment) in his own bedroom, there may be an occasion when the hotel proprietor requests him to put his possessions elsewhere, or the proprietor himself even places the goods elsewhere; in both cases the liability for any ensuing loss falls upon the hotel proprietor. It seems, however, that the hotel proprietor does not incur liability if he merely gives permission for the guest to leave his goods elsewhere than in his bedroom and they are lost through the guest's negligence.

There is no necessity for the goods to be handed over to the hotel proprietor for his safe keeping; it is sufficient if they are within the hospitium. In *Bennett v. Mellor* (1793) the plaintiff put his possessions on the floor behind his chair whilst he took some refreshment in an inn. When he was ready to leave he found that the goods had been stolen. The inn-keeper was held liable for the loss.

Property covered by the rule

The liability owed by the proprietor for his guests' property covers most types of property. Practically all moveable goods are caught by the rule; not merely items such as luggage, clothing and sporting equipment, but also business and legal documents and even money. The guest need not own the goods himself; it is sufficient that he has the right to carry them.

Property excluded from the rule

All vehicles are excluded from the rule together with any property which has been left inside the vehicle. Parliament felt justified in excluding vehicles from the rule as most car owners insure their vehicles against loss and any dispute against an inn-keeper over its loss would merely be a contest between two insurance companies. The only occasion when a proprietor may be liable for the loss of a guest's car is when the guest can prove a 'bailment' of the vehicle. In other words, he must show that the proprietor has come into possession of the car, for example, by receiving the car keys in order to park the car. Once this happens the proprietor is liable for any loss or damage to the car unless he can prove that he was not negligent. But he may exclude himself even from liability for negligence by displaying an appropriate notice which will be effective if it is reasonable. (See U.C.T.A. page 79.)

Also excluded from the rules are 'horses or any other live animals, together with harness and equipment'. It is interesting to realise that the old Common Law rule was formed in the days when people travelled on horse-back and a horse was regarded as a very valuable possession. The inn-keeper was therefore held liable if the horse was lost or damaged whilst on his premises. However, when Parliament modified the rule to exclude motor cars they decided to alter his liability towards animals. Stabling a horse in an inn must be a rare occurrence these days, but 'any other live animal' is still useful as the proprietor does not have to bear liability for lost dogs or other pets.

To whom is the duty of strict liability owed?

Because of the hardship suffered under the Common Law rule whereby the hotel proprietor was liable for losses suffered by all travellers, even those who called in just for a short while to buy a drink or a meal, Parliament decided to limit his liability to certain guests. By s.2(1) of the Hotel Proprietors Act 1956 the hotel proprietors' strict liability extends:

1. Only to those travellers for whom sleeping accommodation has been booked at the time of the loss or damage, and
2. Only if the goods are lost or damaged during the period commencing with the midnight immediately preceding and ending with the midnight immediately following a period for which the traveller was a guest at the hotel and entitled to use the accommodation so engaged. This second point is particularly useful for guests who may have to vacate their rooms early in the day but who wish to leave their luggage in the hotel until later.

If the guest has lost the status of traveller and becomes a boarder the proprietor's strict liability towards his property ceases. Liability, however, may still exist under negligence.

The guest must be a paying guest; either the guest himself or a third party must pay for the accommodation. Strict liability is not owed to a friend staying at the hotel at the invitation of the proprietor.

It is not necessary for the guest to be within the inn when the goods are damaged or stolen. What happens if the guest leaves the inn for a few days but leaves some goods with the inn-keeper? It is submitted that if he is paying for the room then the liability is owed to him still.

Exceptions to the rule

Although the proprietor is generally responsible for the safety of his guests' property, there are some exceptions to the rule:

1. The proprietor escapes liability if the goods are stolen or damaged by the guest's own servant or companion.
2. The hotel proprietor is not liable if the loss is caused by the misconduct or negligence of the guest who actually suffers the loss. The terms 'misconduct' and 'negligence' cover a wide range of actions and behaviour. There are no set rules, however, as to what amounts to negligence in these situations. Most important of all, there is no rule of law that for a guest to leave his bedroom door unlocked and unbolted is negligence. Such cases must depend upon their own circumstances. The court will ask itself the following question: 'Has the guest taken the care of a prudent man towards his possessions?' If the answer is 'no' the proprietor is relieved of his liability and the responsibility is put upon the guest. So the guest who left his money lying around in the open where other people could not fail to see it was acting carelessly (*Armistead v. Wilde* (1851)). On the other hand, the guest who put her jewelry in a jewel box in an unlocked suitcase, but did lock her bedroom on leaving it, was not negligent (*Carpenter v. Haymarket Hotel Ltd* (1931)). So much depends upon the behaviour of the guest and the practice of the hotel in question.

   The hotel proprietor is not liable if a guest has assumed exclusive control over a room or his goods in order to safeguard his possessions, thus indicating to the proprietor that he is relieved from the responsibility. Evidence that a guest has told the proprietor to stay out of his room or not to clean it will be one guideline to determine whether or not the guest has assumed exclusive control.
3. The hotel proprietor is not liable if the loss arises from an act of God or action by the Queen's enemies.

Notice limiting liability

Assuming that the hotel proprietor is liable for stolen or

damaged property he may limit his liability by displaying a statutory notice. The effect of such a notice is that the proprietor's liability to any one guest to make good the lost or damaged property is limited to £50 in respect of any one article, or £100 in the aggregate.

The notice which must be on display when the goods are brought into the hotel must be printed in plain type and be conspicuously displayed in a place where it can be conveniently read by the guests, at or near the reception desk, or, if there is no reception office or desk, at or near the main entrance to the hotel: failure to display it here will render the proprietor fully liable. The notice reads as follows:

NOTICE

LOSS OF OR DAMAGE TO GUESTS' PROPERTY

Under the Hotel Proprietors Act, 1956, a hotel proprietor may in certain circumstances be liable to make good any loss of or damage to a guest's property even though it was not due to any fault of the proprietor or staff of the hotel.

This liability however—

(*a*) extends only to the property of guests who have engaged sleeping accommodation at the hotel.

(*b*) is limited to £50 for any one article and a total of £100 in the case of any one guest except in the case of property which has been deposited, or offered for deposit, for safe custody.

(*c*) does not cover motor cars or other vehicles of any kind or any property left in them, or horses or other live animals.

This notice does not constitute an admission either that the Act applies to this hotel or that liability thereunder attaches to the proprietor of this hotel in any particular case.

This notice is not affected by the Unfair Contract Terms Act 1977.

N.B. The proprietor cannot claim this limited liability protection where:

1. The property has been lost, stolen or damaged through his own or his servants' default, neglect or wilful act;
2. The guest has handed over the property to the proprietor or a

servant for safe custody. The proprietor may ask that it be put into a fastened and sealed container.

3. Although the guest has asked to deposit his property, the proprietor or his servant has refused, or, where the guest has wanted to offer the property for deposit but has, been unable to do so through the default of the proprietor or his servant. It is important for the guest to make it quite clear to the proprietor that he wishes to deposit his property for safe custody. The guest has to prove that the loss or injury is the fault of the proprietor.

In these three cases, as the goods have been lost or damaged through the proprietor's own fault, he remains liable for their full value.

HOTEL PROPRIETOR'S LIEN

By the Common Law, a hotel proprietor may exercise a lien over his guest's property for any unpaid hotel bills. This is a special remedy available only to the proprietor and counter-balances his strict liability towards a guest's property. It is in addition to any other legal rights he may have against his guest, such as a claim for breach of contract; which are discussed in detail in Chapter 7.

The lien gives the proprietor a right to detain the guest's property pending the payment of the bill. Whether or not the lien is worth exercising must depend upon the value of such property.

Extent of the lien

The lien may be enforced against any person who enjoys the facilities offered by the hotel. In this case it is not essential for sleeping accommodation to have been booked.

The lien is a right against property, not against persons or the clothing they are wearing, so it would be quite wrong for the proprietor physically to detain a guest.

All the guest's property (apart from the statutory exceptions) may be detained even though, in its entirety, it may be of greater value than the unpaid bill. The reason for this is that the guest gives one implied undertaking, that he will pay for the services he receives in the hotel, and one lien covers all that he brings with him. It is therefore wrong for the guest to argue that the proprietor should detain only sufficient luggage to cover the value of the bill.

The property may be brought into the hotel by the guest himself or be sent in on his behalf. Even property not owned by the guest himself can be detained provided the proprietor is ignorant of this fact when it is brought into the hotel (*Threfall v. Borwick* (1875)). Therefore, a guest who hires a television during his stay, or who brings in a tape recorder which he is buying on hire purchase, may have such goods detained. Again, so long as the proprietor is ignorant of the fact, stolen property may be the subject of the lien. In *March v. Commissioner of Police* (1944) a hotelier successfully claimed a lien on a stolen ring which had been handed to him as security against an unpaid hotel bill.

When accommodation is booked by a husband on behalf of himself and his wife, the lien extends to her luggage; it does not matter that the husband is solely responsible for the bill or that the luggage is the wife's personal property.

The lien can only be exercised in connection with unpaid food and accommodation bills. It is essentially a right available to a person in his capacity as hotel proprietor. Any other debts or wrongs must be claimed against in the normal way. So if, for example, the proprietor has a separate agreement with the guest to lend him money, and accepts jewelry as security, he cannot exercise a lien over the jewelry for the debt. Again, in *Ferguson v. Peterkin* (1953) a guest refused to pay for damaged bedroom furniture and it was held that the proprietor was wrong in exercising his lien over the guest's luggage until the bill was met.

Property excluded from the lien

The extent of the proprietor's lien has been limited by the Hotel Proprietors Act 1956. It is no longer possible to detain:

1. A car, including any luggage therein.
2. A horse, or other live animal or its harness or other equipment.

Of course, the proprietor may have other legal rights against such property which he would still be entitled to exercise, for example as a bailee of the property.

Duration of lien

Possession of the goods or control over them by the proprietor is essential for the creation and continuation of his lien. The proprietor must act quickly to detain the goods. As a general rule, as soon as the goods are removed from his premises, even if they are only taken as far as the guest's car, he loses his right of lien. The lien cannot be revived concerning a former debt even if the guest returns for a further stay.

However, this right of lien is not lost in the following exceptional cases:

1. If the goods have been removed fraudulently from the hotel in order to destroy the proprietor's lien.
2. If the proprietor has sent the goods away prior to selling them in which case he retains his lien until completion of the sale.
3. If the goods are stolen goods and have been seized by the police as evidence against the alleged thief. In *Marsh v. Commissioner of Police* (1944) a guest staying at the Ritz Hotel who could not pay his bill handed a stolen ring to the proprietor as security. After the ring had been used in evidence to convict the guest of larceny, the proprietor successfully claimed a lien on the jewelry against the true owner. However, it should be noted that by *s*.28 of the Theft Act 1968, upon conviction for theft, a court may order the return of stolen property to its rightful owner who may not necessarily be the proprietor.

A guest who is unable to meet his bill may ask the proprietor to accept an article, e.g. a camera, as security against the bill. If he agrees to do this the proprietor does not lose his right of lien against the guest's property unless the parties have agreed that this should be so.

Enforcement of lien—power of sale

Standing by itself the lien is of little value to the proprietor because he must detain the property at his own expense and take as much care with it as though it was his own property. Should the bill be paid he must repair any damage done to the property caused through insufficient care before returning it.

However, the Innkeepers Act 1878 gives the proprietor a special right to sell by public auction any property over which he has a lien. At least one month before the sale an advertisement must be inserted in one London newspaper and one local newspaper, setting out:

1. Details of the sale.
2. A short description of the goods.
3. The name, if known, of the owner or person who deposited or left them.

Out of the proceeds of sale, the proprietor keeps for himself:

(*a*) the amount of the unpaid bill,

(*b*) any necessary repair costs prior to sale,

(*c*) expenses of the sale,

and hands any surplus money to the guest.

The property cannot be sold until six weeks after the lien is first exercised. However, the property need not remain on the premises all that time so long as the proprietor still retains control over it. In *Chesham Automobile Supply Ltd v. Beresford (Birchington) Ltd* (1913) the proprietor exercised his lien over a car. Within the six weeks' limit, he sent it for repair, but arranged for the sale to take place at the expiry of the six weeks. He was held to be still in control of the vehicle at the time of repairs.

5
Duties Common to all Hoteliers

In recent years, duties have been placed upon owners of catering establishments to inform customers of the services available. Furthermore, restrictions have been imposed upon the same owners in relation to their freedom to choose customers. All categories of catering establishments are covered and therefore hotels, public-houses, restaurants and guest-houses must conform to the following regulations.

NOTIFICATION OF PRICES OF ACCOMMODATION

Part III of the Development of Tourism Act 1969 enabled provision to be made, by Order in Council, requiring hotels etc. to bring their prices for accommodation to the notice of persons seeking to avail themselves of accommodation (s.18). This Order, known as the Tourism (Sleeping Accommodation Price Display) Order, 1977 is now in force. It provides for the display of the maximum and minimum current prices charged per night for sleeping accommodation to guests who have not booked in advance at hotels, private hotels, motels, inns, guest-houses, self-catering and other establishments in Great Britain which provide sleeping accommodation by way of trade or business and which have no fewer than four bedrooms or eight beds. Even though the majority of people being accommodated book in advance, this Order still applies unless *all* book in advance. Establishments which are bona-fide members' clubs, e.g. Youth Hostels Association, and establishments where other services are provided which are not merely ancillary to the accommodation, e.g. holiday camps, are excluded. Bedrooms and beds normally occupied by the same person for more than 21 days are disregarded.

The price notice, which must be legible, should be displayed in a prominent area, or, if there is no reception area, at the entrance.

The notice should include:-

1. The price of a bedroom for one person e.g. '£15 per night' when all such rooms are the same price *or* '£15–£25 per night' if the prices vary.
2. The price of a bedroom for two persons (as above).
3. The price of a bed in any other type of room (as above).

BUT

4. If the prices include VAT this must be stated e.g. '£5.40 per night including VAT'.

OR

If the prices do not include VAT this must also be stated together with the amount of tax e.g. '£5 + 40p VAT per night'.

5. If there is a service charge, it must be included in the price e.g. '£5.94 per night including VAT and service charge'.

OR

'£5.50 + 44p VAT per night, including service'.

6. If the guest has to pay for meals as part of the charge for accommodation, this must be stated e.g. '£6 per night including breakfast, VAT and service charge'.
7. Additional information may be added to the notice provided it does not detract from the prominence of the statutory information e.g. if appropriate 'minimum booking period – 3 nights'.

Any hotelier, etc, who, without reasonable excuse, fails to display the notice is liable to a fine not exceeding £200. The Order is enforced by the local Trading Standards Office, whose officers have a right to enter premises at all reasonable hours.

In the case of a company-owned hotel, not only the company but also any manager, director or secretary will be guilty of an offence under this Act if it is committed with his knowledge or through his negligence.

RACE RELATIONS ACT 1976

This Act, which applies to all Government establishments including hospitals and schools as well as private businesses, makes discrimination on the grounds of race, colour, nationality or ethnic or national origins, unlawful. By 'discriminate' is meant treating a person less favourably than another or imposing conditions upon him which he is less likely to fulfil than another and which cannot be justified on non-racial grounds: it also extends to indirect discrimination and victimisation.

The Act makes it unlawful for any person who provides the public with goods, facilities or services to discriminate against a person by refusing to supply him with such items or by refusing or deliberately omitting to supply him with the same quality of goods, facilities or services as he supplies to other members of the public (s.20). Even to supply separate but equal facilities is to discriminate. It is also unlawful to publish advertisements indicating an intention to discriminate.

Parliament took the unusual step of setting out examples of 'goods, facilities and services'. They include the following:

1. Accommodation in any type of hotel, boarding house, or similar establishment. But small establishments, including hotels and boarding-houses which accommodate no more than six persons in addition to the landlord and any members of his household are excluded from the Act where residential accommodation only is concerned.
2. Access to and use of any place which members of the public are permitted to enter.
3. Facilities for entertainment, recreation or refreshment.

Most social clubs which have more than twenty five members are now caught by the Act (s.25). It is unlawful for a club:

1. To discriminate against a person:
(a) in the terms on which it is prepared to admit him to membership,
or,
(b) by refusing or deliberately omitting to accept his application for membership.
2. To discriminate against a club member and associate member in the provision of its services, or in depriving him of membership etc.

The law now covers social clubs because in some towns they have replaced public houses as the main providers of facilities for entertainment, recreation and refreshment and the objectives of the law would be seriously undermined if its protection did not extend beyond the work place and market place to enable workers and other members of the public to obtain refreshment together on the basis of equality, irrespective of colour and race. Clubs whose main object is to confer benefits on a particular ethnic or national group are excluded from this rule.

The purpose of the Act is to work towards the elimination of discrimination, and to achieve this purpose the Commission for Racial Equality was set up. The Commission may serve a notice upon an offender requiring him to cease the discriminating act. As well as this, the person alleging discrimination may sue the offender for damages.

It is also a criminal offence for any person in a public place to use threatening, abusive or insulting words, which are likely to stir up hatred against any section of the community on the grounds of colour, race, nationality or ethnic or national origins.

SEX DISCRIMINATION ACT 1975

Part III of the above Act makes it unlawful to discriminate, on the grounds of sex, in the provision to the public of goods, facilities or services. Included in this would be hotel accommodation and entertainment, recreation or refreshment. 'Discriminate' has the same meaning as in racial discrimination (see above).

A few exceptions are permitted under the Act, for example where the services provided are of a private nature which might cause embarrassment if used by persons of the opposite sex.

A claimant must bring his claim in the County Court within six months of the act complained of. Damages may include damages for injury to feelings as happened in Sheffield where a woman was awarded £10 damages against an inn landlord who refused to let her play snooker.

6

Duties and Responsibilities
of Private Hoteliers

We must now examine what duty, if any, is placed upon the owners of other catering establishments to receive guests. For convenience we shall refer to such places as 'private hotels', but they include boarding houses, public houses, restaurants, guest houses, in fact, every place which takes in guests even if it be only the occasional guest for bed and breakfast.

The rights and responsibilities of private hoteliers are governed by the Common Law, notably the law of contract and the law of tort. As the basic principle of contract law is freedom between the parties to make their own terms the hotelier may choose his guests. Admittedly, there are some restrictions placed upon him, e.g. he can neither enter into an illegal contract nor contravene the Race Relations Act (see previous chapter) but, in the main, he can decide which guests to accept together with the terms upon which he will receive them. No guest can demand, as of right, to be received into a private hotel, even though there are vacancies. However, once the parties have come to an agreement the terms of the agreement control the rights of both parties. The formation of the booking contract is dealt with in the special chapter on agreements as the rules therein apply to all hotel bookings, whatever category of establishment, as well as being applicable to business contracts in general.

RESPONSIBILITY FOR GUEST'S PROPERTY
IN A PRIVATE HOTEL

The following rules apply not only to private hotels but also to hotels within the meaning of the Hotel Proprietors Act 1956 where the guest has not booked overnight accommodation.

Where guest retains control over his own property

There is no similar rule of strict liability upon the private hotelier for the safety of his guests' property as there is with the public hotelier. The private hotelier is only liable if the property is lost or damaged through the negligence of himself or his employees. This is best understood by appreciating that the hotelier has an implied duty of care, stemming from the law of tort, towards his guests' property. Should he fail to take reasonable care, resulting in lost or damaged property, the hotelier is liable to pay damages. What is reasonable care depends upon the circumstances in each case but one example of unreasonable care would be to leave the front and bedroom doors unlocked and no employee on duty in the hall. In *Scarborough v. Cosgrove* (1905) the plaintiff, a husband and wife who were boarding in the defendant's boarding house, had jewelry stolen from a locked handbag which was left in a chest of drawers in their bedroom. On a previous occasion when they had stayed in the hotel they had been refused a key to the bedroom, and this time had requested a key for the chest of drawers. But this had been refused and they had been assured that the jewelry would be safe as all the guests were known to the defendants. In fact, the jewelry was stolen by a boarder who had been accommodated without supplying character references. This was sufficient evidence for the court to say that the defendant had been negligent. Romer, L.J., stated: 'seeing that the landlord carries on his business of a boarding house keeper for reward, I think he is bound to carry on that business with reasonable care, having regard to the nature and normal conduct of the business as known to the guest'.

However, the hotelier is entitled to exempt himself from liability for negligence. If he wishes to do this it is essential that an appropriate exemption clause be drawn to the attention of the guest at the time the accommodation or services are agreed upon. If the agreement is in writing in advance the correct time is when the contract is made; if the accommodation is booked on the doorstep, the correct time is when the register is signed. If the occasion is a meal in a restaurant then a notice must be prominently displayed. Conditions cannot be imposed by one party to a contract upon the other after the contract is completed, so a notice in a hotel bedroom is of no avail if the contract has already been completed (*Olley v. Marlborough Court* (1949)). The notice must state quite clearly that the hotelier is exempting himself from liability for negligence; if there is any ambiguity in its meaning then the court will interpret it against the interests of the hotelier. Finally, the exclusion clause will only be effective if it is reasonable (Unfair Contract Terms Act). For further details of exclusion clauses see page 79.

Where the hotelier assumes control over the guest's property

Contract of bailment. The following section refers both to private hotels and to hotels within the meaning of the Hotel Proprietors Act 1956.

When a hotelier assumes some control over a guest's property he is, in effect, entering into a contract of bailment. Bailment can take many forms, e.g. simply borrowing goods from a friend without necessarily paying for their use, hiring goods, or pawning them. In the hotel trade common examples of bailment are handing property over to the hotelier for his safekeeping or handing over to a porter the keys to park or move the car. So, a contract of bailment occurs when one person (the hotelier or bailee) comes into possession of goods belonging to another (the guest or bailor): it is essential that the guest hands over possession of his property. The hotelier impliedly promises to return the goods as soon as requested. He also impliedly promises to take reasonable care of the goods. If they are damaged or lost, the hotelier is liable to pay damages for them unless he can show that he or his servants have taken all reasonable care of them. The burden is upon the hotelier to prove that he has acted carefully. If he is handed jewelry for safe-keeping, then he should keep it under lock and key. It is advisable that the package be in a sealed container or the contents be documented and receipted in the presence of the guest. If he provides a cloakroom then it is advisable to have an attendant on duty. In *Samuel v. Westminster Wine Co.* (1959) the plaintiff was awarded £500 damages for loss of her mink coat which was stolen from the defendant's hotel whilst she was dining there. She had left it in the same ante-room where she had left it on two previous occasions, but this time there was no attendant present. Even though she had not physically handed over the coat to another person the court said that there had been a bailment; the provision by the hotel of an ante-room for coats was sufficient to indicate that the hotel held itself out as willing to keep the coat whilst she dined. Their failure to provide an attendant and the fact that the room was easily accessible from the street was sufficient to show lack of care.

In *Ultzen v. Nicols* (1894) the plaintiff had his coat stolen whilst dining in the defendant's restaurant. A waiter, without being asked, had taken the plaintiff's coat and hung it on a hook behind the plaintiff. This action was sufficient to make the defendant a bailee, and, as he had failed to take reasonable care, liable for the lost coat.

In a contract of bailment the bailee can contract out of his duty of care by displaying a notice exempting himself from liability for negligence. Once again, the notice must be reasonable, displayed in a prominent position and be brought to the bailor's attention at the time the contract was made. Furthermore, it must be clearly worded; any ambiguity will be interpreted in the bailor's favour. In neither *Samuel v. Westminster Wine Co.* nor *Ultzen v. Nicols* was there displayed an exemption from liability notice. If the notice is correctly displayed then the bailee will be covered for loss caused by negligence, unless he goes outside the terms of the contract of bailment altogether, e.g. if he allows a third party to borrow jewelry which has been handed to him for safe-keeping. (U.C.T.A. 1977, see page 79.)

A bailment must be distinguished from a licence. A licence merely permits an owner to place his property upon the land of the licensor. It carries no obligations, in particular, no duty of care on the part of the licensor towards the licensee in relation to the property left there. In *Ashby v. Tolhurst* (1937) the plaintiff had paid one shilling to leave his car in the defendant's car park. The attendant allowed a third party who said he had come for the car on the plaintiff's behalf to receive it. The plaintiff did not succeed in his claim for damages for loss of the car as it was held that the relationship between the two was that of licensor and licensee. This decision was followed in *Tinsley v. Dudley* (1951) where the plaintiff failed to recover damages for the loss of his motor-cycle which he had parked in the yard of the defendant's public house. He had not handed the cycle over to the defendant for safe keeping, in fact, the defendant was unaware that the cycle had been put in the yard. He was held to be a licensee and not a bailee of the property and therefore not liable for its loss.

From the four cases mentioned it can be seen that there is a very fine and not altogether satisfactory distinction between bailment and license. In *Ultzen v. Nicols* the decision could have gone the other way if the guest had hung up the coat himself. In *Tinsley v. Dudley* the plaintiff might have recovered damages if the defendant normally employed an attendant in the yard. It could be said that the courts are willing to distinguish between goods left out of doors and those deposited within a building. In any event the hotelier can help himself by displaying an exemption notice.

7
Booking Accommodation: Contractual Agreements

The law of contract is so important in the running of any business that we have devoted an entire chapter to it. Although many of the examples given relate specifically to hotel-booking contracts, it must be appreciated that the rules of law are of general application.

The frequency with which we make contractual bargains in our everyday lives is not generally appreciated. For example, each time we purchase goods from a shop, employ a person in business, make a hotel booking or buy a meal in a restaurant we are entering into a legal relationship with the shop-keeper, the employee, the guest or the restaurant owner. In effect, we are drawing up a contract with these people whereby each side acquires legal rights in respect of the promises or actions of the other party.

DEFINITION OF A CONTRACT

The majority of contracts in English law are known as simple contracts, which means that they can be made orally or in writing. It is often thought that a contract made orally is not a legal contract, but this is not correct Admittedly, an oral contract may be difficult to prove as the court has to decide whose story to believe, but such difficulty does not make the contract illegal or invalid.

Apart from simple contracts there are other contracts which have to be drawn up in writing and made under seal, such as a contract for the sale of a house, but we are concerned only with simple contracts.

Every contract must contain three elements. If one of them is missing no legal contract exists, but only a friendly arrangement which can be kept or broken at the whim of the parties.

The three elements are:

1 The agreement.
2. The intention to be legally bound.
3. Consideration.

AGREEMENT

In order for a contract to exist a definite agreement must be reached. The bargaining and negotiation must be concluded and the arrangements must be certain and final. In the business world very few contracts are cut and dried to such an extent that only one conversation or two letters need be exchanged before the parties reach a bargain; more often than not agreements take time and bargaining to resolve all difficulties. It may be necessary to inspect several documents before being able to say that the parties are in agreement or that there is a *consensus ad idem* (a meeting of the minds). Should essential terms of the agreement be outstanding—perhaps the price, the time or the place are still undecided—then the court would not enforce such a bargain because it would be too vague and the court will not make a contract for the parties.

The agreement is arrived at by a process of offer and acceptance, made in writing, or by word of mouth, or even by conduct as in an auction sale when the auctioneer bangs his gavel on the table shouting 'Going, going, gone'.

Offer

An offer can be made either to a particular person, e.g. a proprietor offers accommodation to Mr Brown, or to a group of persons, e.g. a proprietor offers accommodation to The Wild Cat Association or to the whole world. However, the offer can only be accepted by the person to whom it is made because the proprietor's mind is only directed towards an agreement with that person. So in the above example, an attempt by a third party, Mr Jones, to take the accommodation offered to Mr Brown is not an acceptance, but, in truth, is a fresh offer from Mr Jones.

An offer must be distinguished from the following situations.

An invitation to make an offer. This is really one step further back from an offer. It is only leading up to the agreement and is not the agreement itself. An advertisement giving details either of an auction sale or the services of a restaurant is no more than an invitation to persons to attend the sale or to visit the restaurant and make an offer to do business. Most advertisements in newspapers indicating articles for sale are within this category.

Similarly, goods displayed in a shop window are merely invitations to customers to enter into a bargain with the shopkeeper. In fact, the customer must make the offer to purchase the goods which the shop-keeper may then accept or reject. It is a popular misconception that customers have the right to demand goods they see displayed in a window. However, a shopkeeper who displays goods at other than their correct sale-price is committing a criminal offence under the Trade Descriptions Act 1968 (see page 75). Again, in self-service stores, the offer occurs when the customer hands the goods to the assistant at the cash-desk, who then has the right to accept or reject the customer's offer. If it were otherwise, it would mean that the agreement is reached when the customer picks up the article from the counter and would not be free to change his mind (*Pharmaceutical Society of Great Britain v. Boots Cash Chemists Ltd* (1953)).

A communication of information. Here again, a request for information is really one step further back from an offer: it merely leads up to a possible agreement but is not part of the agreement itself. A guest who enquires of the proprietor if he has vacancies in his hotel is merely requesting information. The proprietor's answer may be general, giving the information, or it may be more definite and include an offer to supply the accommodation. No liability, however, is incurred by either party simply by requesting and supplying information.

An invitation to treat or a communication of information may be difficult to distinguish from a genuine offer. The key to the problem lies in the intention of the party making the statement. Thus, in *Carlill v. Carbolic Smoke Ball Co.*, the company offered £100 to any person who caught influenza after buying and using according to their instructions a carbolic smoke ball manufactured by the company. This offer was made in a newspaper advertisement. Mrs Carlill read the notice, bought the smoke-ball, caught influenza and later claimed £100. The court gave judgment in Mrs Carlill's favour. It was felt that the intention to be bound was particularly clear in this case because the company stated that they had deposited £1000 in the bank to show their good faith.

An offer is terminated:-

1. By the offeree refusing to accept the offer.
2. By the death of either party. If the guest dies, then the negotiations are ended. If the proprietor dies, and if he is running the business personally, and its reputation depends upon the proprietor, the negotiations may cease, but if the hotel is owned by a company the death of the manager will not usually interfere with the bookings.
3. A qualified acceptance terminates the original offer. Strictly speaking, a qualified acceptance is a counter-offer, for example, the proprietor offers Mr Smith accommodation at £20 per week for two single rooms. Mr Smith replies that he wants accommodation at £20 per week but only on condition that he is given one double bedroom. Mr Smith's reply is not an acceptance on the exact terms; it cancels the original offer, becomes a counter-offer and the proprietor is free to accept or reject Mr Smith's request. Furthermore, the proprietor is also free to re-let the two single rooms to other persons.
4. Lapse of time. An offer can be open for a fixed period of time, e.g. a proprietor states that he must have a reply to his offer of accommodation within one week. Once the time has expired the offer lapses automatically. If no fixed period of time is stated in the offer, it will lapse at the expiration of a reasonable time. What is reasonable depends upon the commodity and the custom in a particular trade. In a contract for the sale of perishable goods, two or three days is a reasonable time. In the hotel trade, perhaps a fortnight would be classified as a reasonable time.

Acceptance

In order to complete the agreement the offer must be accepted and the acceptance must be communicated to the offeror. It is not enough for the guest to think that the terms offered are suitable; he must communicate his agreement to the proprietor. We have already seen that a qualified acceptance amounts to a counter-offer. Once, however, an unqualified acceptance is given to the offeror this completes the agreement. So, a letter by a guest stating that he accepts the accommodation offered in the terms quoted means that the parties have reached an agreement. In other words, the contract is concluded even though the time for the guest's visit has not yet arrived.

N.B. Many hoteliers guard against double booking by making it a condition that the booking is subject to the room being available upon receipt of the guest's letter of acceptance.

The booking of hotel accommodation consists really of a mutual exchange of promises, i.e. the proprietor promises to supply the room and board and the guest promises to pay for the services. In agreement such as this a condition that silence shall amount to acceptance cannot be imposed by the offeror upon the offeree without the latter's consent. Thus, when the proprietor offers to accommodate the guest, he must not write: 'I offer you accommodation for one week, etc. If I hear no more from you, I shall take it that you accept the accommodation offered'. Such a clause has no legal effect as there has been no prior agreement between the parties. Neither should a guest try to book accommodation by writing in the following way. 'I wish to book accommodation in your hotel for one week, etc. If I do not receive a reply from you, I shall take it that the booking is in order'. It is submitted that such a letter does not amount to a contract: strictly speaking it is nothing more than an enquiry. There is no way of knowing that the parties have reached an agreement. Should the guest eventually arrive at the hotel only to discover that there is no accommodation for him, he has no legal remedies. The law will not place the offeree in a position where failure to reply to an offer means that he has entered into a contract.

The proprietor may impose a condition regarding the method of communicating acceptance, e.g. 'Please reply by telephone within the next twenty-four hours'. Perhaps the guest replies by telegram which reaches the proprietor within the twenty-four hours' time limit. It is submitted that this will still be a valid acceptance unless the proprietor has made it quite clear that no method other than a telephone call will suffice. But should the guest reply by letter which arrives after twenty-four hours have lapsed there is no agreement as he has not complied with the conditions made in the offer.

In some contracts, known as unilateral contracts, the offer takes the form of a promise to pay money in return for an act, i.e. a reward offered for the return of a lost dog. In such cases after the reading of the advertisement the performance of find-

ing the dog and returning it is a sufficient indication of acceptance: there is no need to warn the offeror in advance. In *Carlill v.
Carbolic Smoke Ball Co.* there was no need for Mrs Carlill to write
to the company saying that she had accepted their offer.

Strictly speaking, an offer cannot be accepted until it has
been brought to the notice of the person to whom it is made. In
'reward cases', should the finder of a lost dog who returns it to
its owner be unaware that a reward exists for its return, he
cannot legally claim the reward at a later stage. However, this
rule is doubtful and somewhat harsh.

Acceptance through the post

In most business transactions the post is taken to be the usual
and normal channel of communication unless the parties indicate a different method.

In postal communications acceptance of the offer is complete
and the contract made as soon as the letter of acceptance is
posted, even though the letter is lost or delayed in the post. If
the loss or delay can be attributed to the Post Office, or to the
fault of the offeror (by mis-quoting his own address, for
example) then this rule can be justified. However, if the loss or
delay is caused through the fault of the offeree (by misdirecting
the letter) it is difficult to accept such a rule. Furthermore, the
rule can easily be displaced by placing conditions in the offer relating to the manner of acceptance; e.g., 'acceptance will be
complete only when your letter of acceptance is on my desk'. In
Holwell Securities v. Hughes (1974) Dr Hughes granted an option to
Holwell Securities for them to purchase his house: if they wished
to take up the option they were to notify him in writing by 19th
April. Although a letter of acceptance was posted on 14th April,
it never reached Dr Hughes. The Appeal Court held that no
contract existed. The express terms of the offer stipulated that
the option was to be exercised by 'Notice in writing' which
meant that the written document had actually to be communicated or notified to Dr Hughes. The claim by Holwell Securities
that they had posted the letter, thereby 'accepting' the offer,
was not sufficient. Thus, the general rule on postal acceptances
was qualified by a condition in the offer.

Acceptance by telephone or teleprinter

Where negotiations are being conducted over the telephone

or teleprinter, the acceptance must be heard by the offeror. It is up to the person accepting to make a proper communication and to make certain that the other party has heard his acceptance. 'Suppose, for instance, that I made an offer to a man by telephone and, in the middle of his reply, the line goes "dead", so that I do not hear his words of acceptance, there is no contract at that moment', *per* Denning, L. J., in *Entores Ltd v. Miles Far East Corp.* (1955).

Revocation of the offer

An offer may be revoked at any time before the acceptance has been given. So, the proprietor who writes offering accommodation to a guest may withdraw that offer at any time before the guest accepts it. (The only exception to this rule is if a sum of money has been received and a promise given in return to keep the offer open for a definite period of time.)

It is not enough for the proprietor to decide in his own mind to withdraw the offer. To be effective, the notice of revocation must reach the guest. It is preferable for the notice to be expressly communicated to him, for example, by a telephone call or letter, but not essential, so it is acceptable for the guest to learn of the revocation indirectly through a reliable third party (*Dickinson v. Dodd* (1876)).

If the notice of revocation is in the form of a letter through the post, the revocation is effective only from the moment the letter is received by the guest and not when the proprietor posts it. Let us examine a simple example:

1st January—Mr Brown writes to Hotel X enquiring about accommodation.

3rd January—Proprietor writes, offering accommodation (offer).

10th January—Mr Brown writes accepting the offer (acceptance).

11th January—Proprietor writes withdrawing offer (revocation of offer).

12th January—Proprietor receives letter of acceptance from Mr Brown.

13th January—Mr Brown receives letter of revocation from Proprietor.

Conclusion: Contract exists. It came into existence as soon as Mr Brown posted his letter on 10th January. If the proprietor refuses to accommodate Mr Brown, he is breaking the contract and can be sued for breach of contract.

INTENTION TO BE LEGALLY BOUND

The parties must be willing to be legally bound by their agreements. In the event of a disagreement they must be prepared to allow a court of law to settle their differences. It is not necessary or even customary in commercial or business contracts for parties to state to each other, at the time they make the contract, that they have such an intention, as this intention is implied between them.

However, if the parties do not wish to be legally bound their agreement must expressly state so, for example:

1. A football pools coupon will usually have a clause in it stating that the parties will not go to court in the event of a disagreement.
2. 'A gentleman's agreement' is an agreement between business men where they expressly state that there is no legal intent behind their bargain.
3. Generally speaking, domestic agreements made between husband and wife who are living together are presumed not to be legal contracts, but financial agreements between separated spouses are usually binding contracts.

CONSIDERATION

Every simple English contract which is not drawn up under seal must be supported by consideration. As very few business arrangements are made through the formal channels of a document under seal, we can concentrate our attention on the meaning of consideration. This is a factor which is peculiar to English law; it is not to be found in other legal systems in Europe.

Consideration can be best be explained by saying it is the price paid for the bargain. In the sale of a suite of furniture, the shop-keeper (the promisor) is offering to supply the customer (the promisee) with furniture in exchange for the customer paying £100. In a restaurant the owner supplies the meal in exchange for the customer paying the price. There must always be a benefit accruing to the promisor (in that he may receive value) or a detriment suffered by the promisee (in that he may give value) to the contract. This is usually, but not necessarily, money. Strangely enough, so long as some price is charged, English law does not worry about whether the bargain is good or bad. The parties are free to make whatever bargain they so choose. A proprietor who charges £1 a day for full board may be a fool but if that is the agreement he made willingly then he has a perfectly legal contract. Furthermore, *the consideration must move from the promisee*, which means that a person can only enforce a promise if he himself promised to do something in return for the other's promise. Or, to put it another way, only the two parties to a contract can sue or be sued upon it.

CAPACITY OF PARTIES TO MAKE A CONTRACT

Having discussed the three basic elements in a contract let us now consider the capacity of persons to make a contract. The law divides people other than normal adults into the following categories:
1. Infants (minors).
2. Mentally sick.
3. Drunkards.
4. Married women.
5. Corporations.
In addition, we shall consider two other categories of persons, namely, managers and agents.

Infants (minors)

Until 1969 the age of majority was 21, but in that year the Family Law Reform Act was passed reducing the age of majority to 18. As a result, the number of infants now entering into contracts must obviously have declined but nevertheless a knowledge of the rule is still vital, for example, for young people starting in full-time employment at the age of sixteen or pop-groups touring the country and staying in hotels who could well be under 18 years of age.

The law aims to protect infants against their own inexperience whilst realising that it should not cause unnecessary hardship to adults who deal with infants.

Although it is not illegal for an infant to make a contract, only certain classes of contract can be enforced against him. An agreement to supply an infant with 'necessaries' is one such contract. Necessaries are goods (*a*) which he needs because he has not sufficient of them when the contract is made and (*b*) which are of a type suitable to his way of life. Thus, a bank-clerk might need a dark suit, and a pop-star a suit covered in sequins. The question is always whether it is reasonable for the infant to buy such an article. It is up to the supplier to prove that the infant needs the goods and that they are suitable to his way of life. Provided he can prove this, then the contract is enforceable against the infant.

Necessaries cover not only material goods but services such as board and lodging. Hotel accommodation could certainly come within the classification of necessaries, e.g. a student who has to live away from home during term time. The infant must pay a reasonable price for the goods received which is not necessarily the contract price.

A contract of service, such as teaching a trade, is also enforceable against the infant. Should the infant break the agreement he may be liable in damages (see also contract of service, Chapter 8).

The infant cannot be forced to repay money he has borrowed or to pay for unnecessary goods unless he has entered into the contract fraudulently. Such agreements are classified as void and unenforceable against the infant.

Mentally sick and intoxicated persons

Such a person must pay a reasonable price if he is supplied with necessaries.

Other contracts can be avoided if he can prove (*a*) the other party know he was sick or drunk and (*b*) that his disability prevented him from understanding the agreement.

Married women

A married woman is free to enter into and be bound by the terms of a contract. Should she book a hotel room but fail to pay then the correct course is to sue her for breach of contract.

Sometimes the wife may be acting as her husband's agent, i.e. she may book a room on his behalf and at his request. In this case, the husband is then liable for any expenses incurred.

Can a husband be made to pay for hotel expenses incurred by his wife? Yes, if the wife has previously stayed at the hotel and the husband has always paid her bill. He will continue to be liable until he expressly notifies the hotel that he will no longer be liable for her debts.

Finally, where a husband and wife or a man and his mistress are living together, there is a presumption of agency arising from co-habitation that she can pledge his credit for necessaries. However, he can escape liability in several ways, e.g. by proving that she had sufficient of the goods or by proving that he had told the tradesman not to give credit to his wife.

Companies

As so many hotels are owned by companies it is important to have some knowledge of the ability of a company to enter into a contract.

A company, being an artificial person, must negotiate through its directors and employees. Acting through such persons, the company may enter into and be bound by contracts in the same way as human beings.

Directors can make contracts on behalf of the company, but they can only make such contracts as they are permitted to make by the documents incorporating the company, i.e. the articles of association and the memorandum. Should they go beyond the powers stated therein, we say that the company is acting beyond its powers or is *ultra vires*. Section 9(1) of the European Communities Act 1972 states that an *ultra vires* contract is now enforceable against the company provided that the third party acted in good faith.

Of course, not every *employee* may bind the company by a contract. It is only those persons who have such authority by the articles of the company; for example, in a hotel a chef would have authority to purchase food and a booking clerk would have authority to make accommodation agreements, whereas a chamber-maid and waiter would have no such authority.

If the articles expressly forbid the employee to make the contract the company is not bound, even if that agreement is of a type normally made by such an employee.

If the employee, in his capacity as an employee, would normally make such a contract, but the articles are silent upon the matter, the company is bound by the agreement even though the employee may not have had such authority.

Managers and other employees

The ability of such persons to enter into contracts on behalf of their employer, acting as their employer's agent, must depend initially on the terms of their personal contract of employment. We are speaking here of employers who are not companies. A restaurant owner who expressly authorises his manager to make a contract on his behalf is bound by the agreement. But the owner may also be bound by those actions which he has not authorised if those agreements are within the normal ambit of a restaurant manager's work. This is so, even though he may have expressly forbidden the manager to make such a contract and provided the other party to the contract is not aware of the prohibition.

Travel agents

It is quite usual for a holiday-maker to book his holiday through a travel agency, especially if he is going abroad.

In the legal sense an agent is a person who makes a contract on behalf of his principal with a third party. Once the contract is made the agent's role is completed.

A travel agent is not always an agent in the legal sense of the word. Speaking generally:

1. a travel agent who helps a customer on an individual basis by booking accommodation, obtaining train tickets or excursion tickets is working as a legal agent. Once the arrangements are completed, his task is over and any dispute over bills is then a matter between the hotelier and the customer. But:

2. the travel agent who arranges package tours may make

    (a) a contract between himself and the hotel proprietor, by which he agrees to take a block-booking of hotel rooms. Any dispute over non-payment of bills is then a matter between the hotelier and the travel-agent, and the prudent hotelier will obtain a written statement from the agent concerning responsibilities for payment of the bill, and,

    (b) a separate contract between himself and the customer, the terms of which are usually set out in the standard form of booking.

Exclusion clauses are very common in the booking forms and the holiday-maker is well advised to read the form carefully before signing as he is taken to have agreed to any conditions on a document to which he has put his signature.

In *Cook v. Spanish Holiday Tours* (1960) the court helped a distraught holiday-maker. Mr Cook booked a Spanish holiday through the defendant company, but when he and his wife arrived in Spain no room was available for them in the hotel. They were offered a filthy room in an annexe where beetles were scurrying around the floor-boards. They had to spend the night in a park, fly back to England the next day, and the remainder of their holiday was spent in Brighton. Damages for breach of contract were awarded to Mr Cook, the Appeal Court saying that the agent could not rely on the argument that his duty was only to book a room and not to provide a room. 'It isn't much good booking room if you can't have a room,' said the Judge.

Some protection has been given to holiday makers by two recent Acts, namely, the Misrepresentation Act 1967 and the Trade Descriptions Act 1968, both of which enable civil actions and criminal prosecutions to be started against persons who mislead others by false descriptions. For further details of these Acts see page 75. Of course, it is not just the fear of a large fine together with the attendant publicity which worries the company. There is also the fact that one false statement in a brochure can give rise to any number of prosecutions (*R. v. Thomson Holidays Ltd* (1974)). Travel agents, in October, 1974, agreed a voluntary code giving more protection to the customer.

At the moment, anyone can set up in business as a travel agent, there being no form of registration. The only control comes under the Civil Aviation Act 1971, whereby, from April 1973, some agents who need an air travel organiser's licence will have to prove that they have adequate financial resources.

PERSUADING A PARTY TO MAKE AN AGREEMENT— ADVERTISEMENTS, BROCHURES, ETC.

The purpose of advertising, whether it be in a newspaper, in a magazine or even on the television is to inform the public of a product with the view to persuading them to buy it. The same is true of advertising accommodation and issuing hotel brochures: they aim to inform prospective guests of the facilities available and to 'sell' the hotel.

Any statement which is made orally or in writing or through the medium of a picture and which persuades a person to enter into a contract is known as a representation. A hotel brochure informing persons of the facilities available at the hotel or a statement in an advertisement that the hotel is situated on the sea-front, or a television picture showing the lounge of a hotel are all examples of representations. Should any such statement be untrue then it is termed in law a misrepresentation and is either an innocent misrepresentation, a negligent misrepresentation or a fraudulent misrepresentation, depending upon the intent behind it.

An innocent misrepresentation is a statement made innocently: a negligent misrepresentation is made carelessly but in neither case is there a malicious intent. A misrepresentation is fraudulent if its maker knows that it is wrong, or without belief in its truth, is careless whether it be true or false. Before any legal action can succeed upon the misrepresentation certain facts have to be proved:

1. The misrepresentation must be a statement of fact, e.g. 'the hotel is situated in an acre of garden' when, in fact, it is hemmed in on all sides by other buildings or 'shower available in every bedroom', when in fact, only a wash basin is available in each room. However, it is not necessary to disclose everything. Silence is permissible so long as it does not amount to a half-truth. So, if the hotel is next to an open prison, the proprietor need not mention such a fact unless he is asked specifically by the guest. Statements of opinion are not misrepresentations, e.g. 'This hotel is the best in the area'.

2. The misrepresentation must have caused the other party to enter into the contract and to have suffered damage as a result: in other words, if he was ignorant of the misrepresentation then he cannot sue upon it.

Remedies for misrepresentation

The party who suffers as a result of the misrepresentation has the following remedies:

1. He may rescind the contract for innocent or fraudulent misrepresentation. This means that he can withdraw from the agreement and is entitled to receive back any money, such as a deposit, which he has already paid over. In a hotel booking agreement rescission is possible either before the guest is due to arrive or immediately on arrival. However, he cannot remain in the hotel, enjoying its benefits and claim rescission.

2. It is possible for damages to be given as an alternative remedy

to rescission in cases of innocent misrepresentation if the court feels that it would be a fairer solution (Misrepresentation Act 1967, *s*.2(2)).

3. He may claim damages for fraudulent misrepresentation.
4. He may claim damages for careless misrepresentation but the hotelier who draws up the brochure containing the misrepresentation might successfully plead that he reasonably believed the statements to be true (Misrepresentation Act 1967, *s*.2(1)).

Damages would include reasonable expenses incurred in finding suitable alternative accommodation and the difference between the costs of the two places.

By *s*.3 of the Misrepresentation Act 1967, as amended, any statement in a brochure or similar document purporting to exclude the hotelier or travel agent from liability for misrepresentations within that document is only effective if it is considered fair and reasonable in the circumstances (See page 81.)

These remedies are available to any person injured as a result of a misrepresentation. They are civil remedies, however, and can be expensive as well as worrying to persons who are not used to pursuing legal claims.

Of far more benefit to the injured person in such cases is the Trade Descriptions Act 1968, because this Act, which makes false descriptions a criminal offence, is enforced by the County Consumer Protection Officers (formerly known as Inspectors of Weights and Measures) at no personal expense to the aggrieved party. In fact, if the prosecution is successful, not only may the accused person be fined but he may also have to pay the aggrieved party a sum of money as compensation (*R. v. Thomson Holidays, The Times*, 28th March 1973).

By *s*.14 of the Trade Descriptions Act 1968 it is a criminal offence to make a false description, in a reckless manner or knowing it to be false, about the nature of any services, accommodation or facilities provided in the course of a trade or business. This section covers a wide field, including services set out in hotel or holiday brochures, travel agents' brochures, advertisements in newspapers, magazines or on television. The statements must be statements of fact. In *British Airways Board v Taylor* (1976), a letter written by BOAC on August 16th to a customer stated that they had pleasure in confirming a flight reservation for August 29th. On August 14, there were sufficient seats to accommodate the customer but BOAC over-booked and the customer was obliged to postpone his journey by one day. The statements in the letter were found to be statements of fact that the customer had a certain and definite booking and that such statements were false, contrary to s.14(1) (a) of the Trade Descriptions Act (On another ground, the airways company was found not guilty of the offence under s.14 of the Act.)

It is not an offence under the Act to make a reckless promise that certain facilities will be provided in the future, or that work will be done wihin a period of time. In *Beckett v. Cohen* (1973) a builder was found not to have committed an offence under s.14 by promising to build a garage for a client within fourteen days. Such a promise may well amount to breach of contract and give rise to an action for damages. Again, in *Sunair Holidays Ltd v. Dodd* (1970), a firm of travel agents were found not guilty of commiting an offence under s.14. The travel agents had advertised in a holiday brochure offering facilities at a hotel in Majorca where it was stated that all twin-bedded rooms had 'private bath, shower, W.C. and terrace'. The travel agents had a contract with the hotel whereby the twin-bedded rooms, which the hotel management kept available for the travel agents to offer to their clients, were rooms with these amenities including a terrace. Two holiday makers and their wives read the brochure and booked twin-bedded rooms at the hotel, but when they arrived there they found that their rooms had no terrace. The travel agents were found not guilty of giving a false trade description because at the time when the statements were made in the brochure they were perfectly accurate. Admittedly, the travel agents were at fault in failing to ensure that the holiday-makers were given the correct rooms and, in fact, did compensate the holiday-makers, but that fault had no bearing upon whether the statement in the brochure was false or recklessly made. It may be that s.14 provides a loop-hole for advertisers. In *R. v. Sunair Holidays Ltd* (1973), although the conviction against Sunair Holidays was quashed on a technical point, it was conceded that statements in the brochure regarding the availability of push-chairs and meals related to the future and no conviction was possible under s.14.

A person can be acting recklessly even though he is not acting dishonestly. In fact, a heavy responsibility is placed upon the advertiser to see that the statement is true. For defences and enforcement of the Act, see page 195.

'Starring' of hotels

Organisations such as the A.A. and the R.A.C. carry out a service of 'starring' hotels for the benefit of its members.

Any hotel may submit an application to the A.A. or R.A.C. requesting that an inspection of their premises be made with the view to being given a 'starred' rating. If the hotel satisfies the necessary standards then the appropriate number of stars will be awarded to it. The purpose of star rating is to indicate the type of hotel rather than the degree of merit: in other words, a star lays down the minimum standards of service to be expected at such a hotel. For example, one star indicates that the hotel has hot and cold water in each bedroom, lounge facilities, etc. Should the 'starred' hotel not provide such facilities an aggrieved member may complain to the A.A. or R.A.C. who will investigate such complaints. However, there is no legal action available to the member against the A.A. or R.A.C. as starring is a recommendation to the member rather than a legal guarantee.

However, a hotel which advertises itself with a star rating but fails to maintain that standard might well be liable to a guest on the grounds of misrepresentation, e.g. a guest, on learning that a hotel has a star rating, perhaps by seeing a sign or headed note paper, may book a room there. On arrival he finds that there is no running water in the bedroom and no lounge facilities. It is submitted that he would be entitled to claim that the booking had been entered into on the grounds of misrepresentation and would be entitled to withdraw from the contract or claim damages.

THE CONTENT OF THE AGREEMENT

Assuming that the parties have entered into a legally binding contract, what terms have they agreed upon? So long as the promise to each other is not illegal, for example, an arrangement to evade the payment of income tax, the parties are free to make any terms they so choose.

It is important, however, for the parties to take care in drawing up the terms of the agreement, because once they have agreed upon the terms no fresh conditions or alterations can be imposed by one party upon the other without the latter's agreement (*Olley v. Marlborough Court* (1949); see page 79).

The terms agreed upon may be both (*a*) expressly stated and (*b*) impliedly understood. Within these divisions the important terms, express or implied, are known as conditions and form the basis of the agreement, whilst less important terms are known as warranties.

Express terms

Express terms are those which are specifically agreed upon and stated between the parties. In a booking agreement the type of accommodation or the price to be charged would be express terms. They can be set out in writing or arranged orally, but in the latter case it is advisable to confirm the arrangements in writing. These examples are not only express terms but are so important that they can be classified as conditions.

Should either side fail to carry out any express conditions they would be breaking their agreement. Later in this chapter we shall discuss the penalties which then follow.

A detailed example of an express condition in a booking agreement is the duration of stay. In the majority of cases the parties will agree upon specific dates for the guest's visit. Any alterations can only be made if both parties agree. However, the terms of the contract may provide for other arrangements. The guest may book accommodation on a day-to-day basis, or a weekly or monthly basis. The length of notice to be given by either side will depend upon the terms in the agreement, or, if it is silent upon the matter, upon the way in which payment is made. A guest paying weekly should receive or give a week's notice; a guest paying monthly should expect to give or receive a month's notice. The notice should be given on the day when payment is due. For example, if the weekly payment is made on Saturday, notice is to be given one Saturday to expire the following Saturday. If notice is given on Wednesday it should expire a week the following Saturday, i.e. ten days' time.

Implied terms

Implied terms are those which are understood to exist without the parties having to mention them specifically. Very often, implied terms came into existence through custom, for example, a hotelier impliedly agrees that the rooms are fit for habitation, or it is impliedly understood that charges can be imposed for room service, early morning tea and newspapers. The former would be classified as an implied condition, the latter as implied warranties. It is also possible for an Act of Parliament to state that implied terms exist in contracts, e.g. it is impliedly understood that when goods are bought in a shop they are fit for the purpose for which they are intended (Sale of Goods Act, 1979, *s.* 14 (3)).

Exemption Clauses and fundamental breach of contract: Unfair Contract Terms Act 1977

Clauses which purport to exempt or limit a party from liability are frequently found in contracts. They too, are terms of the agreement, being classified as express conditions.

But how many people understand the true meaning of clauses such as 'All liabilities expressed or implied whatsoever are hereby excluded'? Furthermore, the bargaining power between the parties is so often unbalanced with many contracts nowadays being made on 'standard printed forms' where one party is the ordinary man in the street and the other is a large company. Here the ordinary man has no choice over the terms: either he accepts them, or tries to do business elsewhere.

To be effective, the exclusion clause must be a term of the contract, which can happen in one of two ways:- If the contract is in writing and signed by the recipient, then he is taken to have read what he has signed and if it contains an exemption clause then he is bound by its terms. This is why it is always so important to read a document before signing it. If the contract is not signed, then the party imposing the clause must take all reasonable steps to bring the exemption clause to the notice of the other party, either by displaying the exclusion clause on a notice board, or by incorporating the clause into a contractual document. Provided the imposing party has acted reasonably, then the recipient will be caught by the exemption clause. In addition, the exemption clause must be incorporated into the contract when it is made: to introduce it later makes it ineffective. Furthermore, a written exemption clause is not effective if an oral misrepresentation is given as to its meaning. Neither is it effective if oral promises are given which over-ride its effect.

Because exemption clauses are often difficult to interpret, guidelines have been developed. Thus,
(a) if the exclusion clause is ambiguous, it will be interpreted against the person who inserted it.
(b) if the purpose of the exclusion clause is to evade

responsibility for negligence, then the clause must state quite clearly that this is what is intended.

Since 1945, concern has grown over the increasing use made by contracting parties of exemption clauses. Before the consumer was given protection by legislation (in the areas of sale of goods and hire – purchase) the courts stepped in to give him protection by saying that certain breaches of contract were so serious that the fundamental purpose of the contract was broken: the innocent party was then entitled to regard the whole contract as at an end including any exemption clause, so that it was of no effect. But once the consumer gained protection through Acts of Parliament, the attitude of the judiciary changed. In 1967, the House of Lords stated (Suisse Atlantique) that in their opinion, it was possible for an exemption clause to cover a fundamental breach of contract. It was necessary to examine the contract and the wording of the exemption clause; if it covered the breach complained of, then the party inserting the clause could claim exclusion of liability. This approach to the validity of exemption clauses has been re-affirmed by the House of Lords in *Photo Production Ltd.* v *Securicor Transport Ltd.* (1980). It may also be necessary in certain contracts to examine the exclusion clause to see if it is reasonable (see below).

An additional safeguard against the onerous exemption clause was given by Parliament to contracting parties through the Unfair Contract Terms Act 1977. Perhaps the gist of the Act can be stated thus – although many exemption clauses are still permissable, they will only be valid if they are reasonable. Most of the provisions of the Act apply only where there is a "business liability" relationship between the parties i.e. a liability arising from things done in the course of a business or where events arise from the occupation of premises used for business purposes. The hotel and catering trade is therefore caught by the Act. Most sections (except *s*.2 on negligence and *s*.8 on misrepresentation) distinguish between:

(a) a person who deals as a consumer and
(b) a person who does not deal as a consumer. A person "deals as a consumer" if he does *not* make the contract in the course of a business.

The Act came into force on February 1st 1978 and affects contracts made after that date. Among areas covered by the Act are the following:-

Avoiding liability for negligence

(a) Death or bodily injury

A person cannot, by inserting a clause in a contract or erecting a notice, exclude or restrict his liability for negligently causing either the death of another person or injuring (including mental illness or bodily shock) that other person. Any such clause is void. Killing or injuring persons negligently covers broken duties under contract, tort or the Occupiers' Liability Act 1957 e.g. a guest killed as a result of a bedroom ceiling collapsing due to the negligence of the hotelier. Thus, decisions such as *Bennet* v *Pontin's Holiday Camps* (1973) (where a widow's claim against Pontin's for her husband's death through drowning failed because he had signed a form excluding Pontin's from liability for any accident) would no longer exist.

(b) Other types of damage

It is permissable to insert an exclusion clause which excludes or limits a person's liability for negligence for other types of damage e.g. damage to goods, possessions or economic loss, provided that the clause is reasonable (see below). It is up to the person claiming the loss to prove that the clause is unreasonable. It is submitted that the statutory notice under the Hotel Proprietors Act 1965 is unaffected by this rule: such a notice is regarded as reasonable and has not been repealed by the Act.

N.B. Even where a person does know about the notice or the term in the contract such knowledge does not necessarily mean that he has voluntarily agreed to accept the risk.

Other exemption clauses

The Act also deals with other types of exemption clauses and modifies their effect: essentially they must be reasonable to be effective. In particular:-

(a) A clause which excludes the contracting party from liability for any misrepresentation he makes prior to the agreement is valid only if it is reasonable at the time the agreement is made. (*s.*8) (page 75).

(b) Where one party deals as a consumer or on the other party's written standard terms of business, that other party when himself in breach of contract, cannot exclude or restrict any liability of his in respect of the breach unless the clause is reasonable. Furthermore any clause which allows the contracting party to perform the contract in a way sub-

stantially different from that which was reasonably expected of him or which claims, in respect of the whole or part of
his contractual obligation, to render no performance at all
will be valid only if reasonable. (*s*.3) This will strike at the
heart of contracts which are made on booking forms found
in hotel or holiday brochures. A clause stating that the
company has 'the right to alter the holiday arrangements'
may no longer permit the company to send visitors to a different country or hotel, or to cancel the whole holiday.

(*c*) In contracts for the sale of goods, and contracts for work
done and materials supplied, any attempt to exclude
implied terms of merchantable quality or of fitness in relation to the goods are (i) void, if the contract is made with a
consumer. (ii) valid, if reasonable, when the contract is
made between two businessmen.

(*d*) A manufacturer cannot exclude himself from liability for
damage caused to the consumer by the negligent manufacture of his product. (*s*.5)

(*e*) Breach of contract. The Act confirms the position stated
by the Court in *Photo Production Ltd*. v *Securicor Transport Ltd*.
namely that a breach of contract, whether fundamental or
not, does not necessarily put an end to the validity of the exemption clause. If the clause, when it is interpreted, covers
the breach which has occurred and if (where the test is
applicable) it satisfies the requirement of reasonableness, it
may be relied upon by the "guilty" party who is in breach of
contract.

The test of reasonableness (*s*.11)
Throughout the preceding paragraphs it has been stressed
that the exemption notice or clause must be reasonable; this
means that it must be fair and reasonable, having regard to the
circumstances:-
a) known to the parties at the time when the contract was
made (in respect of a contract term) or
b) when the liability arose (in the case of a non-contractual
notice).
The Courts will pay particular attention to the knowledge of
the injured party, the freedom he had to negotiate the deal and
whether he had a commercial choice e.g. could he have got the
contract from somebody else without the exemption clause?
Another Act protecting the consumer is the Fair Trading Act

1973, under which a Director of Fair Trading has been appointed. His job is to keep under review consumer trade practice and to investigate practices which may adversely affect the economic interests of consumers. It is envisaged that he will be able to make recommendations when glaring injustices are apparent.

Hotel regulations

It is customary for hotels to display notices to explain the way in which that particular hotel is run e.g. meal times, use of public rooms and the time when the front door is locked. Such regulations are not regarded as terms of a contract but as internal domestic arrangements, and the courts will not interfere with the regulations unless they are too harsh and restrictive.

MISTAKEN AGREEMENTS AND ILLEGAL AGREEMENTS

Mistake can only be pleaded as an excuse to avoid the agreement if the mistake fundamentally alters the whole purpose of the contract. This rarely happens as most mistakes do not go deep enough. Generally speaking, whenever a mistake occurs the contract is still valid and must be performed but the mistaken party is allowed to claim damages.

Contracts entered into for an illegal purpose can usually be avoided, but the knowledge by the parties of the illegality is relevant. So, if a prostitute books into a hotel for the purpose of entertaining clients and the hotelier is aware of her motives, he cannot sue her for breach of contract if she refuses to pay her hotel bill.

Sometimes a contract of employment contains a clause which forbids the employee, on leaving his employment, from working for a rival employer or setting up on his own in competition with the employer. Such a clause is known as a clause in restraint of trade and is generally illegal and void. Exceptionally, it can be classified as valid and effective only if the restriction is reasonable from the point of view both of the parties themselves and also of the general public. The employer does have the right to protect his trade secrets from being passed on to a rival firm. He also has a right to protect his trade connections, in other words, to prevent his customers from being enticed away from him by an ex-employee who was in a position to exercise influence upon the customers. On the other hand, the law does not aim to restrict healthy business competition. Therefore, any clause in restraint of trade must be carefully worded.

DISCHARGING THE AGREEMENT

A contract can come to an end in one of the following ways:
1. Performance of the agreement. (see below).
2. Deciding to end the agreement (discharge by agreement). (see p. 86).
3. Frustration. (see p. 86).
4. Breaking the agreement (discharge by breach). (see p. 87).

Performance of the agreement
By carrying out their individual promises to each other the two parties to the contract are, in effect, discharging it. They must fulfil the exact promises specified in the arrangement. The following points which relate especially to hotel booking contracts need to be noted.

Hotel register
1. *Proprietor's responsibilities*: An obligation is placed upon the keeper of any premises who, for reward, receives and accommodates visitors for one night or more, to keep a record of such visitors (Immigration (Hotel Records) Order 1972). The rule applies not only to hotel proprietors or managers but also to any person, such as the seaside landlady, who takes in the occasional paying visitor. The keeper of the premises has an obligation:

(*a*) to see that the information is given to him, and
(*b*) to keep, for at least twelve months, a written record of the date of arrival of every such person and of all the other necessary information. This record shall, at all times, be open to inspection by any constable or by any person authorised by the Secretary of State.

2. *Visitor's responsibilities*: Every British or Commonwealth visitor, aged sixteen or over, is under an obligation on arriving at the premises to inform the hotel keeper of his full name and nationality. This information can be given personally or through a third person and either orally or in writing. No longer is it obligatory for the visitor to sign the register himself or to give his address. Visitors who are citizens of a British

protectorate, or who are serving in either the U.K. or N.A.T.O. armed forces may also register as British subjects.

Further obligations are imposed upon aliens aged sixteen or over. In addition to his name and nationality, every alien must:

(a) on arriving at the premises inform the hotel keeper of the number and place of issue of his registration certificate, passport or other document establishing his identity and nationality, and

(b) on or before his departure from the premises, inform the hotel keeper of his next destination and, if known to him, his full address there.

Failure to comply with these provisions can result in fines or imprisonment.

NB Ambassadors, staff and families who are within the terms of the Diplomatic Privileges Act 1964 are under no obligation to register at all.

Time of arrival. By custom, guests are not usually permitted to take up residence in their room before noon on the day of arrival and are expected to vacate their rooms by noon on the day of departure. However, a guest may arrive or depart from the hotel at any time within the agreed dates.

As an example, a guest who has booked a room for one week from Saturday to Saturday may arrive at any time on the Saturday or even any time during the week. As he has booked the room, he is entitled to have it kept free for him during that time, but must of course pay the contract price. Should the hotelier re-let the room to a third party, he runs the risk of the original guest turning up late and claiming damages for a broken agreement. It is therefore simpler and safer to make the time of arrival a term of the agreement. All that is needed is a statement in the agreement to the effect that guests are expected to arrive by a certain time, for example, 8 p.m., and that should they fail to do so the proprietor will then be free to re-let the room. In this way the onus is placed upon the guest to inform the hotelier if he will be later than 8 p.m. and an understanding can be reached between the parties.

Payment of bills. It is the duty of the debtor, i.e. the guest, to seek out the creditor, i.e. the hotelier, for the payment of any bill.

It is usual for hoteliers to include rules concerning payment in the contract. A common example is the rule that a cheque must be presented so many days prior to departure. Becoming more common these days is the request by the hotel that the guest pays the price for bed and breakfast immediately on arrival.

So long as the hotelier agrees, payment by cheque, or by banker's card or by giro is in order and discharges the debt. Of course, should the cheque be dishonoured, then the original debt revives.

Discharge by agreement

If the time for performance of the contract has not yet arrived and both parties wish to cancel it altogether or cancel it and enter into fresh terms, there is nothing to stop them legally doing so. In this case both parties mutually agree. If necessary they should return any goods or money such as a deposit already handed over.

Frustration

A contract which begins life as being valid may later be discharged if the contract has become impossible to perform through no fault of either party. In these situations, which are rare, it is said that the contract is frustrated. The parties will not be held to their promises in the light of the altered circumstances. The following are examples of frustrated contracts:

1. Where Parliament has passed an Act or issued an order making the performance of the contract illegal, for example, an order that hotels within a city centre must cease taking in guests because of bomb threats.
2. Where the contract depends upon the personal service of one man his death or serious illness will frustrate it, for example, a small hotel whose business reputation relies upon the service of one man, perhaps the chef.
3. Where the contract depends upon the continued existence of an object, such as a hotel. Should the hotel be destroyed, the contract itself will be frustrated.
4. Where the contract has been made to depend upon the occurrence of one event only, should the event not occur the contract will be discharged. However, the event must be the sole basis of the contract. For example, in *Krell v. Henry* (1903) rooms had been booked overlooking the route of the coronation procession of Edward VII. Owing to the King's sudden illness the coronation was postponed. As the sole purpose of the booking was to view the coronation

procession its cancellation took away the main purpose of the booking and the parties were discharged from their obligations. But, in very similar circumstances in *Herne Bay S.S. Co. v. Hutton* (1903), the contract was not discharged as there the contract had two purposes: (*i*) to see the King review his Fleet, following his Coronation, and (*ii*) to take a trip around the bay and enjoy the sights. Although the Royal Review was cancelled, the outing around the bay could still be undertaken.

Should the contract be frustrated any money already paid over, such as a deposit, can be paid back. However, if the party to whom the money was paid incurred expenses before the frustration for the purpose of performing the contract, he may be allowed to keep some of that money to alleviate the costs he has incurred.

Discharge by breach

A breach of contract can occur when (1) one party to an agreement tells the other party that he has no intention of performing the contract when the time falls due. That other party has a choice open to him. He may either accept the statement and sue immediately for damages or he can treat the contract as still existing and await performance. In this case, however, he runs the risk of some event occurring to discharge the agreement and thus lose his right of action. For example, in a hotel booking agreement the hotel may warn the guest in advance that they cannot take him as promised, because of overbooking. Should the guest treat the contract as existing and hope for a cancellation, if the hotel burns down, thus discharging the agreement in any event, he will lose his right of action.

(2) one party refuses to perform his agreement during the time it should be performed then the other party has a right to sue for breach of contract.

When the conduct of one of the parties makes performance of the contract impossible, or one of the parties simply fails to perform, the contract is immediately discharged and the other side has a right of action, for example, when a hotelier accepts too many bookings, thus making it impossible to fulfil his obligation to a guest.

If the contract as a whole is broken, or if a vital term (a condition) of the contract is broken, the innocent party is entitled to treat the contract as at an end and claim damages. Alternatively, if it is possible, he may continue with his side of the bargain and then claim damages. However, if a minor term of the contract is broken (a warranty) the innocent party must continue to perform the agreement and is entitled to claim damages. A guest who refuses to pay his bill is breaking a condition of his contract entitling the hotelier to sue for damages. A hotelier whose premises or food are sub-standard is breaking a condition of the contract and can be sued for damages.

In the hotel trade the most common instance of breaking a contract occurs when one of the parties cancels the booking without the consent of the other, or the hotel over-books thus making it impossible to carry out the agreement. Let us look at this in more detail.

Cancellation by the guest and rights of the hotelier. Once the hotel booking is agreed upon the contract comes into existence. It follows that if the guest then cancels the booking, he is, in effect, breaking the agreement. The hotelier is entitled to keep any deposit paid by the guest. In addition, the hotelier may claim damages against the guest, which, if the hotel room is not re-let, is usually the amount which the guest would have paid less a sum for food, heating and lighting. Should he re-let the room the damages awarded would be minimal as he has suffered little loss. The hotelier is entitled to await the time for performance of the agreement, and need not go out of his way to re-advertise the room, but if the opportunity presents itself to re-let the room, then he should do so, thus mitigating his loss.

Should the cancellation be due to the guest's illness, or other extenuating circumstances, this may amount to frustration in which case the amount of damages would be much lower, or even non-existent (see p. 86).

Cancellation by the hotelier and remedies of guest. A hotelier who cancels a guest's booking is liable for breach of contract. He must return any deposit paid by the guest. If the cancellation is well in advance of the booking date it is unlikely that the guest could recover more in the way of damages. However, if the cancellation occurs when the guest presents himself at the hotel, or, if the hotelier has overbooked and cannot, therefore, accommodate the guest it is likely that the guest can claim not only the return of any deposit paid but also the financial difference, if any, between the cost of the original accommodation and the cost of new accommodation together with any incidental expenses.

REMEDIES FOR BREACH OF CONTRACT

Whenever a term of the contract is broken, whether it be a condition or a warranty the innocent party is enitled to claim damages. It must be appreciated that damages are intended to act as compensation, not as a punishment.

For what kind of loss can the innocent party claim compensation?

The court will not award damages for every loss suffered by the innocent party after the contract is broken: he may only recover for loss which is not too remote.

Suppose a guest finds that the hotelier has over-booked so he has to go to another hotel, and then the next day he falls down and breaks his leg. Certainly he can claim compensation for changing hotels but not for the broken leg. That injury is too far removed from the hotelier's action; it did not arise naturally from the original broken contract.

What amount of money can the innocent party receive for his loss?

The purpose of awarding damages in a broken contract is to place the injured party, so far as money is concerned, in the same position as if the contract had been performd.

In contracts for the sale of goods if the seller has failed to deliver the goods, the loss to the buyer is the money required to purchase equivalent goods on the open market at the time and place due for delivery. If it is the buyer who refuses to accept the goods the loss to the seller is the difference, if any, between the original contract price and the eventual sale price of the articles.

In hotel booking contracts the amount of damages is not necessarily confined to the actual loss suffered. Admittedly at one time the courts were reluctant to allow an injured party to be compensated for mental distress, annoyance, loss of temper or disappointment. He had to prove a physical loss or inconvenience. But, within the last few years, a change of attitude has come about, and a broken contract or a contract to provide entertainment and enjoyment are considered proper occasions for the court to award damages for mental distress.

In *Jarvis v. Swan Tours Ltd* (1973) Mr Jarvis booked a holiday costing £63 in Switzerland through the defendant company after reading their brochure. He had a miserable holiday as it in no way matched up to the representations in the brochure. The court, in awarding him damages of £125 for the misrepresentations and broken agreement, allowed him this sum for mental distress and inconvenience. The damages were to compensate him for the loss of entertainment and enjoyment which he had been promised but did not receive. Instead of a jolly houseparty with dances and other entertainment which he had been promised, he found himself to be the only guest, the food to be inadequate and the entertainment very poor.

The plaintiff may also recover such damage if he has entered into the contract on behalf of others, such as members of his family. In *Jackson v. Horizon Holidays* (1975) Mr Jackson booked a holiday for himself, his wife and his children on a holiday brochure form specifying that it was a condition of booking that there be an interconnecting door between the children's room and the parents' and also, that he wanted everything in the hotel to be of the highest standard. This was not so: the food and the bedrooms were deplorable and none of the stated amenities existed. He successfully sued the holiday firm for damages for himself, his wife and children for both the diminution in value of the holiday and for the discomfort, vexation and disappointment suffered by them all. *Per* Lord Denning: 'where a person enteres into a contract for the benefit of himself and others who are not parties to a contract, he can sue on the contract for damages for the loss suffered not only by himself but also by the others in consequence of a breach of contract. . . .'

8
Employment of Staff: I

CONTRACT OF SERVICE

The agreement which results in the relationship of employer and employee is a contract which is, in general, subject to the same conditions as any other type of contract. It is known as a *contract of service* and does not embrace those forms of employment which arise from a *contract for services*. The latter involves an agreement between an employer and an independent contractor who agrees to supply a specific service which terminates on its completion and in consideration for a certain payment.

It is important to distinguish whether the relationship is one or the other of these two types. A simple way of determining the employer-employee relationship in the majority of cases is by means of the 'control test', that is, if in addition to the employer being able to tell the employee when, where, what and why he should perform a certain task, he can also control the manner in which it is carried out, whether it be by actual personal control or through the agency of an experienced manager, foreman or chargehand. Control is not a characteristic of a 'contract for services'; one who hires a taxi would not presume to tell the driver how to drive his vehicle.

However, in the contract of service there are situations in which the employer will be unable, either directly or indirectly, to control the work of an employee because of his special expertise. In such cases other tests can be applied to determine the relationship. If it can be shown overall that the employed person is regarded as being permenently on the payroll of the organisation belonging to the employer, this is usually sufficient indication that he is not an independent contractor and thus not a subject of a contract for services.

In the case of *Amalgamated Engineering Union v. Minister of Pensions* (1963) a member of a trade union was appointed its sick steward. His duties as such required him to visit once a week union members who were ill to pay them the union sickness benefit and to keep records of his activities in this connection for the information of the union. He received a payment of one shilling for each visit and travelling expenses. If he were guilty of any neglect in the performance of these duties he could be fined by the union and perhaps removed from his job as sick steward. One day he was injured whilst carrying out these duties. In an action which followed between the union and the Minister of Pensions the court had to decide whether or not a union member in the capacity of sick steward could be an employee of the union and thus entitled to national insurance benefits in respect of the injury he had suffered. The court held that the union controlled his activities as a sick steward in sufficient detail to make him an employee of that union.

However, the court decided otherwise in *Ready Mixed Concrete (South East), Ltd v. Minister of Pensions* (1968). The company employed lorry owners to deliver concrete manufactured by them. The agreement provided that the services of the drivers and vehicles should be at the disposal of the company whenever and wherever it required them, but there were no working time limits and payment was calculated on a quantity-distance basis. The drivers were expected to wear the company's uniform and obey its orders 'as if they were employees'. Here again the court had to decide whether or not the drivers were employees of the company to settle the question regarding the payment of their national insurance contributions. It was held that they were not completely integrated into the organisation, were not employees, and therefore as independent contractors were responsible for the payment of their national insurance contributions.

Several important consequences follow from the recognition of the employer-employee relationship:

1. An employer, in certain circumstances, is vicariously liable to third parties for the wrongful acts of his employee performed during the course of his employer's business (see Chapter 13). The same liability in respect of an independent contractor seldom arises.

2. An employer has a duty to provide a safe system of working

for his employee involving a higher duty of care than that which he owes to other persons.

3. An employer is required to pay national insurance contributions in respect of an employee and to deduct his income tax through the P.A.Y.E. scheme.

4. The conditions of Redundancy Payments benefits apply to employees only.

5. The provisions of the Employment Protection (Consolidation) Act 1978 apply only to a contract of service.

TERMS OF THE CONTRACT

It has already been stated that the contract of service, in general, follows the same rules as those which apply to other forms of contract, for example, there must be consideration, thus the employer pays a remuneration to the employee in return for agreed services. However, the agreement is not one which can follow from unfettered relations between the employer and the prospective employee. Many matters in the eventual relationship which emerges will have been determined already. The wage to be paid for the promised service will be laid down as a minimum by a statutory instrument made under the authority of *s.* 11 of the Wages Councils Act 1959 or will be the subject of a settlement by negotiation between employers or their associations and trade unions sanctioning a wage above the statutory minimum. Certain other conditions which must be regarded as fundamental to the contract will be the subject of statute, for example, the Shops Act 1950, the Offices, Shops and Railway Premises Act 1963, and the Health and Safety at Work Act 1974 provide certain working conditions which must be observed by employers for the benefit of their staff.

However, the contract will only come into existence when there has been an offer and acceptance, and the purpose of the agreement is legal and conforms with public policy.

The general rule regarding the capacity of minors (i.e. persons under the age of 18 years) to be parties to a contract, is not, if all other conditions are acceptable, likely to affect the validity of a contract of employment. If it can be shown that overall the agreement is one which gives benefit to the minor, then it will be binding on him. The benefit need not be an adequate wage, it can be employment into which is built a course of training even though the remuneration paid is relatively small or even non-existent.

Initially, a contract of service can be made in any form, that is, it can be an oral or a written agreement. It is usual, in the employment of permanent staff, that the contract is in writing. The employer presents the intending employee with a form containing as far as possible all the conditions and benefits attaching to the employment, and his agreement and signature with that of the employer or his representative will complete the contract.

However, the Employment Protection (Consolidation) Act makes provision that in all cases of permanent employment written evidence of the agreement shall be made available to the employee.

s.1, EMPLOYMENT PROTECTION (CONSOLIDATION) ACT 1978

This section provides that an employer must give 'written particulars' of the terms of the employment to the employee within thirteen weeks of the employee's commencing work. The particulars which must be included are the following:

1. The names of the parties to the contract.
2. The date when employment began.
3. Whether employment with a previous employer counts as part of the employee's continuous period of employment and if so, the date commencing the period of continuous employment.
4. The scale or rate of pay or the method of calculating it, the intervals at which remuneration is paid and any terms or conditions relating to hours of work.
5. Any terms or conditions respecting:
    (a) holidays, including public holidays and holiday pay together with particulars to enable its calculation including accrued holiday on termination of employment;
    (b) sickness or injury;
    (c) pensions rights if any, except where provided by Act of Parliament;
    (d) The length of notice required to terminate the employment;
    (e) the title of the employee's job
6. A note:

(*a*) specifying or indicating the availability of any disciplinary rules applying to the employee;

(*b*) describing persons to whom application can be made if the employee is dissatisfied with any disciplinary action relating to him and to whom an application can be made to seek redress respecting any grievance arising out of his employment, together with the way in which the application should be made and any further steps required to be followed.

7. In the case of a fixed term contract, the date of termination of the contract.

Particulars relating to disciplinary and grievance procedures do not include those relating to health and safety at work.

If there is any change in the conditions outlined above the employer must inform the employee in writing of that change within one month of the change taking effect.

If an employer fails to comply with any of the provisions of *s*.1, an employee affected must apply to an Industrial Tribunal who will determine what the terms should have been and the employee can then regard these as served upon him.

It is not necessary for the employer to give a detailed account of every particular. In fact, it is sufficient if, in the written notice, he draws the employee's attention to the existence of documents which contain the necessary information. On the other hand, where no provision for a fundamental particular is made, for example, provision for pension, this must be stated.

The provisions of *s*.1 Employment Protection (Consolidation) Act do not apply to the following employees:

1. Those who normally work less than 16 hours weekly.
2. Those employed by the Crown.
3. Those employed wholly or mainly outside Great Britain.
4. Those who are employed for less than 13 weeks.
5. Those who are related to the employer, i.e. father, mother, wife, son or daughter.

Employment in the hotel and catering trade is greatly affected by one of the above exemptions. The employment of temporary and seasonable labour in the field is quite considerable. An employee engaged in a temporary capacity will often work less than an average of 16 hours weekly. In such cases the agreement resulting in employment will be an oral one, including the periods to be worked. Seasonal employment is necessary to supplement permanent staff during peak sessions at holiday resorts and tourist centres. There is no doubt that seasonal employees, in most cases, work in excess of sixteen hours per week average, and after thirteen weeks must be supplied with 'written particulars' even though it is understood that the duration of the contract is of a limited nature. These circumstances are dealt with by the insertion of a clause in the 'written particulars' or the original written contract, if there is one, showing that it has been agreed that the employment is of a 'seasonal nature' and can be terminated when the need for it ceases to exist.

However, *s.*3 of the Employment Protection (Consolidation) Act provides that where an employee who has normally worked sixteen hours per week alters his contractual relationship with his employer so that he continues to work normally for less than sixteen hours but more than eight hours per week, his employer shall, for twenty six weeks, treat him in accordance with the written particulars originally served upon him under *s.*1 of the Act. Provision is also made that *s.*1 of the Act will apply to employees who are governed by a contract which normally involves less than sixteen hours but eight or more hours weekly who have been continuously employed for a period of five years or more.

STATUTORY RIGHTS ARISING OUT OF THE CONTRACT OF EMPLOYMENT

As soon as the contract of employment is agreed, the employee becomes entitled to certain rights and protections provided for him by statutes such as the Offices, Shops and Railway Premises Act 1963, the Health and Safety at Work Act 1974, the Race Relations Act 1976, the Sex Discrimination Act 1975 etc. and the Employment Protection (Consolidation) Act 1978. We are concerned here with the last Act. The provisions of the other Acts are discussed at a later stage in the book.

Concerning pay

The Employment Protection (Consolidation) Act 1978 provides for guarantee payments, payment whilst suspended from work on medical grounds and maternity payment. In each case the employee concerned, to benefit, has to fulfill certain conditions. With regard to the first two, the employee must have been employed for more than four weeks, not be the husband or wife of the employer, and normally have worked for sixteen hours per week, or more than eight hours per week after five years continuous employment. In relation to suspension on medical grounds, no payment will accrue when the employee is otherwise incapable of work because of physical or mental illness or has not made himself reasonably available for work. In the third case relating to maternity pay, the employee must have been continuously employed for two years or more up to the eleventh week before the estimated time of confinement. The calculation of the two years period does not include any week of less than sixteen hours or eight weeks after five years continuous employment.

1. *Guarantee Payment*

*s.*12 of the Act provides that where an employee is not provided with work during any part of a day in which he would be required to work according to his contract of employment because

(*a*) there has been a diminution in the requirements of his employer's business for the kind of work which the employee is employed to do, or

(*b*) there are other occurrences affecting the normal working of the business in relation to that kind of work,

he shall be entitled to a guarantee payment.

The formula for the calculation of the payment is based upon an hourly rate in relation to the weekly pay and allows up to £6·60 per day where there are hours without work. The number of complete day's pay are limited to five in one quarter of a year (quarters commencing on the first days of February, May, August and November). So a maximum of £30 guarantee payment is allowed each quarter.

Workless hours or days caused by work being unavailable due to any industrial dispute involving the employer or an associate employer are not subject to guarantee payment. Also the employee concerned may deny himself of his right if he unreasonably refuses suitable alternative employment or where he does not observe agreements made with his employer to make himself available for work.

The industrial tribunals have jurisdiction to determine disputes arising out of guarantee payments and can assess the amount to be paid by the employer in the particular circumstances.

Guarantee payments are not a new innovation. In the past Wages Council Orders have made similar provisions and such an order can, on application to the Secretary of State, take precedence over the new statutory provision.

2. *Payment whilst suspended from work on medical grounds*

A statutory provision or statutory instrument or even a code of practice resulting from the Health and Safety at Work Act 1974 can contain a provision compelling an employer, in certain circumstances which could be a risk to the health or safety of his employees, to suspend the affected employees from work until the risk is eliminated.

*s.*19 of the Act provides that an employee suspended from work in these circumstances shall be entitled to be paid a remuneration by his employer for the period of suspension up to twenty six weeks. Suspension in this context means that the employee in his continued employment with his employer is not provided with work or does not perform the work he normally did before the suspension. The remuneration is not available to an employee who has been offered suitable alternative employment which he has reasonably refused or if he does not comply with reasonable requirements laid down by his employer with regard to his availability for work.

The remuneration to be paid is a normal week's wage, i.e. that related to his normal hours of working.

3. *Maternity Payment*

*s.*33 of the Act provides than an employee who is absent from work wholly or partly because of pregnancy shall, subject to other provisions of the Act, be entitled to be paid by her employer a sum to be known as maternity pay and be entitled to return to work. We are here concerned with maternity pay; the right to return to work is discussed later (p. 120).

The entitled period is limited to six weeks and she must continue in employment until the beginning of the eleventh week before the calculated week of confinement. Three weeks notice of her intended absence must be given to her employer or, in emergency cases, as soon as is possible.

The payment is calculated as nine tenths of her normal week's pay but account is taken of any maternity allowance she is paid out of public resources.

As with redundancy payments (p. 114), the initial payments are made by her employer who eventually claims a refund from the public Maternity Fund which is maintained by contributions paid by the employer with the normal national insurance contributions.

Payments can be recovered directly from the Maternity Fund if the employee concerned can show that, despite all reasonable approaches made by her, the employer has not paid, or that the employer has become insolvent. Where the Secretary of State is of the opinion that the employer's default in payment was unreasonable, he may recover from the employer an amount which he considers to be appropriate in the circumstances, but not exceeding the amount of the relevant maternity pay. The sum recovered is paid into the Maternity Fund.

Time off work

The 1978 Act makes provision giving employees the right to take time off work to carry out certain specified activities, *viz.*

1. *To carry out trade union duties*

s.27 gives an employee, who is an official of an independent trade union recognised by his employer, the right to expect that his employer will allow him time off work in order that he can carry out his official duties concerning industrial relations between his employer or any associated employer and their employees, or to attend any course of training relating to industrial training and relevant to those duties and approved by the Trade Unions Congress or his own union.

The time off must be with pay but, the period allowed is negotiable. The Code of Practice in referring to this simply mentions 'reasonable time off'.

2. *To carry out trade union activities*

s.28 relates to the right of employees, ordinary members of a recognised trade union, to expect their employer to allow them to take time off from work for trade union activities. This, of course, does not apply to industrial action. No entitlement to pay accompanies this right and the extent of the time off allowed is, according to the Code of Practice, what is reasonable in the circumstances.

3. *To carry out public duties*

s.29 provides that an employer shall permit time off to employees to perform duties in connection with the holding of a specified public office. Such offices are justice of the peace, councillors of local authorities, members of tribunals, school or college governors, members of health and water authorities. The period of time off is again within the discretion of the employer but must be reasonable and payment is not mandatory. Unreasonable refusal to allow time off can be the subject of a complaint to an industrial tribunal.

DISCRIMINATION IN EMPLOYMENT

On grounds of race

The Race Relations Act 1976 makes it unlawful for an employer or any person concerned with the employment of others to discriminate against another person:

1. if he is seeking employment, by refusing or deliberately omitting to employ him on work of any description which is available and for which he is qualified or
2. if he is employed or seeking employment or work of any description, by refusing or deliberately omitting to afford or offer him similar terms of employment, similar conditions of work, and similar opportunities for training and promotion as he makes available for other employees who are similarly qualified or
3. if he is employed on work of any description, by dismissing him in circumstances in which the other employees doing the same kind of work are not dismissed. (s.4)

It is not only the employer who is caught by this section. It also refers to 'any person concerned with the employment of others' and so includes hotel managers, head-waiters and other such persons.

A person discriminates against another on racial grounds if he treats that person less favourably than others, or imposes conditions on him which because of his racial origins he is less likely to be able to fulfil and which are not justified.

It is also unlawful for an employer who hires staff from an agency to discriminate against such staff in their working conditions.

It is not unlawful however to select a person of a racial group if 'the job involves working in a place where food or drink is provided to and consumed by members of the public in a particular setting for which in that job a person of that racial group is required for reasons of authenticity' (*s.*5). The classic example is, of course, the Chinese restaurant employing Chinese chefs and waiters. Nor is it regarded as unlawful if there is discrimination but it is done in good faith in order to achieve an integration of nationalities.

Complaints against racial discrimination in employment are dealt with in the same way as complaints against sexual discrimination (see below). In addition, the Commission for Racial Equality may issue a 'non-discrimination' notice against the employer requiring him to stop committing the discriminating acts.

The Sex Discrimination Act 1975
(Throughout the text, discrimination against a woman is used as an example but the rules apply equally to discrimination against a man.)

This Act makes unlawful:-
1. Discrimination on the grounds of sex in the field of employment.
2. Discrimination against a married person on the grounds of her marital status in the field of employment.
3. Victimisation.

Sex discrimination and marital discrimination can be direct or indirect. Speaking generally, a person directly discriminates against another when he treats her less favourably on the grounds of her sex and marital status: he would treat her better if she were a man or if she were unmarried. A person indirectly discriminates against another where he imposes conditions or requirements for a job which make it difficult or impossible for her to perform the job and where such conditions or requirements are not really necessary e.g., a 'six foot tall chef'—there are not so many women as men who are six feet tall and in any case, height has no bearing upon the qualities of a chef.

Sex discrimination and marital discrimination both direct and indirect apply to the field of employment. Thus:-
1. When recruiting an employee there must be no discrimination
   (*a*) in the arrangements an employer makes for determining who shall be offered a job—advertisements and application forms must be carefully worded, interviews and

selection must be conducted with care. (It is preferable to keep a record of questions asked at the interview.)

(*b*) in the terms on which employment is offered e.g. generally, pay, hours of work etc.

(*c*) by deliberately omitting to offer the job to the woman, e.g. where the woman is the more suitable candidate.

2. With regard to existing employees women must be treated equally with men when offering opportunities for promotion, transfer or training: similarly with fringe benefits. There must be no unfavourable treatment of a woman, e.g. by dismissing her, in circumstances where one would not have dismissed a man. In *McLean v. Paris Travel* (1976) a female clerk was dismissed because she married the assistant manager, but her husband was not dismissed. She was awarded damages.

NB (1) Special treatment is allowed to women re maternity leave, and an equality clause does not operate to terms in relation to death or retirement.

(2) Jobs which carry a genuine occupational qualification are exempt from the sex discrimination rules e.g. cloakroom attendant.

(3) Employers will be responsible if they instruct their employees to act contrary to the Act and the employers will be held vicariously liable if the act is in the course of the employee's employment.

When a woman feels that she has been discriminated against, she may write to her employer and ask him to reply to her questions (special forms are available for this purpose). The answers will help her to decide whether she has a good case against him and can be used at the hearing. She then places her complaint before an industrial tribunal within three months of the act complained of.

Every endeavour is made to settle the dispute amicably with the help of a conciliation officer but if that fails, the claim goes to a hearing. The remedies available, if the case is proved are any or all of the following:

1. To declare the rights of the parties.
2. To recommend that the employer takes certain action to obviate or reduce the effect of his discrimination.
3. To grant compensation to the injured party.

Equal Pay Act 1970 (as amended by Sex Discrimination Act 1975)

The purpose of this Act is to end discrimination between men and women with regard to pay and work opportunities and to ensure that men and women who are employed on similar work will have terms and conditions of work which are equally favourable to them.

It applies to both men and women (although examples given below refer to women). It covers employment contracts or contracts for services. What must be appreciated is that it is *not* confined to pay but covers all the terms of the employment contract, e.g. holidays, sick leave etc.

The Act implies an equality clause into the contract of every woman employed at an establishment in Great Britain when such a clause is not already expressly included *s*. 1 (1). An equality clause is 'a provision which relates to terms (whether concerned with pay or not)'.

If the woman's contract includes a term of similar kind to the man's (e.g. to pay her a wage) but her term is less favourable than his (e.g. to pay her less than him) then the woman's contract is modified so that her pay will be increased to his level. *s*. 1 (4). In *Sorline v. Trust Houses Forte* (1979) waitresses who were employed in a hotel restaurant doing the same work as a waiter were paid 85p per hour in comparison with his wage of 97½p per hour. The employees attempted to avoid paying the increases to the women when the Equal Pay Act came into force by promoting the waiter to the post of banqueting supervisor: there was a difference in time of one week between the Equal Pay Act coming into force and the waiter being promoted. The Industrial Tribunal modified the women's contracts to increase their pay to 97½p per hour and the Court held that once the modification had occurred it was not right to return their pay to the original figure after the waiter had been promoted.

Again, any beneficial clause which is included in his agreement but not hers will be implied into her agreement. These rules apply only in two situations, namely, where she is employed on 'like work' and work 'rates as equivalent' with that of a man in the same employment. (There is nothing to stop an employer paying a man more for a different job even though it is less responsible than a woman's.) 'Like work' means work in another job which is the same or of 'a broadly similar nature'. The difference in a job which is of a broadly similar nature must be of no practical importance.

A woman's job is 'rated as equivalent' with a man's if her job and his job have been given an equal value, in terms of the demand made on a worker under various headings (e.g. effort, skill, decision), on a job evaluation study. Up to this point, the emphasis is on the work she does. But even where a woman is doing like work or work rated as equivalent, her claim will fail if the employer can prove that 'the variation is genuinely due to a material difference (other than the difference of sex) between her case and his'. The emphasis now switches to the employee: so, if he has more experience or better qualifications than she then that is a material difference.

Normally the comparison when the claim is 'like work' or 'work rated as equivalent', is between employees in the same establishment, but it may extend to employees in different branches of the company if the employees have common terms and conditions of employment.

If certain categories of an employer's pay structure apply to men only and the women fall into a lower pay category, the Central Arbitration Committee may make a declaration that the higher rate of pay for the male workers shall apply to women workers as well. (Some employers try to evade this by stating that all categories are open to both men and women.) Wages Councils in the catering industry have written into their Orders provisions for equal pay so staff who are paid in accordance with such Orders are covered provided that their work grading is correct.

As with the Sex Discrimination Act, certain exceptions exist where the equality clause does not operate: women can be given special treatment in connection with pregnancy or childbirth, and may have different death and retirement benefits.

A claim under the Act goes to an industrial tribunal. A claim only lies if the woman has been in the employment of the employer within the six months preceding the date of the reference. The maximum that can be recovered by way of arrears of remuneration or damages is limited to an amount in relation to a time of two years before the date on which the proceedings were instituted.

TERMINATION OF CONTRACT OF SERVICE

The special nature of a contract of service allows it to be

terminated in ways additional to those which apply to contracts in general.

By giving notice

The contract may be terminated by either party giving notice to the other. The length of notice must be stated in the initial contract and the 'written particulars' when issued, and although the subject of agreement cannot be less than the minimum laid down in *s*.4 of the Employment Protection (Consolidation) Act 1978. The Act provides a table of periods tied to the lengths of service of the employees.

1. The notice to be given to an employer to terminate the contract of employment of a person who has beeen continuously employed for four weeks or more:

(*a*) shall not be less than one week if his period of continuous employment is less than two years, and

(*b*) shall not be less than one week's notice for each year of continuous employment if his period of continuous employment is two years or more but less than twelve years, and

(*c*) shall not be less than twelve weeks notice if his period of continuous employment is twelve years or more.

2. The notice required to be given by an employee who has been continuously employed for four weeks or more to terminate his contract shall not be less than one week.

3. *s*.53 of the Act provides that where an employee has been continuously employed for a period of twenty six weeks, and his contract is terminated (a) with notice, (b) without notice or (c) an agreed fixed term of employment expires without being renewed, he can request that his employer should supply him, within fourteen days of the application, with a written statement giving reasons for his dismissal.

The agreement can cater for periods different from the above, but these will be recognised only if they are longer periods. If shorter periods are agreed, these will give way to the statutory minimum.

Very often the agreement will provde that the notice to be given by the employee is the same as that to be given by the employer.

It will have been noticed that the qualifying service for any length of service must be continuous. This means that in general the employee must have worked for an average of more than sixteen hours each week for the unbroken period of time required. Schedules 13 and 14 of the Employment Protection (Consolidation) Act 1978 provides details for the calculation of continuous employment and provides exceptions to the general rule. Briefly, the period or its continuity is not broken when there is absence from work because of sickness or injury, and where the employee is on strike, the continuity is not affected, but any week during which he is on strike is excluded in calculating the qualifying period for a particular length of notice.

One important provision relating to the computation of periods of employment arises from paragraph 6 of Schedule 13 of the 1978 Act. Where an employee has worked under a contract of employment requiring normally sixteen hours or more per week and then after five years of conformity with this contract, with the agreement of his employer, continues to work at a reduced weekly period of eight hours or more, he shall be treated as though he had at all times worked sixteen or more hours weekly.

The statutory minimum periods of notice do not apply to those employees who are not qualified to enjoy the provisions of the 1978 Act, for example, temporary staff, in some cases seasonal staff and those whose period of employment is less than four weeks.

However, in these cases the courts, where the matter is in issue, insist upon a reasonable period of notice and will decide what is appropriate after having considered the facts in each individual case. It will take into consideration such factors as the length of the wage period which is normally taken as the reasonable notice period or what is customary in the particular trade; but this latter would normally be used only in the absence of other positive factors.

In *Richardson v. Koefod* (1969) the respondent had been employed by the appellant as manageress of his cafe. It was agreed that she would be paid monthly and that her contract could be terminated by notice as provided in the Contracts of Employment Act 1963. The employer terminated the contract after seven weeks by giving the manageress one month's salary in lieu of notice. She sued for wrongful dismissal and the issue was eventually heard in the court of Appeal which held that her dismissal was in no way wrongful. She had worked for less than twenty-six weeks (the initial qualifying period in 1969) and in these circumstances one month's notice was reasonable.

Wages in lieu of notice

It is recognised that an employer can give the equivalent wage in lieu of notice. The employee, however, cannot expect to receive more than his agreed wage. The employer is not bound to include emoluments that were given over and above the agreed wage, for example, lodging allowance, car allowance and *ex gratia* bonuses.

Expiration of an agreed term

The contract can be one in which it is agreed that employment will exist for a stated period, for example, one month or two months, etc. In such cases the contract will come to an end at the end of the stipulated period without the need to give any length of notice; the period of employment is a fundamental condition of the contract and is satisfied upon its expiration. On the other hand, dismissal without good cause before the expiring date arrives will constitute a breach of contract.

Termination for breach of contract

A total breach of the contract by either the employee or the employer will allow the other party summarily to terminate the employment. The breach must, however, be one which completely undermines the original purpose of the contract.

The employer may summarily dismiss the employee in the following circumstances.

Misconduct. What is misconduct depends entirely upon the facts of each case. Generally it is that behaviour which fundamentally impairs the employee's recognised performance of his work. Whether or not the behaviour would warrant summary dismissal is dependent upon the standard of duty expected of the employee and his degree of responsibility within the employing organisation. The degree of careful behaviour expected increases with the degree of responsibility carried by the employee. Summary dismissal for this cause is, in general, confined to the performance of duties inside working hours, but occasionally it can be good grounds for dismissal when performed outside working hours if the trustworthiness of the employee with respect to his employment is, as a consequence, automatically questioned.

Wilful disobedience. Wilful disobedience can include an unwarranted refusal to obey a lawful order given by an employer or someone in a supervisory capacity or wilfully neglecting to carry out an agreed task appreciating that this conduct could result in loss or injury.

What is a lawful order in this context will depend entirely upon the contractual agreement. An employee can certainly refuse to do something which he recognises as being outside the law in general, but here the word 'lawful' is used in respect to its being consistent with the employee's recognised duties. He certainly can validly refuse to carry out an order which is not a part of those duties, or one which he recognises would endanger his life or health unless, of course, the nature of his work is such and he recognised this when he took up the employment.

Nevertheless, one simple act of disobedience is not sufficient to justify summary dismissal. There must be a major incident or a history of several refusals.

In *Laws v. London Chronicle* (1959) Miss Laws was employed as secretary to the manager of a department of the *London Chronicle*. She accompanied her boss to a meeting with the managing director of the newspaper. A quarrel developed between the two men and her immediate supervisor left the office. She started to follow him but was ordered by the managing director to remain. After a pause, she left the room. She was summarily dismissed by the managing director for disobeying a lawful order.

It was held that the act of the secretary was trivial and did not indicate a wish to terminate her contract. One single act of this nature was insufficient to warrant instant dismissal.

Incompetence. Incompetence will be a good reason for summary dismissal only when the employee obtained his employment by claiming competency in the relevant field. So an employee cannot be summarily dismissed if he shows a lack of ability in a field of work he never claimed he was able to do.

Illness. Normally the contract or the written particulars will contain details of the effect of illness upon the contract of employment. In the absence of any positive statement the Common Law position in this circumstance must be taken into account. In order to apply the Common Law correctly the facts of each case must be taken into consideration, for example, the length of the engagement, the time elapsed since it started, the expected duration of the illness and whether or not there is someone employed by the same employer who can easily replace the sick person. Only when the employer can show that it was essential to employ a replacement to do the work will the court hold that termination of the employment was justified. Seldom, in the absence of this necessity, will the court find that the contract of employment has been frustrated.

In *Condor v. The Barron Knights Ltd* (1966) Condor, aged 16, was employed as a drummer by the group of musicians known as The Barron Knights. The agreement provided that for five years he would perform for them whenever he was directed and he was to devote all his time to serving them. The contract could be terminated, by six months' notice, by either side, except if Condor was in breach of his obligations or misconducted himself. Condor collapsed through over-work and was ordered by his doctor to limit his appearances with the group to three or four nights a week instead of seven as agreed. The group, the employers, decided that it was not practicable to employ a substitute drummer for the other nights of the week and dismissed Condor summarily.

The court held that the summary dismissal was justified.

In *Story v. Fulham Steel Work Co.* (1907) Story was employed on a five-year contract. He became ill after two years and was absent from work for five months. His employers dispensed with his services. The court decided that, in the circumstances, the employers had no good reason for discharging the contract.

In the latter case the contract could not, in the absence of justified cause, be terminated before the end of the agreed five years. In a contract of service subject to notice an employer can always end the relationship by giving the appropriate period of notice.

Frustration. A contract of service must obviously end when either party, for some reason, is incapable of performing his obligations, for example, if the employee is convicted and sentenced to imprisonment; obviously if he dies; and in the case of an employer in the form of a partnership or a corporate body, i.e. a company, if there is a dissolution of the former or a liquidation of the latter.

When a business is sold to another concern the contracts of its employees will not be immediately terminated. Employees, unless they re-assign their services to the new owner, are entitled to pay in lieu of their notice entitlement.

The employee has a corresponding right to terminate his contract without notice:

1. Where the employer has been guilty of misconduct, e.g. improper advances towards a female employee.

2. Where the employment has caused the employee to become ill and a return to work would be detrimental to his health.
3. When the employer has neglected to carry out his obligations under the contract.

If the employee leaves his employment without giving the required notice and not having good cause as authorised above, theoretically he can be sued by his employer for breach of contract. Whether it would be profitable for the employer to maintain such an action is a matter of fact; most employees would be men of straw, and to commence litigation would be a waste of time. Nevertheless, a delinquent employee would not be able to claim wages or benefits such as accrued holiday remuneration for the part of the agreed wage period which he had completed before he summarily terminated his employment.

REDUNDANCY

Part VI of the Employment Protection (Consolidation) Act 1978 makes provisions for payment of redundancy compensation to an employee who loses his employment through no fault on his part. Previous to the 1965 Redundancy Payments Act, in general, the employee would only receive unemployment benefit.

A statutory obligation is now placed upon an employer to make a redundancy payment to his employee who becomes unemployed because of redundancy, who is laid off work or who is kept on short time.

The Act, as is the case respecting other statutes concerning employment, applies only to persons employed under a contract of service and who, in the case of a male is under sixty-five and in the case of a female is under sixty years. Excluded from the provisions of the Act are Crown servants; employees employed in a domestic capacity in a private household by their father, mother, grandfather, grandmother, stepfather, stepmother, son, daughter, grandson, granddaughter, stepson, stepdaughter, brother, sister, half brother, half sister, or in all types of employment where the employer is the husband or wife of the employee; employees working less than sixteen hours per week (less than eight hours after completing five years at more than sixteen hours per week); employees under a contract for a period of two years or more in which it is agreed that there shall be no claim to redundancy benefits; and employees who have agreed a private redundancy scheme with their employers which has governmental approval. Disputes relating to redundancy can be referred to Industrial Tribunals.

Dismissal

Dismissal by reason of redundancy is presumed to exist if the dismissal can be attributed wholly or mainly to the fact that:

1. the employer has ceased or intends to cease, to carry on business for the purpose for which the employee was employed, or has ceased, or intends to cease, to carry on that business, in the place where the employee was employed;
2. the requirements of the business for the employee to carry out work of a particular kind, or of a particular kind in the place where he was employed, has ceased or diminished or is expected to cease or diminish.

The employer can plead that although the circumstances outlined above exist he should not pay redundancy payment because he has shown a willingness to retain the service of his employee in conditions different from those which originally existed, i.e.:

(a) *At a different place.* Whether or not the offer of similar employment at a different place can amount to redundancy depends upon the disturbance caused to the employee and can only be determined by examining the facts of each case and the presence or absence of relevant conditions in each individual contract of service.

In *R. H. McCulloch v. Moore* (1967) the South Eastern Gas Board in Sussex resolved that it no longer could provide work for a semi-skilled employee at that place but offered him alternative employment in Reading, the East Midlands or Scotland. He refused to move. The tribunal held that his dismissal was due to redundancy.

On the other hand, in *Noquet v. Essex Publishing Co. Ltd* (1966) the applicant was informed by her employers that the office where she worked in Walthamstow was being closed and that she would, in the future, work at new premises about two miles away. She refused and her employment came to an end. She claimed a redundancy payment.

The tribunal decided that the termination was not a dismissal but a transfer of employment. The applicant had left because her personal circumstances made the transfer not to her liking.

However, personal circumstances have been taken into consideration. In *Cahuac v. Allen Amery Ltd* (1966) an offer of employment to women working at premises in Hackney, London E.2, in a similar capacity in premises in E.C.1., a forty minutes' journey from their homes, was held by the tribunal to be unsuitable; with regard to one of the women, the fact that she had to care for her widowed mother at home was taken into consideration. Similarly, in *White and Others v. John Boulding Ltd* (1966), a married woman's refusal to move because it would break up her marriage was accepted as reasonable.

(*b*) *Change in the type of work.* Slight changes in the type of work cannot be interpreted as a dismissal from the former type of employment and so qualify for redundancy payment. However, again, each case must be judged upon its facts.

In *Cooper v. Fiat (England) Ltd* (1966) the applicant was employed in a fragmented capacity; about one-third of his time was spent as a 'body-work inspector' whilst the remainder of his time was spent driving and on body-finishing work. He was told by his employers that in future he would work entirely as a body finisher; and he would continue to receive the same rate of pay and benefits. He refused the offer and when dismissed claimed a redundancy payment. It was held by the tribunal that he had acted unreasonably in refusing the offer. The work which he had been offered was substantially similar to his former work and was therefore suitable.

In cases where the character of work is changed the Act in *s.*2 requires that such an offer of alternative employment must be made in writing and as can be seen from the above cases, if it is suitable and refused without good reason, the payment of redundancy money cannot be demanded. The employee has the task of proving that the offered employment is not suitable for him at the time when the offer was made. In determining suitability or otherwise a tribunal will take into account travelling alterations, family circumstances, affect upon the employee's health, diminution in wages, etc.

In all cases of dismissal it is the intention of the Act that a presumption will subsist that the cause of the dismissal was through redundancy. Initially, the burden of disproving this lies upon the employer. If he disposed of the services of an employee for some other reason, for example, misconduct, it is up to him to prove it. If there is any evidence of his business declining or being about to be moved to another location the employee is usually in a relatively strong position, unless of course it can be shown that he has, without good reason, refused suitable alternative employment.

(*c*) *After confinement.* Where a woman is entitled to return to work after her confinement and is denied her right to exercise this entitlement, she will be treated as though she was dismissed and entitled to redundancy payment, and employed for the purpose of calculating such payment up to the notified date of return.

In general, the employee who gives notice to terminate his employment does not qualify for redundancy money, but if he can show that he had good reason for taking his action, for example, because of his employer's misconduct or because he has been subjected to 'short time' working or 'lay off', he will retain his redundancy pay entitlement.

Reduction in agreed working hours

1. *Short time.* An employee is considered to be on short time if his working hours are reduced so that he receives less than one half of his ordinary weekly pay.
2. *Lay off.* An employee will be taken to be laid off in respect of any week during which he is not provided with the work which he requires to earn his pay.

If he has been subject to short-time working or has been laid off for four or more consecutive weeks or six or more weeks (of which not more than three were consecutive) within thirteen weeks, he is entitled to give notice terminating his employment without prejudice to his redundancy entitlement. The calculation of the periods must be up to the date when the notice is given.

Employer's counter-notice

The employer can at this stage serve a counter-notice upon the employee to avoid liability to pay redundancy. The notice must contain an assurance that employment and pay will be available to the employee in the future. If that assurance promises a reasonable expectation that, if he continues in his employment, the employee would within the next four weeks 'enter upon a period of employment of not less than thirteen weeks during which he would not be laid-off or kept on short time for any week,' the employee will not receive redundancy payment if he refuses to withdraw his notice.

Change of employer

A contract of employment cannot be assigned to another employer at Common Law without the consent of the employee concerned. The termination of the contract in these circumstances is regarded as a dismissal which would qualify for redundancy payment. The 1978 Act, however, makes provisions for amalgamations, reorganisations and take-overs. In these events, in order that the transferred employment should come within these provisions, the employing business must be transferred in its entirety as a going concern, including plant, customers and employees.

Section 94 of the Act provides that if the transfer of the business is a complete handing over as above, although theoretically the existing contracts of service are terminated at the time of transfer, if an employee agrees the new owner can renew the contract and this will be recognised as a continuity of the former contract. However, if the employee refuses the renewal of his contract without good reason, he will lose his entitlement to redundancy payment.

Redundancy payments

Redundancy payment is available to employees who have completed at least 104 weeks' employment but the period of time upon which calculation is based commences from the applicant's eighteenth birthday or afterwards. The total redundancy payment is calculated by taking account of the employee's length of continuous service and the rate which the Act provides according to his age and normal salary:

1. For each year completed before the age of twenty-one years (inclusive) the employee will receive one half of his normal weekly wage.
2. For each year between the ages of twenty-two and forty (inclusive), one week's pay.
3. For each year between the ages of forty-one and sixty-four (fifty-nine in the case of women) (inclusive), one and a half weeks' pay.

The maximum period over which a calculation can be made is twenty years and weekly pay in excess of £110 is not taken into account. Therefore the maximum redundancy payment which can be obtained is that in respect of an employee who has completed twenty years' service from the age of forty-one at a salary at or in excess of £100 per week, i.e., £3300 free of income tax. Whether overtime payment will be considered where £110 per week is not exceeded depends upon the terms of the contract. It will be included in the calculation only when overtime is compulsory.

Continuous service

The fact of continuous service is again important and is defined in the same way as for the purposes of the 1978 Act. As the calculation of the redundancy payment is based upon the total service of the employee a few details must be noted.

1. Absence due to sickness or injury up to a limit of twenty-six weeks does not break the continuity of the employment or cause a reduction in the time actually worked.
2. Strike action does not break the continuity of service, but the time during which the employee is on strike is deducted from the period of time which represents his employment with the employer concerned.
3. Temporary lay-offs caused, for example, by strike action in another sector of employment which affects the supply of materials necessary for work to continue and also, of course, holidays, do not break the continuity.
4. Absence of a female employee because of her pregnancy or confinement does not break continuity.
5. Continuity of employment is based upon the employee being employed for at least sixteen hours in each week (eight hours after five years).

In *Kincey v. Pardey and Johnson Ltd* (1966) Mrs Kincey was employed in a sub-post office for seven years until January 1966. She worked on a two-week system, i.e. Mondays, Wednesdays and Fridays, between 9 a.m. and 5.30 p.m. during one week and Tuesdays and Saturdays between 9 a.m. and 5.30 p.m. and Thursday between 9 a.m. and 1 p.m. in the second week. She was allowed a lunch period of one hour on the days she worked until 5.30 p.m.

Therefore during one week she worked twenty-two and a half hours and nineteen hours in the other. It was held by the tribunal that, because of the nineteen-hour week, she had not been continuously employed and was not entitled to redundancy payment when the sub-post office was closed down and her employment ceased.

It must be noted that the Redundancy Payments Act 1965 which governed the situation at that time, required a minimum of twenty one hours per week.

Administration

Each employer has to pay a contribution, additional to national insurance contributions, in respect of every male and female on his staff. The payments are in the first place collected by the Department of Health and Social Security and then passed over to the Department of Employment who maintains a special redundancy fund.

When an employee becomes entitled to redundancy payment he is initially paid by his own employer who may then claim a rebate from the fund. Schedule 6 of the 1978 Act has provided that the rebates are 123/200 of a week's pay for each year of employment from the age of forty-one until one year before redundancy, 41/100 of a week's pay from forty to twenty-two and 41/200 of a week's pay from twenty-one to eighteen.

The Department of Employment and Productivity must be informed of the redundancy in advance, otherwise the employee might not receive the full rebate.

If the employer refuses to pay redundancy money the employee can apply directly to the Minister who, if he is satisfied that the employee is entitled to the payment, can make that payment to him. In such circumstances, if the Minister considers that the employer has failed to pay without good reason, the rebate can be withheld in whole or in part and the employer can be made to reimburse the fund.

The Minister can also pay redundancy money directly to an employee who has lost his employment because of his employer's insolvency.

UNFAIR DISMISSAL

An employee who has been dismissed without sufficient cause or, by reason of redundancy, has the right to claim compensation. In the case of wrongful dismissal, the employee can institute an action for damages in the High Court, but the assessment of the compensation awarded will take into account whether or not he has taken reasonable steps to mitigate his loss. In *Brace v. Calder* (1895), Brace who was employed by a firm of solicitors operating as partners, claimed that an alteration in the partnership members operated as a termination of his contract of employment. The new partnership offered to re-engage him on the terms which had prevailed before, but he refused. The court held that although the dissolving of the former partnership operated as a breach of contract, he had refused to minimise, that is, to reduce his loss. He was awarded nominal damages only.

Schedule 4 of the 1978 Act provides the scale of compensation when it is established by the courts or tribunals that dismissal was due to redundancy. (See page 114.)

The now repealed Industrial Relations Act 1971 provided a further right of action based upon 'unfair dismissal' in the industrial tribunals. The Trade Union and Labour Relations Act 1974 re-enacted this provision in its First Schedule with amendments, and the Industrial Tribunals (Labour Relations) Regulations 1974 replaced the procedure, provided by the Industrial Relations Act, to be used in the industrial tribunals.[1] These provisions are now consolidated in the Employment Protection (Consolidation) Act 1978. The purpose of this remedy is to safeguard employees against arbitrary dismissal, that is, dismissal in which, although the formalities of the pre-1971 law have been observed, for example, by the giving of sufficient notice or for good cause, it is held that the employer has acted unreasonably in the circumstances.

The meaning of dismissal

A dismissal within the meaning of the provision means:

(*a*) a termination of the contract of employment by the employer with or without notice, or

(*b*) a termination of a contract of employment which is for a fixed term, at the expiration of that term, without there being an offer of a renewal, or

(*c*) a termination of the contract of employment by the employee, with or without notice where the circumstances are such that he was entitled to terminate it without notice because of the employer's conduct.

In the last category, the employee must show that the employer's conduct was such as to entitle him to leave or resign without giving notice. This is commonly known as constructive dismissal. In *Wales v. Caithness Leather Products* 1972, a supervisor lost his temper when reprimanding a female em-

[1] SI 1974/1386

ployee. She resigned. The industrial tribunal held that the supervisor's attitude and language far exceeded anything which was reasonable and that the resignation would be recognised as a constructive dismissal.

The employer's behaviour however must be such that resignation by the employee is recognised by the tribunal as enforced. In *Anderson v. Northgate Group* 1972, a waitress, who worked in the directors' dining room, was told that the room would, in future, operate on a self-service basis and that she would be employed in the executives' dining room a few yards away. She refused to obey these orders and resigned. The tribunal refused to recognise this as constructive dismissal; her application for compensation was refused.

But in *Hanlon v. Allied Breweries (UK) Ltd* 1975, Mrs Hanlon, a barmaid, was suspended from work for refusing to work under new conditions. The company failed to pay her for part of the period of suspension and she resigned. The tribunal held that in the circumstances, this amounted to a constructive dismissal.

In the first two categories, the burden of proving that the dismissal was fair rests upon the employer who must show the reason and establish that it is one which related to:

1. the capability or qualifications of the employee for performing the kind of work which he was employed to do, or
2. the conduct of the employee, or
3. the fact that the employee was redundant, or
4. that, because of a statutory provision, the employee could not continue in his employment without contravening it.

In the first group of reasons above, 'capability' means capability assessed by reference to skill, aptitude, health or any other physical or mental quality and 'qualifications' means any degree, diploma or other academic, technical or professional qualification relevant to the position held by the employee.

Fair or unfair dismissal

The industrial tribunal must decide the question of reasonableness or otherwise, in accordance with justice and the circumstances of the case and, in many cases which have so far been settled, it is obvious that, whilst tribunals have relied upon the Common Law and statutory provisions, that is, the Contracts of Employment Act 1972 and the Redundancy Payments Act 1965, (both now repealed), relating to dismissal, they have, when necessary, interpreted them in a way which shows a desire to conform with the expressed intention of the then existing *s*.1 of the Industrial Relations Act, that is, to improve industrial relations. In fact, the Act itself had provided that where proceedings are based upon both redundancy and unfair dismissal, the statutory presumption that a dismissal by an employer is attributable to redundancy unless the employer can show otherwise, will not be allowed to fetter the separate issue of unfair dismissal.

Inadmissible reason

The 1978 Act provides a term in unfair dismissal which it calls 'inadmissible reason'. This applies in a dismissal where the reason or the principal reason, if there are others, is based upon certain behaviour in connection with trade union membership or non-membership or in respect of activities connected with a trade union. The Act also includes within inadmissible reason, in certain circumstances, dismissal as a result of a lockout or a strike or other industrial action.

With regard to trade union membership, it is an inadmissible reason to dismiss an employee who:

(a) was, or proposed to become, a member of an independent trade union;

(b) had taken, or proposed to take, part at any appropriate time in the activities of an independent trade union; or

(c) had refused, or proposed to refuse to become or remain a member of a trade union which was not an independent trade union.

An independent trade union for the purposes of the Act is one which is not under the domination or control of an employer or a group of employers or one or more employers' associations; and is not liable to interference by an employer or any such group or association, arising out of the provision of financial or material support or by any other means which might suggest control of that union.

However, a special provision has been made for the situation in which there exists a union membership agreement, that is, that all employees of an employer or all employees of the same class should be members of a specified independent trade union or to be members of a number of specified independent trade unions. The dismissal of an employee because he is not a member or has refused to become or remain a member of such a

union is deemed by the Act to be fair unless the employee affected by the dismissal can adduce a genuine objection, based
upon religious belief or some other reasonable ground, to being
a member of that particular trade union.

The Act also includes within the meaning of inadmissible
reason, dismissal by way of lock-out unless the employee is
offered re-engagement as from the date of resumption of work
and dismissal of an employee because he was taking part in a
strike or other industrial action if it can be shown that one or
more of his fellow employees who took part in the strike were
not dismissed because of that participation or that other
employees who had been dismissed had been offered re-
employment. It must be shown, however, that the participation
in the strike or industrial action was the sole or principal reason
for the dismissal.

Recent legislation, now consolidated in the 1978 Act, has provided further grounds for unfair dismissal. This relates to the
dismissal of a woman because of her pregnancy or any other
reason arising out of the pregnancy except:

1. that at the date of the dismissal she is or would become, because of the pregnancy, incapable of adequately doing her
   contract work;
2. that her pregnancy will, if she is allowed to continue to work
   after the dismissal date, involve her or her employer in the
   contravention of a duty or restriction provided by any enactment.

The employer can however escape liability for unfair dismissal if he can show that before or on the date of dismissal an
offer was made of a new contract of employment involving
work of a kind suitable to the employee and her circumstances and that it is not substantially less favourable to her
with regard to capacity and place than that provided in her
previous contract. The employer is not obliged to make
such an offer if no suitable vacancy exists.

Unfair dismissal can also be claimed by an employee who
has been absent from work because of pregnancy or confinement and whose employer denies her the right to return to
work at any time before the termination of twenty-nine
weeks from the date of the confinement to refill her previous
job and on terms not less favourable than those which applied to her under her original contract of employment.

Complaint of unfair dismissal

An application for an examination of a complaint by a tribunal, which must be presented within three months of the dismissal or an extended time in excess of three months where the tribunal considers that it was not reasonably practical for the complaint to have been presented earlier, must first of all be scrutinised by a conciliation officer of the Department of Employment and Productivity. A considerable proportion of the cases are settled at this stage and are usually disposed of by:

1. re-engagement by the employer, or
2. a voluntary payment by the employer upon the employee agreeing to withdraw his complaint, or
3. a settlément which appears on the record of the tribunal, or
4. the conciliation officer being able to satisfy the employee that the circumstances of his case would not entitle him to compensation.

When a tribunal has to decide a case, it will give full consideration to the Code of Practice on Industrial Relations issued by the Department of Employment, especially the sections dealing with disciplinary procedures.

Experience of cases decided in the industrial tribunals when considering appropriate dismissal procedures gave rise to the publication of amended Codes of Practice for the guidance of employers and information for the employees. The current Code was issued in June, 1977. It must be regarded simply as a set of conventions to be observed by employers; they are not mandatory.

The main provisions of the current Code are:

1. A copy of the discipliniary code should be made available to all employees and it should be couched in specific terms and facilitate speedy disciplinary procedures.
2. Employees should be made aware of complaints made against them and allowed an opportunity to give their versions of the circumstances with the support of a trade union representative or a friend.
3. Before discipliniary action is taken every case should be fully investigated. Instant dismissal should not be allowed by immediate superiors; reference should be made to senior management.
4. A first breach of discipline should not warrant dismissal unless it amounts to gross misconduct.
5. A reason for the discipliniary action taken should be given to

the employee concerned and appeal procedures should be made available giving a disciplined employer an automatic and known right of appeal.

6. Where the discipliniary action will not involve dismissal, the employee should be given an oral warning or a written warning according to the severity of the offence.

7. Where the employee's working conditions are such that he is divorced from application of the normal procedures, special provision should be made, e.g. for employees working night shifts.

8. A delinquent trade union official should be given an oral warning only unless there has been prior consultation with a senior trade union official.

9. The commission of a criminal offence which has no direct effect upon the employment of the employee concerned should not normally be reason for dismissal.

One of the most important conventions in the Code is that the employee affected should always be given the opportunity to present his case before his employer makes the ultimate decision and that, where misconduct is the cause of a consideration of dismissal, one act of misconduct should be the subject of a warning in preference to dismissal. In *Earl v. Salter and Wheeler* (1973), it was held that an employee had been unfairly dismissed when that dismissal was due to bad workmanship but he had not been given the opportunity to state his case.

The same decision was given in the case of *Burrows v. Ace Caravan Co.* (1972), when an employee was dismissed for incompetence but successfully claimed that this was due to his employers' neglect in the provision of adequate training. Again in *Bendall v. Pain and Betteridge* (1973), even though the employee had been warned about his disobedience with respect to a regulation concerning smoking at work, it was held that he had been unfairly dismissed when he ignored the warning because it had never been specifically pointed out to him that the continuance of his conduct would lead to dismissal.

There is no doubt that the decisions which have flowed from 'unfair dismissal' cases have mitigated the relevant law of pre-1971. The desire to reflect the intention of the Industrial Relations Act in improving industrial relations has also influenced the decisions in cases which were not based upon unfair dismissal, for instance, in those where actions were brought because of redundancy dismissal or dismissal because of illness.

For example, in the case of *Marshall v. Harland and Wolff* (1972), it was held that a fitter who had been away from work for eighteen months due to illness was not to be considered to have had his contract terminated because of his lengthy illness and was thus entitled to redundancy payments when his employers closed the yard where he worked. A new principle regarding the position of a sick employee appeared in the judgment. Besides the recognised Common Law rules relating to sickness, the decision produced the notion that an employee who has been employed by the same employer for twenty years is entitled to a longer sickness absence than one whose period of employment is a matter of months and also, that such an employee whose original situation had had to be filled, might be put into a 'special holding' department by his employer with the intention that every effort would be made to re-engage him when he returned to work.

On the question of illness, there is also the case of *Burdekin v. Dolan Corrugated Containers* (1972), in which a woman who was employed to make tea was dismissed when she had been away from work through sickness for two months with no certainty when she would return. The tribunal decided that this amounted to unfair dismissal and recommended that she should be re-engaged at a specified date two months from the date of the hearing.

Where misconduct is the reason for dismissal the tribunal must be satisfied that it was serious and related to the work of the employee concerned. Thus in *Comerford v. Swel Foods* (1972), it was held that dismissal was justified in the case of an employee who, to his knowledge, allowed the machine for which he was responsible to continue to operate with a fault with the result that the food which it produced was spoilt.

On the other hand, in *Rosenthal v. Butler* (1972), it was decided that an employee who had used bad language to a foreman had been unfairly dismissed when his services had been terminated without his having been warned respecting his conduct. This decision was upheld in *Wilson v. Racher* (1974) when the Court of Appeal held that the use of bad language was insufficient to warrant summary dismissal. In this case a gardener had used bad language towards his employer with whom he had never really been on good terms and the court held that such a case involving a gentleman and a competent gardener in the circumstances should be considered against the principle adopted in *Laws v. London Chronicle Ltd* (1959); 'one act of disobedience or misconduct can justify dismissal only if it is of the nature which goes to show (in effect) that the servant is repudiating the contract or one of its essential conditions'.

The misconduct of an employee outside working hours must also be established as such as will affect his job to warrant a fair dismissal. In *Robb v. Mersey Insulation Co* (1972) it was held that a conviction of theft justified the dismissal of a dock-worker because his retention might detrimentally affect his employer's business.

For another reason a conviction can be recognised as a reason for fair dismissal. In *Appleyard v. Smith* (1972), a driver, on conviction, lost his driving licence. He could not continue to drive for his employers without contravening the relevant provisions of the Road Traffic Acts, and they could not continue to employ him in any other capacity. It was held that his dismissal was fair.

In the trade with which we are concerned, very often employment is dependent upon a man and wife joint participation. In such situations the case of *Henry v. Scottish Liberal Club* (1977) is interesting. Mr and Mrs Hendry were employed as joint managers of the club. The club management received a number of complaints about the performance and attitude of Mr Hendry. There were no complaints against Mrs Hendry. A subcommittee of the club considered the complaints and also took into consideration a past conviction based upon Mr Hendry having possessed drugs. They decided that Mr Hendry should be dismissed and that in the circumstances Mrs Hendry's dismissal was inevitable. A full committee of the club confirmed the dismissals and here the 'spent' conviction was again mentioned. The industrial tribunal held that the 'spent' conviction had to some degree influenced the club's decision and that the dismissal of Mr Hendry was unfair and consequently that of Mrs Hendry was unfair. It however appears to be reasonable to suppose, that if the first dismissal had been judged to be fair, where the employment is joint, the misconduct by one partner can be treated as a valid reason for the dismissal of the other.

Bearing in mind the tolerance which has been shown in respect of dismissal cases since the Industrial Relations Act, it would be interesting to speculate about the possible outcome, if examined in the present climate, of the circumstances of *Vaux v.*

Ward which was decided in 1969. In that case, the management of a public house dispensed with the services of a middle-aged barmaid and employed, instead, a young woman because it wanted to attract a younger type of customer. The tribunal decided that this was not a case of redundancy and of course did not, in 1970, have to decide the issues of unfair dismissal, which would, no doubt, be favourably considered at the present time.

Limitations governing a complaint

In general, in any application to the tribunal regarding unfair dismissal, the application must be shown to comply with the recognised qualifying conditions provided in the 1978 Act, that is, he or she must be below the statutory retirement age, (sixty-five years in the case of a man and sixty years in the case of a woman), or an agreed earlier retirement age and that he or she had been continuously employed for a qualifying period. The Act also made arrangements to allow the qualifying period of employment to gradually reduce from the 104 weeks required by the Industrial Relations Act to 52 weeks for the six months following the adoption of its unfair dismissal provisions, and then to twenty-six weeks at the end of the six months' period. The 26 weeks period became operative from 16th March, 1975 and is now a provision of *s*.64 of the 1978 Act.

However, in the case of a dismissal based upon an inadmissible reason, the Act provides an exception to the general rule in that the age limit and continuous service conditions do not apply when redress is sought from a tribunal.

s.142 of the Act also makes special provisions with regard to dismissal from employment when the contract is for a fixed term. In contracts for a fixed term of two years or more, an agreement in writing with the employee concerned will preclude an unfair dismissal complaint when he is dismissed at the expiration of the agreed term without an offer of renewed employment being made.

With regard to the hotel and catering industry, an important exception to the unfair dismissal provisions must be noted. They do not apply to any employment where the employer is the husband or wife.

Remedies for unfair dismissal

Where the tribunal finds that the grounds for the complaint

are well founded, it can avail itself of one of the following remedies; it can:

1. make an order of reinstatement, i.e. an order that the
   employer treats the complainant in all respects as if he had not
   been dismissed; and can specify an amount which the
   employer should pay to restore any loss of benefit caused by
   the dismissal such as arrears of pay, and the restoration of
   any rights and privileges such as pension rights and seniority
   and the date by which he should comply with the order.
   In respect of this order the tribunal has to consider—
   (*a*) whether the complainant wishes to be reinstated;
   (*b*) whether reinstatement is practicable as far as the
   employee is concerned;
   (*c*) whether reinstatement is just in the circumstances.
   Where the tribunal decides against reinstatement it can consider of order for reengagement.
2. make an order for reengagement; that the complainant be
   engaged by the employer or his successor or an associate
   employer in employment similar to his former employment
   or other suitable employment and specifying the terms upon
   which the reengagement is to take place.
   Again the tribunal in making the order must apply considerations similar to those above.
3. grant compensation;
   (*a*) if the terms attached to an order of reinstatement or reengagement cannot be complied with, the tribunal can make
   an award to be paid by the employer to the complainant of
   an amount it decides will compensate for the failure to
   comply.
   (*b*) if there is an absolute failure to reinstate or reengage as
   ordered by the tribunal, an award for unfair dismissal
   must be made and unless the employer can show that it
   was not practical to comply with the order, the tribunal is
   empowered to make an additional award of compensation.
   The calculation of the additional award is governed by the
   circumstances of the complaint, viz.
   (i) it shall not be less than twenty-six and not more than
   fifty-two weeks pay where the dismissal is unfair because it was caused by trade union activities; it is an act
   of discrimination made unlawful by the Sex Discrimination Act 1975; it is an act made unlawful by the Race
   Relations Act 1976.

(ii) in any other case it shall not be less than thirteen nor more than twenty-six weeks pay; maximum £5 720[1].

The 1978 Act provides rules to be followed in calculating compensation for unfair dismissal. It consists of a basic award and a compensatory award. The maximum in the latter is £5 750.

The basic award is generally calculated by reference to the last twenty years or if less, the total employment of the employee, and allows one and a half weeks pay for each year of employment in which the employee was not younger than forty-one; one weeks pay for each year below forty-one and not below twenty-two; and half a week's pay for each year below twenty-two and not below eighteen. The basic award cannot be less than two weeks pay. Where the complaint is based upon other causes besides or together with unfair dismissal i.e. redundancy or under the Sex Discrimination Act 1975 or the Race Relations Act 1976, the basic compensation awarded must take into account those other causes even if compensation based upon them has been granted by another tribunal, and can never exceed £3 300 based on a maximum of £110 per week.

However, the Act makes provision for a reduction in the assessed compensation because of contributory fault, that is, although the dismissal was unreasonable, if the employer can establish a good ground for dismissal, the employee can expect that his compensation will be reduced, for example, in *Clapton v. Ketton Foundry* (1972) the compensation assessed was reduced by 25% in the case of an employee who was dismissed for taking time off without permission and had not been given the recommended first warning. It was unfair dismissal in the circumstances, but taking time off without permission was recognised as contributory by the employee.

The theoretical total of compensation is £14 770, this operative from February 1st, 1979 by virtue of The Employment Protection (Variation of Limits) Order, 1978 and The Unfair Dismissal (Increase of Compensation Limit) Order 1978.

---

[1] Calculated on 52 weeks pay at £110 per week

9

Employment of Staff: II

DUTIES ARISING FROM THE CONTRACT

A well constructed contract of service, added to by the written particulars required by the Employment Protection (Consolidation) Act 1972, should make provision for all the agreed rights and obligations which pass between an employer and an employee.

The Common Law, however, over a long period of time has, through interpretation of the relationship, created numerous duties which must be observed by both employer and employee. These duties could not be made express provisions of every contract because of their complexity; nevertheless, they are implied whenever a contract of employment is shown to exist.

So far as the hotel and catering industries are concerned, the relevant duties can be summarised as follows.

Duties owed by the employee to the employer
1. To give personal service.
2. To obey lawful orders.
3. To give careful service.
4. To be loyal to his employer.
5. To account to his employer for any secret profit to himself or loss caused to his employer by his negligence.

These duties arise out of the essentially personal nature of the contract of employment. Most important is that the contract cannot be assigned to a third party without the consent of the party who would be affected by the assignment. Therefore, theoretically the employee should give personal service. This duty obviously applies to the services of a highly qualified chef but it is doubtful if a short-staffed licensee would refuse a competent replacement sent by a barmaid who has been taken ill.

The personal nature of the contract also gives rise to the other duties listed above. Those that come within the meaning of obedience to lawful orders and the giving of careful service have already been discussed in Chapter 8 in the section concerning termination for breach of contract.

The duty of loyalty to an employer implies that the employee will not make any profits out of his employment without the permission of his employer; nor will he take other employment which will conflict with his employer's interests.

In the hotel and catering trade it is recognised by tradition that staff can accept 'tips' for service rendered to customers, so this in no way infringes the duty of loyalty, but if a barmaid, for example, consistently makes a profit for herself by a manipulation of the drinks which she serves, the duty of loyalty is breached and besides the criminal liability which she has incurred, she can be called upon to account to her employer for the profits she has made.

Whether or not other employment conflicts with the interests of the employer depends upon the facts in each case. In the majority of cases the employment of bar staff is in itself a form of secondary employment. In the industry with which we are concerned a conflict of this nature would only involve staff who provide a special expertise or who carry special responsibility. Therefore a chef whose reputation is an attraction offered by a hotel or restaurant would be in breach of his duty of loyalty if he worked in his off-duty time for a competing establishment.

In *Hivac Ltd v. Park Royal Scientific Instruments Ltd* (1946) the plaintiffs were engaged in the manufacture of hearing aids. Several of their employees took up part-time work in their spare time with the defendants who had started a business in opposition to Hivac Ltd. It was held that the employees' contracts of service had been breached and the court awarded an injunction to restrain the defendants from employing Hivac's employees in the future.

The employee could also be in breach of his duty of loyalty over recipes which had been used by him in his part-time employment and which were recognised as a proprietary right by his true employer and consequently attracted customers away from his true employer's hotel or restaurant.

Loyalty also involves giving the best personal service of which the employee is capable. He must therefore be diligent and not idle and must work the agreed number of hours, not being guilty of persistent lateness or leaving his employment without permission before the end of his agreed period of work.

The duty to account can also require an employee to recompense, either partly or fully, for compensation which his employer has to pay a third party for injury caused through his, the employee's, negligence.

In *Lister v. Romford Ice and Cold Storage Co. Ltd* (1957) the Romford Ice and Cold Storage Co. Ltd employed Lister as a lorry driver. His father was also employed by the company and travelled with Lister as his mate. Lister's lorry was involved in an accident caused by his negligence and his father was injured. The company was held to be vicariously liable and was ordered to pay compensation. The company, however, successfully claimed that, as Lister junior had failed to provide careful service, he must compensate it for the loss he had caused to it.

It must be appreciated that the delinquent employee could be sued as an individual and also, besides his liability to contribute for not giving careful service, could be treated as a joint tortfeasor with his employer under the Law Reform (Married Women and Tortfeasors) Act 1935. A joint tortfeasor is a person who is alleged to share responsibility with other blameworthy parties.

Duties owed by the employer to the employee
1. To pay the agreed remuneration.
2. To account for all expenses incurred by his employee on his behalf, i.e. to indemnify him.
3. To provide safe working conditions for his employees.
4. To observe all statutory provisions relating to the maintenance of recommended welfare and safety conditions.

To pay the agreed remuneration. An employee must be paid the agreed remuneration. The means by which the wages of persons employed in the hotel and catering industry are determined have recently moved in some sectors from statutory provision of minimum standards to agreements, finalised between employers or their associations and trade unions representing various sections of employees, establishing levels in excess of the statutory minimum. These levels of remuneration, when incorporated into a contract of service, must be observed by the employer (see Chapter 7).

This implied duty also places an obligation upon an employer to pay the wage at the agreed or customary time.

Other forms of remuneration such as payment of bonuses and the provision of accommodation are generally incorporated into each contract of service and, in the absence of such provision, it is difficult to envisage any situation in which there is an implied duty to provide these extra facilities; for example, where staff have for several years been paid a Christmas bonus for good service voluntarily by an appreciative employer, this does not give rise to an implied duty to continue this practice at every future Christmas.

To indemnify for all expenses. An employer must indemnify an employee for all expenses he incurs whilst carrying out the employer's lawful business following instructions from a person authorised to control the employee's work. Therefore travelling and subsistence expenses must be paid when an employee is ordered to travel to fulfil a service to his employer's business.

To provide a safe system for working. The employer has an implied duty to exercise reasonable care to ensure that the employee is provided with a safe system for working. This Common Law duty is supplementary to numerous statutory provisions which also lay down standards of safety and welfare. The whole field of the employer's Common Law and statutory duties in this respect are discussed in detail in Chapter 12.

Finally, two other aspects of the relationship between an employer and his employee must be discussed.

Provision of work. In general, an employer is under no duty to provide his employee with work. Provided he pays him the agreed wage, he can retain him on his staff but order him to stay away from the business premises. There are, however, exceptions to this general rule:

1. If the employee is dependent upon doing work to earn his remuneration, e.g. he relies upon commission for having accomplished a result, he must be given a reasonable opportunity to earn that commission.

2. When the employee's profession is such that his chances of future employment depend upon his professional reputation, the employer would be in breach of the contract of service if he denied the employee the work to maintain or improve that reputation. This applies to journalists and writers, and in particular, in the hotel and catering industry, to entertainers and chefs.

In *H. Clayton and J. Waller Ltd v. Oliver* (1930) Oliver was contracted to take part in a show. The promoters of the show then decided that they did not require him for the part but offered to pay him the agreed salary. The court held that the promoters would be in breach of the contract if they did not supply the part and would have to pay damages as well as the salary.

3. Under the Wages Councils Act 1959 where minimum wages are laid down by a Wages Councils Order an employee must be given an opportunity to accept available work in order to earn the minimum wages, or, in the absence of a written declaration by him of his inability to accept, be paid the minimum wage.

Supplying a reference. Unless there is a specific provision in the contract of service relating to an employer's duty to supply a reference in respect of his employee, the employer is, at Common Law, not obliged to do so.

If he does decide to make any oral or written comment upon an employee's efficiency and character, he must be careful that he does not make any statement which might lead to an action for defamation.

Defamation is a tort and is defined as a statement which tends to bring the person to whom it relates into contempt, hatred or ridicule in the opinion of reasonable thinking members of the public. Defamation can be either:

1. Libel, that is, a permanent record of the offending reference, e.g. in writing or on tape, or,
2. Slander, in which the form of reference is of a transitory nature, e.g. an oral statement either directly made or by a telephone message.

In each case the aggrieved employee must show that the statement had the effect which makes it defamatory; the statement was intended to refer to him; and, the statement was published to a third party, i.e. a person other than the employer and the employee. This would obviously include an intended second employer or anyone representing him. Frequently the reference is handed to the employee to pass it on to the recipient. If the third party received it unopened this would constitute the required publication for defamation, but not if the employee had received it as an open reference.

There is one important distinction between libel and slander. Libel is actionable *per se*, that is an action can be taken for defamation even though no damage to the employee has resulted; proof of publication is sufficient. An action for slander, can, in general, only be taken where damage can be proved. There are, however, exceptions to this general rule, and an action can be taken on publication only in the following cases:

1. That the employee had been guilty of an offence punishable by imprisonment.
2. That the employee is suffering from a disease which makes him an undesirable companion or workmate.
3. That the employee, a female, is unchaste.
4. That the employee's conduct impairs his trade, profession or occupation.

It is obvious, then, that extreme care should be taken when a reference is supplied. Fortunately the law provides defences which the employer, who has acted properly, can use to combat an action for defamation. He can prove:

1. That the statement is substantially true. This defence is known as justification. Since the Defamation Act 1950 it is not necessary to prove that the statement or statements are totally true. If on balance they are substantially true, that is sufficient.
2. That the statement, although based upon opinion only, was made honestly and without malice to be received by a person who had a justifiable interest in its contents. The defence is called qualified privilege and would cover a statement, detrimental to the employee, based upon suspicion and not fact; but it must have been made honestly and without malice and directed to the person having an interest.

A reference irresponsibly made can also incur liability if it causes damage or loss to the person to whom it is addressed. Such would be the case where the statement is made recklessly or with knowledge as to its truth and the recipient acts upon that statement to his detriment; for example, a person is employed because his employer relies upon a 'puffed up' statement respecting his efficiency or character and subsequently suffers loss because of a lack of either quality.

The ownership of a written reference or testimonial belongs to the person to whom it is given, to the employee when it is directly issued to him, and to the intended employer to whom it has been specifically directed.

10

Factors Affecting Wages

STATUTORY CONTROL

Statutory provisions relating to minimum wages are considered to be necessary in certain trades and industries where negotiating machinery for the settling of wage levels by collective agreement is non-existent or not adequate. The Catering Wages Act 1943 dealt with the remuneration and conditions of employment of people employed in the relevant industry. A permanent commission, the Catering Wages Commission, was set up by the appropriate Minister, with powers to inquire into conditions relating to remuneration, employment, health and welfare of employees. It could also consider the needs of the industry as a whole *vis-à-vis* the public which it served. Recommendations could be made to Government departments on the matters considered including the establishment of wages boards. Five such boards, the Catering Wages Boards, were set up to deal with different areas of the industry.

Legislation, culminating in the Wages Councils Act 1959, caused the abolition of the Commission and converted the boards into Wages Councils. The councils currently operating are the following:

1. The Industrial and Staff Canteen Undertakings Wages Council (I.S.C.).
2. The Unlicensed Place of Refreshment Wages Council (U.P.R.).
3. The Licensed Non-Residential Establishment Wages Council (L.N.R.).
4. The Licensed Non-Residential Establishment (Managers and Club Stewards) Wages Council (L.N.R.M.).
5. The Licensed Residential Establishment and Licensed

Restaurant Wages Council (L.R.).

Each council comprises an equal number of members representing employers and employees together with a maximum of three independent members, two of whom are appointed by the Minister to act as chairman and deputy chairman. The independent members are appointed from persons who have no connection with either side of the industry.

A Wages Council can submit proposals to the Minister upon matters in the following areas:

1. The minimum remuneration to be paid, the hours of work and overtime rates.
2. The fixing of holidays, holiday remuneration and rest days.

The proposals must be circulated by the Minister to all those who will be affected in the industry and each employer is required to post a copy in a convenient place in his premises, accessible to all his employees, so that it can be read by them. A period of time, not less than fourteen days from the publication of the notice, must be specified on the notice during which employers and employees can comment upon the proposals. After amendments, if any, the proposals are then embodied into a 'Wages Regulation Order' and become law when published by the Minister in the form of a statutory instrument, under a power vested in him by *s*.11 of the Wages Councils Act 1959, as from a specified date.

Wages Council Order

The matters dealt with in each Order are legally binding upon all employers in the sector of industry to which they are referred, and must be included as positive terms in every contract of service as from the commencement date of the Order.

If an employer fails to implement the new proposals immediately, he can be fined £20 and, in the case of a minimum wage requirement, can be ordered by the court to pay the accrued arrears in wages for the relevant period and up to three years.

The Minister has appointed inspectors whose duties are to enforce the legal requirements of the Wages Councils Act 1959 and its statutory instruments. The powers of each inspector are as follows:

1. He can enter any premises where the employees are within the provisions of a Wages Council Order, provided he does so at a reasonable time, and can question employees and employers on matters which are the subject of an Order.

2. He can inspect records which the Act requires an employer to maintain and can demand to have access to such records compiled during the previous three years.
3. He can ensure that all notices issued by the Minister are displayed in a conspicuous position.

If the employer obstructs the inspector in the fulfilment of his duties or is found to have failed with the requirements of the Act, the inspector can institute proceedings against him which could result in a fine of £20.

The Council Orders dealing with the conditions of employment in the various sectors of the industry vary in detail but the main provisions cover grounds common to all. Each Wages Council issues an Order with reasonable frequency. Recently representation of staff in some employment areas, by trade unions or associations, has increased and the determination of employment conditions by agreement with employers has become more advantageous to those concerned. Nevertheless, the continued existence of Wages Councils is essential because of their influence on actual rates paid; they are maintained at a reasonable minimum level.

It is necessary to give a general summary of the purposes of the various Orders.

Minimum remuneration

The minimum wage referred to in any Order refers to the minimum gross wage which must be paid by the employer. Certain deductions may be made from the wage, for example, income tax, national insurance, graduated pensions and deductions allowed by the Truck Acts (see Chapter 11) where they apply. One qualification in connection with remuneration is that where an employee is available for work for the full stipulated weekly hours and no work is available, the guaranteed minimum wage must be paid. The employee who, for personal reasons, does not want to work a complete week, is usually requested to give a written statement to the employer stating his or her inability to be available for the total number of hours.

The Orders also detail the wage rates for shift workers, night workers, split duty or 'spreadover' hours and emergency duty where these are required in any one of the sectors of the industry. Under the Wages Council Order, L.N.R.M., club stewards only and not hotel managers are entitled to overtime pay.

In those employments where full board and lodgings are provided or where an employee receives a guaranteed certain weekly amount in gratuities the salary can be reduced by a fixed amount.

A Wages Council can make a special case in respect of a worker where it is satisfied that the worker is incapable of earning the minimum remuneration specified in a Council Order. It can in such cases grant a permit authorising his employment at a rate less than the statutory minimum.

Holidays

The holiday entitlement provided by the Orders is generally based upon the employee's length of service during the previous twelve months and also upon the length of his working week.

If an employee terminates his employment before his holidays have been taken, he is entitled to accrued holiday remuneration for that season only, unless of course his termination is due to the following:

1. His leaving without giving at least his contractual or statutory notice. Theoretically his holiday remuneration could be reduced by a sum representing the amount of notice he failed to give.
2. His dismissal is due to misconduct and he is informed of this fact when dismissed. In such a case he loses all accrued holiday remuneration.
3. His previously having been allowed to take holidays to which he was not then entitled. The accrued holiday remuneration is amended in these circumstances to take the length of that holiday into account.

The Licensed Non-Residential Establishment (Managers and Club Stewards) Wages Council (L.N.R.M.)) provides for holiday entitlement with pay in the same way as the other Council Orders in respect of managers and club stewards, but makes an exception of club stewards who normally work for less than eighteen hours per week.

COLLECTIVE AGREEMENT

Industrial and staff canteens

The collective bargaining arrangements which exist in the industry as a whole vary in their efficiency from one sector to another. Where catering is an ancillary part of another industry most of the employees are represented by the same trade unions or associations which cater for the conditions of the workers in the parent industry; for,example, schools catering staff are covered by the National Joint Council for Local Authority Services and the hospital catering staff by the Ancillary Staff's Council.

Unlicensed restaurants and cafés

The trade union representation of employees who work in unlicensed places of refreshment, on the other hand, is very fragmented; such representation which does exist is insignificant. This is due to many factors; this sector of the industry is made up to a great degree by small establishments and many family-owned businesses displaying a high proportion of women, foreign and part-time workers. The position of these employees is unlikely to change significantly in the near future and consequently the statutory determination of minimum wages by a Wages Council is necessary. The Wages Council (U.P.R.) will continue to operate for a considerable period of time in the future.

Boarding-houses

For similar reasons the position of staff in boarding-houses is unsatisfactory and this state is further complicated by considerable seasonal fluctuations. This sector, because of the very great problems attached to identification of the establishments and enforcement of statutory provisions, has not been brought within the ambit of the Wages Councils Act 1959 and consequently wage levels are dependent almost absolutely upon individual agreement and recognised local custom.

Public-house managers

The position of employees in public houses is somewhat better, but even then is only satisfactory in the case of managers. In general the actual salaries paid to managers are substantially better than the minimum laid down by the Wages Council (L.N.R.M.). This has been achieved through national voluntary agreement between the Brewers Society, whose membership consists of practically all brewery companies operating a tied trade, and the N.A.L.H.M., the National Association of Licensed Hotel Managers. This negotiating machinery has existed since October 1969 and can agree such matters as salaries of managers, payments to their wives, annual holidays and holiday remuneration, allowances in respect of board and/ or accommodation, weekly rest days and public holidays, etc. The *Report of the Commission on Industrial Relations Part III, The Hotel and Catering Industry*, published by H.M.S.O. in March 1973 (Report 36), states that the N.A.L.H.M. and the Brewers' Society intend in future to conduct their negotiations at company level, rather than on a national basis, and that in fact this method has commenced to a small degree.

In view of the apparent success of this negotiating machinery the report of the C.I.R. recommends that eventually public house managers should be removed from the scope of Wages Council Orders.

Public-house bar staff

The position of bar staff is not satisfactory, however. Again the influences of low rates of pay, although very often in excess of the statutory minimum, cause a high staff turnover and do not encourage workers to become full-time employees. The C.I.R. recommend in its report that Wages Council Orders (L.N.R.) should be reviewed on a more regular basis. It found, however, that in the northern part of the United Kingdom the Transport and General Workers Union had, through its own initiative, attracted a considerable proportion of bar staff into union membership, and recommended that the Trades Union Congress Industrial Committee for Catering 'should review the existing sphere of influence for bar staff in the public house sector', and that the review should lead to 'the trade unions concerned taking steps to expand their membership among bar staff . . . recruitment being most likely to be conducted successfully on a company-wide scale and might be directed initially towards full-time staff who represent the most stable element of the labour force'.

The report of the C.I.R. also drew attention to the fact that bar staff representation on the L.N.R. Wages Council, reconstituted from the 1st December 1972, did not reflect its trade union membership and that the T.U.C. Industrial Committee for Catering should revise this situation and make appropriate recommendations to the Department of Employment.

Club stewards and other staff

Evidence shows that there is a low level of trade union membership and a lack of voluntary collective bargaining in the club sector of the industry. Again it appears that the initiative lies with the trade unions. The United Federation and Union of Club Stewards (U.F.U.C.S.) and the Union of Shop, Distributive and Allied Workers (U.S.D.A.W.), through their activities, have shown that club stewards are interested in trade union membership. The report of the C.I.R. (Report 36) recommends that trade unions should take that initiative by developing organisation on an area-by-area basis.

The employment in clubs mainly comprises full-time club stewards, their wives and stewardesses. The remainder of the staff is made up of bar staff, cleaners, doormen, etc., the proportion of full-time employees is relatively small, mostly concentrated in the large clubs. The greater proportion of other staff is made up of women and old-age pensioners mostly employed only seasonally or at weekends. Consequently the organisation of trade union membership is difficult if not impossible.

Usually the only positive contracts of employment are with club stewards, etc., and are in most cases based upon model contracts supplied by the various club associations, the majority just observing the minimum provisions of the relevant Wages Council Order (L.N.R.M.), whilst some occasionally (about 10 per cent in 1971), as discovered by the Wages Inspectorate, infringe the relevant Order, either in respect of minimum wages or accrued holiday pay.

The C.I.R. recommends that the present position necessitates the continued existence of the Wages Council (L.N.R.).

Hotels and restaurants

There is very little collective bargaining on rates of pay in this sector of the industry. Wage rates are usually determined by management and vary from area to area according to the fluctuating factor of the labour market. Whilst there is not an established principle for the determination of wages throughout the country as a whole, it is clear that the provisions of the relevant Wages Council Order (L.R.) have an effect upon levels in that its regulations with respect to holidays and holiday remuneration are adhered to, whilst actual wages paid are above the level provided in the Order and are adjusted in accordance with any upward trend in new Orders.

One area of remuneration peculiar to this sector of the industry seems to cause difficulty, that is, the supplementation of the basic wage by the service charge system which has replaced to a large extent the practice of 'tipping' for the service given. The manner in which this is done is in most cases the prerogative of the manager and consequently it varies from one hotel or restaurant to another. Evidence accumulated by the *Report on Hotels and Restaurants* by the C.I.R. (Report 23, published by H.M.S.O. in October 1971) shows that generally the service staff tend to get a very high proportion and in some cases the total amount. The C.I.R. is of the opinion that this could cause discontent amongst kitchen staff and others who play a part in providing the end product.

The administration of the distribution also varies. In some establishments it is averaged over a yearly period whilst in others it is paid out at the end of each week thus causing considerable fluctuations in total weekly wages according to the time of the year. In some cases, only all-the-year-round staff are allowed to participate; the seasonal worker receives nothing.

The variations in this matter alone call for a more positive system of negotiation and agreement.

The C.I.R. found some encouragement in that the hotel sector has recognised the need for negotiation by creating machinery involving the British Hotels and Restaurants Association and the General and Municipal Workers Union to provide wider areas of discussion on conditions of employment, including pay.

Developing from this first step, it is recommended by the C.I.R. that trade unions should make selective recruitment drives on an area and a company basis.

TERMS AND CONDITIONS OF EMPLOYMENT ACT 1959

The provisions of *s*.8 of the Terms and Conditions of Employment Act 1959 are the sole reminder of the various Orders which were made during World War II to compel adherence to collective agreements between employers and employees even if they were not parties to the agreements. Originally intended to apply only to collective agreements, the scope of the provisions was broadened by *s*.152 of the Industrial Relations Act 1971 to include the enforcement of conditions made to benefit workers' remuneration or minimum remuneration fixed under the Wages Councils Act 1959; but no other enactment. The repeal of the Industrial Relations Act by the Trade Union and Labour Relations Act 1974 does not affect this extension of *s*.8.

The purpose of the provision is to eliminate the possibility of manufacturers and other employers undercutting the price of others in the same industry by failing to pay the recognised rate of remuneration to their employees.

The Terms and Conditions of Employment Act 1959, as amended, provides that where terms and conditions of employment are established in any trade or industry, or section of a trade or industry, either generally or in any district by an agreement, an award or a Wages Council Order, a written claim can be submitted to the Secretary of State requesting that the activities of an employer who is failing to comply with the established terms and conditions be investigated.

The claim can be submitted only by organisations or associations which are parties to the agreement, etc., or representative of such parties, who form a substantial proportion of the employers or employees in the relevant trade or industry or a section of it. The employer who is the object of the claim need not be one represented by the claimants.

The Secretary of State will only consider whether the claim contains sufficient detailed information and can send it back to the initiators for clarification. When he is satisfied that a case has been properly reported he can utilise whatever means appears to him to be appropriate to settle the claim and as a last resort submit it to one of the commissions of enquiry, which, if satisfied that the claim is well founded and that the employer concerned is observing terms and conditions which are less favourable than those required, will make an award requiring the employer to observe the established terms and conditions in respect of all relevant employees in his employment.

The award will become an implied term of each contract of employment concerned from a date specified by the commission, that date not being earlier than the date when the employer was initially made aware of the award which gave rise to the claim to the Secretary of State.

The commission's award, of course, ceases to have effect when the basic agreement or award is altered by a subsequent agreement, award or Wages Council Order.

The activities of public or local authorities are treated as a trade or industry for the purposes the Terms and Conditions of Employment Act 1959.

Employer's Responsibility to make Deductions from Wages and to Pay Levies

THE TRUCK ACTS

The main purpose of the Truck Acts, 1831–96, is to prevent the exploitation of employees by employers by prohibiting the payment of wages in kind, to prevent the use of 'tommy shops' owned by the employers in which the employees were compelled to spend a proportion of their wages and to lay down provisions which have to be complied with if deductions are made from wages.

However, the Acts apply only to workmen as defined in s.10 of the Employers and Workmen Act 1875 and are thus limited to those engaged in manual labour. They do not include domestic servants, that is, those whose services are directed towards catering for the personal needs of residents of a household or any other residential establishment. Even if an employee's work can be said to be manual, if the end product is one of catering it is doubtful if he would be a subject of the Truck Acts.

It was held in *Cameron v. Royal Ophthalmic Hospital* (1941) that the Truck Acts did not apply to a hospital worker whose job was to stoke the furnaces of the hospital central heating apparatus.

However, in the industrial climate which now exists a wise employer, if he deems it necessary to make any deductions from his employees' wages, should ensure that that possibility is the subject of an agreement with his employees either in the initial contract of service or in some subsequent written form, for example, an agreement that a deduction from wages will be made in lieu of breakages. In this case the agreement must detail the circumstances in which such deductions will be made and would obviously be dependent upon the breakage being caused by some negligence on the part of the employee concerned.

The various Catering Wages Councils Orders make provision for deductions where full board or living accommodation is supplied but, as collective bargaining between employers' associations and employees' unions increases, this factor must be clearly provided for in the final agreement.

Other than the above, where wages are governed by a Wages Council Order, deductions from wages can only be made as follows:

1. To deduct income tax under the Pay As You Earn (P.A.Y.E.) scheme.
2. To extract contributions in respect of the National Insurance and National Insurance (Industrial Injuries) Acts' provisions.
3. By written agreement, to extract contributions in respect of superannuation or any other scheme in which the employer is not beneficially interested.

INCOME TAX

The Income Tax Acts, operating through the P.A.Y.E. scheme, provide that all employees subject to a contract of employment should pay their income tax by deductions made from their main sources of income. The employer is responsible for the calculation and extraction of the deductions which must be forwarded to the appropriate Inland Revenue department.

NATIONAL INSURANCE

The Social Security Act 1975 as amended by the Social Security Pensions Act 1975 provides a scheme of compulsory insurance to cater for an employee's absence from work during sickness and unemployment. Also the Act provides benefits in respect of maternity and widowhood, retirement pensions and death grant.

The overall effect of the Act, therefore, is to provide a scheme of social insurance which affects and is beneficial to every person resident in Great Britain.

Subscribers to the scheme

The scheme demands that every individual should, during

his or her working life, become insured. The Act provides, therefore, that every person over school-leaving age and under pensionable age, i.e. under sixty-five in the case of men and sixty in the case of women, must be contributory members to the scheme or covered by the contributions of the person upon whom they are dependent. Therefore, children under school-leaving age are covered by the contributions of their parent.

Insured persons

Persons insured can be classified into three groups.

1. Employed persons, i.e. those gainfully employed under a contract of service (or employment) or apprenticeship.
2. Self-employed persons, i.e. those who are gainfully employed, but not under a contract of service.
3. Non-employed persons, i.e. all other insured persons.

The difference between (1) and (2) rests on the distinction between a contract of service and a contract for services (see Chapter 8).

The term 'gainfully employed' is important. It means that some payment is received for services given even if that payment proves to be inadequate when the overall cost of giving the service is accounted.

Thus, in *Vandyk v. Minister of Pensions and National Insurance* (1955) it was held that a person who was paralysed because of polio and who accepted a research appointment to keep himself occupied was gainfully employed although the cost of his special transport arrangements to go to and from his work exceeded his wages.

Contributions

Contributions in respect of each individual are, in the case of employed persons, deducted from the employee's wages by the employer to represent the employee's stipulated contributions for each week of employment. On 6th April 1975 the method of collecting national insurance contributions by the purchase of stamps ceased and was replaced by the P.A.Y.E. procedure, as with income tax. The contributions payable are related to the employees' earnings in the form of a percentage of all wages between a lower limit per week and an upper limit per week, these being adjusted from time to time.

The contributions consist of two classes:

1. Primary Class I contributions from employed earners, and

2. Secondary Class I contributions from employers and others paying earnings.

The employee's contributions are classified into two rates:

1. A standard rate which applies to most employees, i.e. 5.5 per cent of the earnings up to the maximum of £120 per week, £520 per month or £6240 per year, according to the method by which earnings are paid.

2. A reduced rate payable by certain married women and most widows receiving national insurance widow's benefit, after they reach retiring age (i.e. the end of the tax year following their 59th birthday) unless they are non-liable. This rate also applies to newly widowed women during the first 26 weeks of widowhood. The rate of contribution is 2.0 per cent.

Employees who are over retirement age and retired from regular employment are non-liable for payment of contributions, but if they work their employers are still liable. This also applies to an employee over maximum pension age, who has not qualified for a national insurance pension and one who continues to work after 70 in the case of a man and 65 in the case of a woman.

The employer's contributions are the same irrespective of whether the employee pays the standard or reduced rates or is non-liable. The employer's contribution is 8.5 per cent in every case.

No deductions or payments are made in respect of employees under 16 years of age.

Contribution rates and the earnings limits which govern them will be renewed every year and made the subject of legislation for the following year.

The total contribution covers not only unemployment and sickness benefit, etc., but also contributions in respect of the Industrial Injuries Scheme and the Redundancy Payments Fund.

The National Insurance contribution is not due, but will be credited instead, in any week in which the employee is,

1. absent from work because of illness, or
2. unemployed and not in receipt of any wages.

Only one employer in respect of an employee is required to take the responsibility of making deductions. Therefore, if an employee works for more than one employer during the week, it is the first employer with whom he works for a wage in excess of £17.50p who must assume the necessary administrative function.

In cases where two or more employment contracts in respect of one person qualify for the deduction of the national insurance contribution, an arrangement can be agreed between the employers concerned. However, in the majority of cases the employee will only take part-time employment to supplement his income from a recognised complete employment contract and then it is the usual practice for him, in respect of his part-time employment, to sign a certificate to the effect that his full-time employer is deducting the necessary contribution from his wages.

Self-employed persons are required to make their own contributions, at a different rate. A self-employed person is not entitled to unemployment benefit.

A non-employed person is not required to pay contributions and is not entitled to unemployment benefit. The important groups in this category are those undergoing full-time education or full-time apprenticeship for which no payment is received. Although contributions are not required in respect of persons in either group, they will be credited with them instead.

The insurance card in respect of each employee must be retained by the employer during the period of employment but it must be returned to the employee, with the required number of insurance credits, immediately upon termination of the employment, or within fourteen days by forwarding it to his known address or, if his whereabouts are unknown, to the Department of Social Security.

NATIONAL INSURANCE INDUSTRIAL INJURIES

The Social Security Act 1975 also provides an insurance scheme in respect of an employee who is absent from work as the result of an injury sustained out of and during the course of his employment or because he suffers from a disease or illness which has been subscribed by the Department of Employment as being incidental to his type of work. Obviously the claimant must bring forward medical evidence to support his case.

The contributions towards industrial injuries insurance are deducted from the employee's wages along with those for national insurance. In general all persons employed under a contract of service or apprenticeship must be insured against industrial injury, illness or disease.

The contribution of the employee is payable irrespective of

the hours he might work at the beginning of each contribution week so that the employee becomes immediately insured against accidental injury; an accident might cause such an injury at any time. The contribution should then be deducted from the employee's wages when they fall due. An employee must continue to be insured under the scheme for any week when he is on paid holiday, but not when he is absent through sickness, injury or unemployment. The employer pays a contribution for each employee.

When a person is employed by more than one employer during the week, the one employing first is responsible for crediting him with the contribution, but, as with national insurance, several employers can arrange to share the cost.

There are several exceptions to the general rule that every person employed under a contract of service must be insured under the industrial injuries scheme. The most important are the following:

1. Where a person is engaged in casual employment, as distinct from part-time employment, and the purpose is not connected with the employer's business or trade.
2. Where the employee is the husband or wife of the employer.
3. Where a relative is employed as a household help.

The 1975 Act provides that when an employer employs more than ten persons on his premises he must keep an accident book in which every accident must be recorded. Apart from this, every employer must investigate each accident reported to him and must, when requested by an insurance officer, supply him with all relevant information concerning an accident.

VALUE ADDED TAX

Value Added Tax was introduced into Great Britain on the 1st April 1973 to replace Selective Employment Tax and Purchase Tax. The change involves all those businesses which sell goods or supply services whose annual turnover in taxable goods and services exceeds £5000. Businesses in this category should have registered with H.M. Commissioners of Custom and Excise from the 1st October 1972 by completing form V.A.T. 1 and forwarding it to them.

At the present time, apart from 'zero-rated' commodities (see below), the standard rate of V.A.T. is 15 per cent. Provision is, however, made for this rate to be altered, if necessary.

When V.A.T. was introduced procedures were created through which named goods and services could be exempted form the tax.

1. *Zero-rated supplies,* i.e. supplies which should be taxed but on which for any stated period of time the rate of tax is nil and V.A.T. charged on inputs relating to them can be reclaimed in the normal way.

2. *Exempt supplies,* i.e. supplies which are outside V.A.T. Input tax must not be deducted or reclaimed for them.

Each stage in the manufacture or supply of goods or services attracts V.A.T. and is paid by the person who receives at any one stage. The receiver identifies these supplies as his 'inputs' and the tax as his 'input tax'. He in turn charges V.A.T. on the goods and services called 'outputs' which he supplies. His collected tax is called 'output tax'. When he is required to forward a return to H.M. Commissioners of Customs and Excise he must total all his input and all his output tax and determine the difference. This will represent the amount which he should pay to Customs and Excise or the amount which should be repaid to him. Certain administrative duties in connection with the charging and paying of V.A.T. must be observed; for example the receiver must:

1. keep a record of his outputs and the V.A.T. charged on them;
2. when required, must supply invoices showing the V.A.T. charged;
3. keep a record of his inputs and the V.A.T. charged on them;
4. complete his V.A.T. return showing the difference between his output tax and his deductible input tax;
5. organise an adequate system of records and accounts in connection with the above.

In the hotel and catering industry some of the commodities supplied, i.e. liquor and cigarettes, are still subject to a direct excise tax[1]; but the addition of V.A.T. will apply to the supply of meals and the provision of accommodation. Food is zero-rated at the present time, but the supply of sandwiches, crisps, etc. for consumption on the premises is subject to V.A.T. as a service is being provided.

Other exemptions from the payment of V.A.T. arise from the interpretation of the term 'business'. This includes the carrying on of any trade, profession or vocation and is broad

[1] Plus 15% V.A.T.

enough to embrace the activities of clubs and associations. However, trade and professional associations are not recognised as businesses for V.A.T.; the services they provide from subscription income are outside the V.A.T. scheme.

Customs and Excise officers are granted powers to visit registered businesses from time to time to examine their records and accounts and the methods used to calculate and pay V.A.T. Their powers are provided in the Finance Act 1972 and anyone who obstructs an officer in entering a premises at a reasonable time to exercise his powers or who witholds information, documents or samples of goods when requested by the officer, will commit an offence.

Other offences can be committed where there has been failure to make a return, falsity in a return, where false information has been given to an officer and where a person has knowingly been concerned in the fraudulent evasion of V.A.T. whether by himself or by anyone else.

INDUSTRIAL TRAINING

The Secretary of State for Employment has the power, under the Industrial Training Act 1964, to create industrial training boards in respect of industries where it is considered that a need exists to establish an authority to ensure that the training in that industry is sufficient and adequate and to recommend future schemes for training.

The Hotel and Catering Industrial Training Board, established in 1966, supervises all sectors of the hotel and catering industry except registered clubs, hospitals, nursing homes, aircraft and ships.

The Board's representation comprises eight members from the employers' association, eight members chosen from the relevant trade unions and five professional educationalists. The Ministries involved supply assessors to augment the Board.

The finances required to cover the activities of the Board are acquired by means of levies imposed upon employers in proportion to their annual payrolls where these payrolls exceed a certain figure. Employers exempt from the scheme may be admitted voluntarily with the consent of the Board.

The levies form a fund from which an employer who has contributed to the scheme can, on application, be awarded a grant to finance the training of his staff on an educational course which has the approval of the Board. The employer, or a person responsible to him, must maintain a record of each trainee's progress whilst he is pursuing the course.

Safety and Welfare of Employees

An employer has a legal responsibility to provide for the safety and welfare of his employees. These duties are imposed upon him by the following:

1. The Common Law, which implies that a duty to provide a safe system of working arises out of every contract of employment.

2. Various statutes such as the Factories Act 1961, the Offices, Shops and Railway Premises Act 1963, Health and Safety at Work Act 1974, and the Shops Act 1950, which lay down standards of safety and welfare in respect of persons employed in the type of premises catered for by the statute. The hotel and catering industry is covered by the above three last-named Acts.

It might appear that statutory provisions have replaced the need for the Common Law duty, but in practice it is found that, although in many cases both cover similar circumstances, actions deriving from both sources are brought to a court.

A Common Law action allows an employee who has been injured because of his employer's negligence to seek compensation in respect of that injury. However, although the court, if satisfied of the alleged negligence, will grant adequate damages, it cannot order the employer to be more careful in future to prevent a similar occurrence.

The statutory provisions, on the other hand, detail positive actions which must on all occasions be implemented by an employer and failure to do so, even though no injury to an employee has resulted, can result in a criminal action punishable by a fine. Although originally intended to enforce the constant maintenance of safe and ideal welfare conditions through a threat of prosecution, the courts have since *Groves v. Wimbourne* (1898) allowed the injured employee to base a civil action for the recovering of compensation upon what has become known as a 'breach of a statutory duty'.

In the above case it was held that the plaintiff could recover damages in tort as Parliament, having passed an Act for the benefit of factory workers, could not have intended that the infliction of a small fine should be the sole remedy.

The Common Law action is retained because, being based upon the tort of negligence, it is elastic and not dependent upon the detailed circumstances that the relevant statute might require. If the circumstances of the incident do not conform with those of the statutory provision, an action for breach of statutory duty could fail, whereas an action for Common Law negligence would be successful.

THE COMMON LAW DUTY

The Common Law duty to maintain a safe system of working is not an absolute one. If an employer can show that in the circumstances of the incident in dispute he had exercised reasonable care, an action based upon negligence, seeking compensation for an injury caused to an employee, will not succeed.

In *Latimer v. A.E.C. Ltd* (1953) Latimer brought an action against A.E.C. Ltd alleging negligence when he slipped on a patch of wet flooring in their factory. The factory premises had become flooded when a nearby river overflowed. The employers had spread as much sawdust and sand on the floor as they were able but several patches had been left uncovered. It was held that the employers had acted reasonably in the circumstances. The only alternative would have been to close the factory to entirely eliminate the risk of injury.

The duty of care with regard to safety can be classified as follows:
1. To provide safe premises.
2. To provide safe plant, equipment and materials.
3. To provide a safe environment.

To provide safe premises
The premises include all parts that make up the fundamental

structure of the building, i.e. the floor, walls, roof, insulation against power installations and ventilations.

To provide safe plant, equipment and materials

Plant is defined as 'fixed assets' as opposed to fluctuating stock and includes such assets as counters and such things as are physically fixed and form a part of the permanent establishment, to be replaced when worn out. It is not necessary that the asset should be of the latest design; whether or not an outmoded model could be regarded as giving rise to negligence can only be judged by taking all the surrounding circumstances into account. The duty of care does not prohibit an employer from installing apparatus which could cause injury, but he must take care to reduce the risk to a minimum by providing protective equipment or at least by giving warning of the danger to his employees. It would be an act of negligence on the part of an employer to allow an inexperienced employee to handle dangerous apparatus without giving him adequate training as to its use.

On the other hand, the equipment must be suitable for the purpose for which it is intended to be used. Improvisation must be avoided. Also, the equipment must be free from any defect, and any defect drawn to the attention of the employer must be repaired.

Before 1969 the employer was relieved of responsibility when equipment was proved to have a latent defect. In this case an injured employee could only bring an action against the manufacturer.

The Employer's Liability (Defective Equipment) Act 1969 provides that the responsibility must be borne by the employer who must pay compensation whether the defect which caused the injury was patent or latent. The employer is also required, by the Employer's Liability (Compulsory Insurance) Act 1969, to cover all future claims in respect of personal injuries to employees by an approved insurance contract.

There can be, of course, an action between the employer and the manufacturer who produced the defective equipment.

To provide a safe environment

The employer's Common Law duty under this heading can be broadly divided into two sections.

To provide safe fellow employees. An employer is liable to pay compensation to an employee who has been injured as a result of the foolhardiness or incompetence of a colleague. This duty comes within the employer's vicarious liability but must be discussed apart from that liability with respect to persons not parties to a contract of employment.

Obviously an employer cannot initially guarantee that a new employee will not endanger his fellow employees, but as soon as he has evidence that his behaviour is likely to do so, he must warn him to correct that behaviour and if no heed is taken of the warning he should dismiss him.

In *Hudson v. Ridge Manufacturing Co. Ltd* (1957) the employers, the defendants, became aware that one of their employees indulged in horse-play. They had warned him several times but still retained his services. Hudson, a fellow employee, broke a wrist when he was tripped by his delinquent colleague. It was held that as the employers had continued to employ a person with knowledge of his dangerous conduct, they were liable to compensate Hudson for his injury.

To provide reasonable protection against unnecessary risks. Where the employment is inherently dangerous an employer has a duty to provide protective measures to reduce the danger to a minimum and to make these measures readily available. However, he is not obliged to supervise the use of the appliances as long as his employees are aware of their availability.

In *Woods v. Durable Suites Ltd* (1953) the employers were manufacturers of furniture and used a glue which could cause dermatitis when it came into contact with the skin. They provided a means to protect employees against this danger. However, supervision became slack following the appointment of a new foreman and Woods failed to make use of the protective measure and contracted dermatitis. The court held that the employers were not liable; having provided the necessary equipment they were not bound to ensure that an experienced employee made use of it.

When exercising his duty of care an employer will not be held to have acted reasonably if he did not make allowance in his safety measures for a particular susceptibility of an injured employee. It is not sufficient for him to show that he had adopted precautions which were commonly recognised in his trade or industry in similar circumstances. If, in the peculiar conditions, he omitted to do something which the court considers to be a folly on his part he can still be in breach of his duty.

In *Cavanagh v. Ulster Weaving Company* (1959), although it was common practice in the building trade not to provide a handrail for use by workmen working on a sloping roof, the House of Lords held that an employer had not acted reasonably when he failed to do so and an employee who was carrying a bucket of cement fell from a roof.

Again, in *Paris v. Stepney Borough Council* (1951) it was held that the council were liable when a garage fitter, who had only one good eye, lost that one when a splinter of metal entered it whilst he was hammering a bolt. It was shown that it was not a custom for protective goggles to be issued to employees engaged in this kind of work. Nevertheless, the court was of the opinion that the employers should have appreciated the risk of much greater injury and loss to the plaintiff and provided him with goggles.

The employer's Common Law duty of safety applies only to premises under his control and to the person of the employee; it does not apply to the employee's personal property.

In *Williams v. Grimshaw* (1967) the stewardess of a club claimed damages from her employers for breach of their Common Law duty of care when she was injured during an attempted robbery whilst carrying the club's takings along a lonely road to her home. It was held that the employers were not in breach of their duty of care because the attack on the stewardess had taken place outside their premises.

In *Deyong v. Shenburn* (1946) the clothes of an actor were taken from his dressing-room whilst he was performing. It was held that his employer had no duty to provide a lock for his dressing-room or to afford other means of protection.

This rule also applies to the property of employees who are required to 'live in'.

THE DEFENCES AVAILABLE TO AN EMPLOYER

The employer has several defences available to him to combat an action for negligence based upon injury to an employee.

Volenti non fit injuria

He may plead *volenti non fit injuria*, that is, that the employee knew of the risk involved in the incident leading to his injury and accepted that risk. Proof of acceptance is important; that the employee appreciated the danger involved is not sufficient.

In *Alveran v. Phillip Leonard Catering* (1965) the assistant manager of a Wimpy Bar broke his leg whilst assisting the manager to eject some obstreperous youths from the bar. He had without hesitation gone to the manager's assistance when summoned, and was held to have accepted as well as appreciated the risks involved. His action against his employers failed.

Contributory negligence of employee

The employer may plead that the employee had contributed to his injury by his own negligence, that is, he was guilty of contributory negligence. The Law Reform (Contributory Negligence) Act 1945 provides that, in a case where the court is satisfied that both parties to an action have been negligent in the issue before it, it can divide the total loss suffered by the plaintiff between him and the defendant in the ratio of their degrees of negligence as assessed by the court, and in extreme cases can assess the plaintiff's proportion at 100 per cent.

In *Uddin v. Associated Portland Cement* (1965) the plaintiff was injured when he climbed to the top of an extractor fan whilst chasing a pigeon. The injury necessitated the amputation of his arm. The court was of the opinion that he had acted with 'incredible folly which could not reasonably have been anticipated by any prudent employer'. The degrees of blame were assessed at 80 per cent in respect of the employee and 20 per cent in respect of the employer.

STATUTORY PROVISIONS

The statutes which regulate the employment of persons in the hotel and catering industry are the Shops Act 1950 as amended by the Shops (Early Closing Days) Act 1965, the Offices, Shops and Railway Premises Act 1963, and the Health and Safety at Work Act 1974. The first deals primarily with the regulation of periods of work whilst the latter two are concerned with provisions for health and comfort.

For the purposes of this book the legal definition of 'shops' must be given as these statutes apply to them.

Definition of a shop

A shop includes any premises where any retail trade or business is carrried on (*s*.74, Shops Act 1950) and includes the business of a barber or hairdresser, the sale of refreshments or intoxicating liquors, the business of lending books or periodicals when carried on for purposes of gain and retail sales by auction, but does not include the sale of programmes and catalogues and other similar sales at theatres and places of amusement.

As with every statutory definition, considerable litigation has followed to define whether or not certain premises fall within its ambit. Thus in *Fine Fare Ltd v. Brighton County Borough Council* (1959) it was held that a supermarket must be regarded as one shop and not a number of smaller shops, but in *George Hotel (Colchester) Ltd v. Ball* (1938) it was decided that the dining-room of a residential hotel in which non-residents were provided with meals came within the definition.

Therefore the definition of a shop includes any premises which cater for the sale of food and drink to members of the general public, that is, public houses, public bars and dining-rooms in a hotel, cafés and restaurants.

The statutory provisions exist for the benefit of persons employed in such premises, i.e. 'any person who is wholly or mainly employed in a shop in connection with the serving of customers, the receipt of orders, or the dispatch of goods'.

Therefore, in the catering trade the provision would cover kitchen staff, waiters, cashiers and managers employed in any premises within the definition of a shop (*Melluish v. London County Council* (1914) and *Prance v. London County Council* (1915)). Those employed in registered clubs and fully residential hotels are outside the terms of the statute whilst those employed in industrial canteens are normally covered by the provisions of the Factories Act 1961.

Shops Act 1950

The provisions of the Shops Act 1950 and the Shops (Early Closing Days) Act 1965 are primarily intended to govern employees in normal retail establishments where the hours of working are fairly conventional. The irregular opening hours of public houses, cafés and restaurants have made special provisions necessary.

The Shops Act provides for this special position of catering establishments by the following:

1. Compromising over the general provisions of the Act to make them suitable for catering premises, especially the provisions

relating to half-day closing on one weekday and full-day closing on a Sunday.

2. Drafting an entirely separate scheme tailor-made for the requirements of employees in the catering industry.

An employer can choose the scheme which is more suitable in his special circumstances and can change from one to the other after an interval of twelve months, but he must exhibit a notice in a prescribed form in a prominent position in his premises. In the absence of choice an employer will have to operate the compromised general provisions.

A comparison between the compromised scheme and the catering scheme can best be shown as follows:

ADULT EMPLOYEES

Compromised Scheme	*Catering Scheme*
Hours of work	
No maximum hours of work.	Not to exceed 65 hours exclusive of meal times.
One weekly half day free from 1.30 p.m.	No provision for free half day.
Meal Breaks	
One hour for lunch or ¾ hour if taken on premises between 10.30 a.m. and 3.30 p.m. ½ hour for tea between 4 p.m. and 7 p.m. There must be a 20 minute break at least every 6 hours.	Two hours at any time or ¾ hour where hours do not exceed 6 and end before 3 p.m. There must be a 30 minute break at least every 6 hours.
Sunday Working	
For every 4 hours there must be a full day in lieu in the week before or after and not on an allotted ½ day. Not more than 3 Sundays to be worked in each month. Where under 4 hours worked ½ day in lieu as above. Applies to those employed in sale of refreshments but not in the main sale of liquor.	There must be 26 Sundays per year completely free with at least 1 free in every 3. Applies to all catering staff.

Annual Holidays

No provision for annual holidays.

There must be 32 weekdays per annum; 6 to be consecutive to form an annual holiday and remainder spread to give 2 a month. Two half days in one week equal one day.

The Shops Act also makes special provision for the employment of persons under the age of eighteen years who come within the definition of shop assistants and who are employed in the catering industry. Again there is a choice between the compromised scheme and the catering scheme, but additionally an employer can adopt the scheme provided by the Young Persons (Employment) Acts 1938 and 1964.

In the absence of a notified preference, it is presumed that the catering scheme is to prevail.

EMPLOYEES UNDER 18 YEARS

Compromised Scheme	*Catering Scheme*	*Young Persons Scheme*
Hours of Work		
16-18 years, maximum 48 hours per week excluding meals. Under 16 years, 44 hours per week excluding meals.	16-18 years, maximum 48 hours per week, but during 12 specified 2 week periods maximum 96 hours for 2 weeks and maximum of 60 in either week. No overtime in these periods. Under 16 years, maximum 44 hours per week but during 2 weeks including Christmas Day, maximum 88 hours in 2 weeks with maximum 48 hours in one week.	16-18 years, maximum 48 hours per week except meals. Under 16 years 44 hours per week except meals.
Overtime		
16-18 years, maximum 50 hours per annum over maximum of 12 weeks. Not more than 12 hours in one week. Under 16 years no overtime.	16-18 years, maximum 50 hours per annum, not more than 8 hours per week. No limit with regard to number of weeks involved. But refer to above.	16-18 years, maximum 50 hours per annum over maximum of 12 weeks. Not more than 6 hours in one week. Under 16 years no overtime.

Night Work

No work between 10 p.m. and 6 a.m. Must be an unbroken 11 hours break in 24 hours from 12 noon.	No work between 10 p.m. and 6 a.m. except 16-18 year males can serve meals between 10 p.m.-12 p.m. 11 hour break applies.	As in compromised scheme.

Half Day

Half day in weekday from 1.30 p.m. where 25 hours or more worked per week.	No provision.	Half day in weekday from 1.0 p.m.

Sunday Working

As in Adult Employees table.	As in Adult Employees table.	For any period worked there must be a whole day in lieu in the weeks before or after and not on an allotted half day.

Meal Breaks

As in previous table but there must be a break of 20 minutes in every 5 hours.	As in previous table but there must be a break of 30 minutes in every 6 hours.	Meal breaks of 45 minutes between 11.30 a.m. and 2.30 p.m. Rest break of 30 minutes every 5 hours.

The provisions of the Young Persons (Employment) Acts 1938 and 1964 apply to persons who are employed in residential hotels or clubs as messengers or receiving guests, or in licensed hotels and registered clubs where liquor is sold or supplied after 11 p.m. The Licensing Act 1964 provides that persons under the age of eighteen years are prohibited from being employed in the bar of licensed premises during permitted hours. They may, however, be employed in licensed premises as waiters in the restaurant.

It is a statutory duty of an employer of staff under the age of eighteen years to keep a record of their hours of work, meal breaks, etc., or more usually, to record any deviations from the laid-down standard which must be contained in a notice exhibited by him.

The local authority which is responsible for supervising compliance with the provisions of the Acts appoints inspectors who have the right to enter premises and inspect relevant records and documents and interview staff about any matter concerning working hours, etc. The penalty for failure to observe the provisions of the Shops Act and the Young Persons (Employment) Acts is a fine upon conviction by a Magistrates' Court.

The Offices, Shops and Railway Premises Act 1963

The Offices, Shops and Railway Premises Act 1963 together with the Factories Act 1961 and the Mines and Quarries Act 1954 form a series of statutes which through their provisions define minimum standards of working conditions for those employers who work in the types of premises defined in each act.

The 1963 Act is the one which applies to the catering industry. For its purpose a shop is defined as in the Shops Act 1950 (see page 157). An office is a building or part of a building the sole or principal use of which is as an office or for office purposes. Office purposes are defined as including administration, clerical work, handling of money and telephones or telegraph operating. Clerical work is further defined as including writing, book-keeping, sorting papers, filing, typing, duplicating, machine calculating, drawing and the editorial preparation of matter for publication.

In order that the provisions of the Act should apply to the premises the workers should not exclusively be near relatives of the employer and the sum total of work performed by all employees must exceed twenty-one hours per week.

Consequently, the Act covers the majority of persons employed in the catering industry except those in solely residential hotels and registered clubs. Three classifications of workers result:

1. Shop assistants who serve the general public in restaurants and bars of hotels, kitchen staff, and those who are engaged in a subsidiary retailing capacity in the larger hotels, such as hairdressers, florists, etc.
2. Administrative staff such as office staff, receptionists, cashiers, telephonists, etc.
3. Canteen employees who are engaged in the work of supplying and serving refreshment and food for the benefit of employees in offices, shops or railway premises. In this instance it must be appreciated that a canteen which exists for the purpose of serving meals to the workers in a factory could come within the very similar provisions of the Factories Act 1961.

The provisions of the Act exist only for the welfare and safety of the employees and do not apply only to the rooms in which people work; they also cover other parts of the premises used by them, i.e. stairs, passages, landings, storerooms, entrances, exits and yards.

The responsibility for complying with the provisions is usually that of the occupier, except where the premises are leased to the occupier and do not take up the complete building. In such a case the owner of the building will bear the responsibility.

The conditions which must be observed in all relevant premises can be classified as follows.

General health and welfare

1. *Cleanliness.* Section 4 of the Act requires that all premises, furniture, fittings and furnishings must be kept in a clean state. Accumulations of dirt and refuse must be eliminated and floors and steps must be cleaned at least once a week by the most effective means, i.e. washing, sweeping or by some other method. This latter requirement is obviously designed to prevent accidents which arise because of slippery floors, etc. The provision relates only to the cleanliness of the premises; the fit state of the commodities sold in a catering premises is governed by the Food and Drugs Act 1955.

2. *Overcrowding.* Section 5 provides that a room solely used by work people, and to which members of the public are not invited to resort, must not be overcrowded to a degree which would cause a risk of injury to health.

   To achieve this, the Act provides that for each person who habitually works in a room at one time, there must be 40 square feet (3.7 square metres) of floor space, or where the height of the room is less than 10 feet (3 metres), 400 cubic feet (11 cubic metres). In arriving at these figures, allowances must be made for the space taken up by furniture, cabinets and machinery in the room.

3. *Temperature.* Section 6 requires that a reasonable temperature shall be maintained in a work room where people are occupied otherwise than for short periods, and who are not involved in severe physical effort. The standard required is that the temperature must not be less than 16°C (60.8°F) after the first hour of working.

   There are exceptions to this condition, for example, office rooms which must be used by the public and therefore it would not be practical to maintain the required standard, or where the temperature would cause a deterioration of goods. In these cases employees must be given reasonable opportunity and access to means of warming themselves.

Where used, the means of heating must be safe, i.e. it must not be one which could cause injurious or offensive fumes and a thermometer must be provided in such a position as to permit the employees concerned to check the temperature.

4. *Ventilation.* Section 7 lays down a general requirement that all workrooms must be effectively and suitably ventilated to allow the circulation of fresh or artifically purified air.

5. *Lighting.* Section 8 relates to suitable and efficient lighting. It concerns the whole of the premises in which people work or commute and can be either natural or artificial lighting provided it is efficient. To achieve the required efficiency windows and skylights must, as far as is practical, be cleaned to keep them free from obstruction, but they can be treated to mitigate heat and glare.

6. *Sanitation.* Section 9 requires occupiers to provide sufficient and suitable sanitary facilities for both sexes. Such facilities must be properly maintained and kept in a clean condition. The requirement also includes the availability of adequate washing facilities, i.e. hot and cold water, soap and drying materals or equipment (s.10) and a sufficient supply of drinking water together with adequate drinking vessels (s.11).

The number of conveniences to be provided is governed by the numbers of workers of both sexes employed on the premises and the type of convenience it is intended to install.

7. *Seating arrangements.* Section 13 provides that employees who have reasonable opportunities for sitting without detriment to their work should have available for their use suitably situated seats. In shop premises the seats provided must not be less than one for every three workers.

8. *Accommodation for clothing.* Section 12 partially fills a Common Law deficiency. Arrangements for the accommodation of clothing must be made. This applies to clothing not worn during working hours as well as for clothing not taken home. Also where practicable, reasonable provision must be made for drying clothing.

Safety

1. *Floors, passages and stairs.* Section 16 relates to the construction

of floors, etc. These must be of sound construction and properly maintained and where practical kept free from slippery substances and obstructions. Suitable handrails must be provided on every staircase on both sides if necessary if there is a special hazard, and sufficiently well constructed to prevent people from accidentally falling through.

2. *Fencing dangerous parts of machinery.* Section 17: all dangerous parts of machinery must be fenced to prevent the operator from coming into contact with that dangerous part. This can be accomplished by either a guard which is fixed or, when this is not practical, by an automatic device. The guard must always be in position when the dangerous part is in motion or in use to guard against all foreseeable injuries. Section 19 confirms the Common Law duty that operators of dangerous machinery must be trained to operate the machine and warned of its potential danger. Section 18 prohibits persons under 18 years from cleaning any machine which might expose him to injury from a moving part of that or an adjacent machine.

3. *Heavy work.* Section 23: the Act prohibits an employee being required to lift, carry or move a heavy load which would be likely to injure him.

First-aid. Section 26 requires that an adequate first-aid box or cupboard must be made readily accessible to employees. If the staff exceeds 150 a second box must be available and each box must be placed in the charge of a responsible person. When the size of the staff warrants more than one first-aid box, one of the responsible persons must be trained in first-aid and be available during working hours.

Where a permanent first-aid room is available for the treatment of injured or sick people, the premises may be exempted from the need to maintain first-aid boxes.

Fire precautions. Sections 27 and 28 deal with the precautions which must be observed in all premises and lay down a standard of satisfaction which must be achieved, following inspection, to enable premises employing more than twenty people or more than ten above ground-floor level, to obtain a fire certificate without which it would be unlawful to operate as a business. These obligations are now dealt with by the provisions of the Fire Precautions Act 1971 (p.173). Sections 27 and 28 are repealed.

Health and Safety at Work Act 1974

Before the passing of the Health and Safety at Work Act 1974, it had for some time been recognised that existing industrial legislation suffered from defects which impeded its proper enforcement, viz.

1. Previous statutes are directed to defined categories of workplace such as factories, offices, shops, mines and quarries and in order that a particular provision should be capable of being enforced, it has to be established that the workplace concerned exactly comes within the statutory definition of a factory, office, shop, etc. contained in the statute supplying the provision.

2. The provisions themselves are drawn up in precise terms and concentrate upon specific items, e.g. the safe guarding of machinery, adequacy of heating, provision of sufficient lighting and ventilation, etc. and subsequent rulings by the courts tend to limit their application further.

The Robens Committee on Safety and Health at Work recommended a statutory framework applying to all workplaces, laying out in a broad framework the general duties of those involved in safety in employment so that in the course of time more detailed legislation could be enacted. The Health and Safety at Work Act 1974 follows the recommendations of the Committee's Report.

*s.*2 of the Act provides the duties of any employer:

1. It shall be the duty of every employer to ensure, so far as is reasonably practicable, the health, safety and welfare at work of all his employees.

2. Without prejudice to the generality of an employer's duty under 1. above, the matters to which that duty extends includes in particular:-

   (*a*) the provision and maintenance of plant and systems of work that are so far as is reasonably practicable, safe and without risks to health;

   (*b*) arrangements for ensuring, so far as is reasonably practicable, safety and absence of risks to health in connection with the use, handling, storage and transport of articles and substances;

   (*c*) the provision of such information, instruction, training and supervision as is necessary to ensure, so far as is reasonably practicable, the health and safety at work of his employees;

(*d*) so far as is reasonably practicable as regards any place of work under the employer's control, the maintenance of it in a condition that is safe and without risks to health and the provision and maintenance of means of access to and egress from it that are safe and without such risks;

(*e*) the provision and maintenance of a working environment for his employees that is, so far as is reasonably practicable, safe, without risks to health and adequate as regards facilities and arrangements for their welfare at work.

These provisions follow very closely the pattern formulated by the Common Law to compensate an employee for injury caused to him by his employer's failure to maintain a safe system of work and the Act has made provision that, contrary to the decision in *Groves v. Wimbourne* 1898 (p.153), an injured employee cannot base a civil claim for compensation upon a breach of a provision of the 1974 Act. For this purpose he can however utilise a provision of an earlier protective statute e.g. the Offices, Shops and Railways Premises Act 1963 where it remains unrepealed or any specific regulation eventually made under the authority of the 1974 Act. He also can continue to take an action based upon the continuing Common Law provision.

The 1974 Act extends the promotion of health and safety at work beyond the responsibility of management. No longer is it a management prerogative. The establishment of health and safety requirements must now involve the full cooperation of all employees and to this end they must be able to take part in making and monitoring arrangements for health and safety at their place of work. *s.2 s.s.*(4) of the Act allows the Secretary of State to make provision for the appointment of safety representatives by recognised trade unions from among the employees. Such safety officers must be consulted by employers to enable them and their employees to cooperate in formulating procedures to ensure health and safety and also to check the effectiveness of these procedures. An employer who fails to cooperate in this respect could be obliged to do so by the application of an improvement order (p.168).

The employee's responsibility in health and safety is also further emphasised in *s.*7 which lays down the general duties of employees at work. Every employee must take reasonable care for the health and safety of himself and of other persons who may be affected by his acts or omissions at work and he must cooperate with his employer so far as is necessary to perform or comply with any duty imposed by law. A breach of *s.*7 amounts to a criminal offence and this would result simply where the employee by his act or omission endangers the health or safety of other persons. Hitherto, commonsense obligations imposed upon employees have been implied into their contracts and frequently specifically imposed by the employer. *s.*7 reinforces the employer's right to take disciplinary action for disobedience of safety practices and certainly makes more secure his position when actions are taken by employees for unfair dismissal.

Codes of practice in relation to health and safety may be issued by the Health and Safety Commission or it may approve already existing or proposed codes of practice. Non-observance of an approved code does not of itself form the platform for criminal or civil proceedings, but in criminal proceedings it can be admitted as evidence where the provision contained in the code appears to the court to be relevant to the alleged breach of statute or regulation.

The Robens Committee recognised the diverse systems of inspectorate created by the other protective statutes and its suggestion that their functions should be amalgamated into a single department has been acted upon. The Act has created the Health and Safety Commission and the Health and Safety Executive, both of which are supervised by the Secretary of State. These bodies are responsible for encouraging measures to ensure health and safety and to investigate and prosecute when an employee has been injured in circumstances which appear to be in breach of the Act or other protective legislation, e.g. the Offices, Shops and Railway Premises Act. Such executive action will be taken by the Executive, which also through its inspectors has the already established powers of entry, inspection, interview and sampling. Where the Act is breached without incurring injury, provision is made for the serving of an 'improvement notice' with time limits respecting the implementation of a specified improvement or in more extreme cases, the serving of a 'prohibition notice' which has the effect of ordering the stoppage of the stipulated practices regarded as being potentially dangerous until safe conditions have been restored. An even more extreme measure is made available in that items which, in the opinion of the inspectors, constitute an immediate danger to personal safety, may be removed by them from the premises.

The Act provides powers of appeal from improvement and prohibition notices to an industrial tribunal.

DEFENCES TO BREACH OF STATUTORY DUTY

Where an action is brought based upon a breach of a duty imposed by the Offices, Shops and Railway Premises Act, the defendant, as in the case of a Common Law action, has defences available to him.

The defence of *volenti non fit injuria* does not apply to a breach of statutory duty because it is based upon consent and acceptance and no person can consent to waive a provision provided by statute. However, the defence based upon the plaintiff's contributory negligence will apply in exactly the way it does in an action in Common Law negligence (see page 157).

13
Employer's Responsibility for the Safety of Third Parties

The employer, in this case the owner of a hotel or restaurant, is not under the same duty to protect other persons who enter into his premises, as he is where his employees are concerned. However, the law does place some responsibility upon him for the safety of his guests and other persons, such as independent contractors, who come into his premises to work. The duties which apply in these cases are laid down in the Occupiers' Liability Act 1957 and the Fire Precautions Act 1971.

Also, an employer can be liable for injury caused to a third party by his employee when that employee is conducting the employer's business. This liability is imposed upon him through the doctrine of vicarious liability (see page 177).

THE OCCUPIERS' LIABILITY ACT 1957

Section 2 of the Occupiers' Liability Act 1957 provides that, to persons entering on his land with his permission, whether expressed or implied, the occupier has a duty 'to take such care as in all the circumstances is reasonable to see that the visitor will be reasonably safe in using the premises for the purpose for which he is invited or permitted by the occupier to be there'.

This duty is owed to everyone, therefore, except a trespasser, and includes guests, workmen carrying out repairs, tradesmen delivering commodities to the premises and entertainers contracted to perform on the premises.

In the case of contractors, the 1957 Act provides that 'an occupier may expect that a person, in the exercise of his calling, will appreciate and guard against any special risks ordinarily incidental to it, as far as the occupier leaves him free to do so'.

So where the occupier employs, for example, an electrician to carry out his work in connection with his trade, he is entitled to expect the electrician to be competent to deal with and guard himself against, the dangers which could arise from working with an electrical installation.

The Act also anticipates the fact that injury could be caused to a guest because of the faulty work of an independent contractor, and relieves the occupier who employed him from liability if, first of all, it was reasonable that the work should be carried out by the contractor, and secondly, that the occupier had satisfied himself that the contractor was competent in his professed trade. Where injury is caused to a guest in these circumstances his action should be taken against the contractor.

Therefore the occupier's duty involves only those factors which are under his control, except where the doctrine of vicarious liability is concerned (see p. 177) and includes the security and proper maintenance of safe carpets, stair bannisters, lifts and efficient lighting. Whether or not an occupier will be liable in any case will depend upon the relevant facts. Normally an action for negligence will succeed if the guest is injured in a part of the premises to which access is allowed. The occupier, therefore, must give clear notice that certain parts of the premises are not accessible to persons other than staff. If no notice is given he could be liable for an injury caused to a guest irrespective of the situation of the accident.

In *Campbell v. Shelbourne Hotel Ltd* (1939) the lights in a passageway of the hotel were switched off at 11 p.m. Campbell, a guest, searching for a toilet at 11.20 p.m., walked down the unlit passageway, opened a door leading into a private part of the premises, fell down some steps and was injured. It was held that the hotel management had been unreasonable in switching off the light in a passageway which might be used by a guest and, therefore, Campbell was entitled to damages.

The same degree of care must must also be observed with notices explaining procedures to be followed in an emergency, especially in the event of a fire.

In *McLenan v. Segar* (1917) fire broke out in a hotel during the night. A guest who had arrived late and who had been taken immediately to her bedroom had no knowledge of the emergency procedure to be followed and was injured when she tried to escape from the premises through a second-floor window. It was held that the proprietor was liable.

The case of *Stone v. Taffe* (1974) illustrates that a duty under the 1957 Act is owed even when the injury is caused to a visitor who is on the premises in circumstances which are contrary to the law and against the orders of the owner of the premises. Mr and Mrs Stone attended a party at a public house and the licensee continued to serve drinks until after midnight although no extension of the licence beyond 'closing time' had been obtained. When they left at 1.0 a.m. they had to negotiate a stairway which was in complete darkness. Mr Stone fell down the stairway and suffered head injuries from which he died. The Court of Appeal held that there had been a breach of a duty of care under the 1957 Act since, at the time of the accident, Mr Stone was a visitor on the premises and had no knowledge that an extension to the licence had not been obtained to allow the party to continue and drinks to be sold after 10.30 p.m. Also in this case it was held that, although the negligence in failing to light the stairway was that of the licensee, an action against the owners of the public house must succeed because they were vicariously liable for this negligence even though the licensee, their servant, had in the circumstances acted contrary to an agreement between them. The compensation awarded took into account Mr Stone's contributory negligence.

We must also consider the duty of care which is owed by an occupier of hotel premises to children allowed on the premises. Dangers which may be obvious to an adult may be concealed or be a temptation to a child. Therefore it is not sufficient to give a warning if the child would not profit by it; the occupier must take due care to protect the child from all dangers to which he might be exposed by entering the premises. However, this greater duty of care applies only to obviously dangerous situations. These apart, the occupier's duty, as in all other cases, is a duty of reasonable care. There is no obligation to ensure that the premises are absolutely safe before allowing a child to enter. 'There is nothing with which a child cannot hurt himself' (*Morley v. Staffordshire C.C.* (1939)). However, even in the case of trespassers, especially children, the occupier has a duty to afford protection against known potential dangers; *British Rail Board v. Herrington* (1972) followed in *Southern Cement Ltd v. Cooper* (1974).

In *Panett v. P. McGuinness Ltd* (1972), Lord Denning laid

down four guidelines to be observed.
1. A commonsense assessment of the gravity or likelihood of probable injury must be borne in mind.
2. Account must be taken of the character of the intrusion by the trespasser or allowance made for the thoughtlessness of little children.
3. Regard must be made to the nature of the place where the trespass occurred.
4. Account must be taken of the knowledge which the owner or occupier has or ought to have of the likelihood of trespassers coming onto the premises.

DEFENCES AVAILABLE TO THE OCCUPIER

The same defences that are avialable to Common Law actions based upon negligence are available to occupiers of premises. The defence of *volenti non fit injuria* is rarely accepted by the court; the offending danger should not have existed, but if it did, it would be difficult to prove that the injured person had accepted the risk, although he had been warned about it.

Contributory negligence as explained in Chapter 12 is a more likely defence as is one based upon evidence that the plaintiff was injured whilst doing something which was not within the occupier's intention when he was allowed into the premises; for example, a guest in a hotel injures himself whilst trying to repair a faulty television set without the knowledge of the occupier.

Clauses in contracts which are intended to exempt the proprietor from liability for personal injury to third parties are not now recognised by a court; Unfair Contract Terms Act 1977 (p.80).

THE FIRE PRECAUTIONS ACT 1971

Before the Fire Precautions Act 1971 the necessity for the occupier of a premises to obtain a fire certificate from the local fire authority showing its approval of the adequacy of the fire escape facilites applied only to those premises which came within the definitions in the Factories Act 1961 and the Offices, Shops and Railway Premises Act 1963. Parts of a hotel used as bedrooms or for the entertainment of guests were not subject to the requirement of certification.

The 1971 Act now makes provisions which cover these deficiencies.

The premises subject to the Act

Section 1 of the Act requires that a fire certificate must be issued by the fire authority for premises which are put to a use designated by that section. The premises which concern the catering industry are:

1. Those used for the provision of sleeping accommodation.
2. Those used for the purposes of entertainment, recreation or instruction for the purposes of any club, society or association.
3. Those used for any purpose involving access to the premises by members of the public, whether on payment or otherwise.
4. In certain circumstances the living quarters of a premises can be made subject to the provisions of a fire certificate. It is the intention of *s*.3 of the Act that this should apply to living accommodation in hotels, restaurants, etc., where that accommodation is:
   (*a*) below the ground floor of the building containing the premises; or,
   (*b*) two or more floors above the ground floor of that building; or,
   (*c*) a room, the floor of which is six metres or more above the surface of the ground on any side of the building;
   (*d*) a part of a building which stores explosives or highly inflammable materials in greater quantities than the maximum prescribed in relation to materials of that type.

Control over the categories of premises mentioned has been gradually implemented by 'designating orders' issued by the Secretary of State and eventually has extended to premises carrying on the business of an hotel or boarding house providing sleeping accommodation for staff and/or sleeping, dining room, drawing room, ball room, or other guest accommodation. Prior to the passing of the Health and Safety at Work Act 1974 certain hotel premises where sleeping accommodation for six or less guests and staff was provided, and all restaurants, were excluded from the Act's control. However *s*.78 of the 1974 Health and Safety at Work Act extended the premises listed above by the qualifying words 'used as a place of work' and an order by the Secretary of State in 1976 made this effective so that any place of work now requires a fire certificate. So certain shop premises now come under the authority of the fire safety officers. This means that all catering establishments which fall within the definition of a shop must seek a fire certificate if they employ in excess of twenty persons on the premises at one time or more than ten persons above ground floor level.

The application

Section 5 provides that an application for a fire certificate must be made to the fire authority and must contain the following:

1. Details of the particular use or uses of the premises which it is desired to have covered by the certificate.
2. Relevant information required about the premises or any matter connected with them, and, if the premises are a part of a building, similar information respecting the rest of the building.

The fire authority can require the applicant to supply a plan of the premises which is the subject of the application or whenever possible a plan of the building of which the premises forms a part. The time within which the plans are to be submitted will be stipulated and failure by the applicant to comply with the request or to apply for an extension of that time will lead to a presumption that the application has been withdrawn. From a practical point of view it is desirable that plans should be made available to the fire authority. It is easier to indicate accurately on the plan what modifications should be made to satisfy the fire authority than to detail them in a written report.

Following the receipt of all the required information, it is then the duty of the fire authority to carry out an inspection of the premises and any relevant adjacent building or part of a building to satisfy itself that the following provisions are such as may reasonably be required in connection with the proposed use of the premises:

1. The means of escape in case of fire; and
2. The means (other than that for fighting fire) for securing that the means of escape can be safely and effectively used at all material times; and
3. The means for fighting fire, whether in the premises or affecting the means of escape, for use in case of fire by persons in the building; and
4. The means for giving persons in the premises warning in the case of fire.

If the fire authority is satisfied with the adequacy of these factors it will issue a certificate covering the intended use of the premises.

In a case where the factors are, in the opinion of the fire authority, not adequate, it must inform the applicant of that fact and the steps which must be taken, whether by making an alteration or installing a new device which would then satisfy the standards it requires, and that a fire certificate will not be issued unless those steps are taken within a specified time.

An extension of time can be granted by the fire authority or by an order of a court if the applicant decides to appeal as provided under s.9 of the Act. A failure to complete the required adaptations at the end of the original or extended period of time will result in a refusal of the application for a fire certificate.

The fire certificate

The fire certificate for any premises must specify the use of the premises covered by it and also the factors which were the subject of the inspection. In the cases of fire fighting and means of giving warning, details of the number and location of the apparatus must also be specified; if possible, reference to a plan is desirable.

Additionally, the certificate must impose other requirements which the fire authority considers to be necessary in the circumstances, for example, that the means of escape are properly maintained and free from obstruction, that employees are given appropriate fire training and that records be kept relating to this, that there be a limitation upon the number of persons on the premises at any one time, and that other precautions should be observed.

In December 1973 the two following additions were added to the requirements to be included in fire certificates issued for premises covered by the first designating order made under the Act:

1. Bedroom doors should be self closing as well as fire resisting at the discretion of and to the satisfaction of the fire authority.
2. An automatic fire detection system should be provided and maintained in certified premises as considered necessary by the fire authority.

   This applies also to premises not employing the required number of persons, i.e. less than twenty etc.

s.78 of the 1974 Act also inserted into the Fire Precautions Act an additional section, s.9A, which provides that all premises covered by the Offices, Shops and Railway Premises Act 1963 shall be provided with an adequate means of escape from fire having regard to the persons working in those premises.

The fire certificate, when issued, is sent to the occupier of the premises and must be kept in those premises whilst it is in force.

Section 8 provides that as long as a fire certificate is in force, the fire authority can inspect the premises at any reasonable time to ascertain if there has been a change of the conditions making them inadequate for the specified use.

Schedule 8 of the 1974 Act provides that fire certificates obtained under the provisions of the Factories Act or the Offices, Shops and Railway Premises Act, shall continue in force but shall be deemed to be 1971 Act certificates.

Offences

It is an offence under *s*.7 to use any premises when that use by *s*.1 requires the issue of a fire certificate and none has been issued.

It is also an offence, even though a fire certificate is in force in respect of a premises, to contravene any specified requirement whether in a positive or negative manner, for example, to fail to keep a means of escape free from obstruction.

A person guilty of such a offence shall be liable:

1. On summary conviction, to a fine not exceeding £400.
2. On conviction on indictment, to a fine or to imprisonment for a term not exceeding two years, or both.

Powers of a court

A complaint can be made to a court by the fire authority, if it is satisfied that there will be a risk to persons by fire, that until the premises have been satisfactorily adapted its intended or actual use should be prohibited. The court, if satisfied with the evidence supporting the complaint, can make an order prohibiting or restricting the use of the premises to the extent appropriate in the circumstances until the necessary alterations or additions have been completed.

VICARIOUS LIABILITY

An employer can be liable in tort for the actions of his employee which cause injury to a third party, even though he had no knowledge of those acts and perhaps had actually forbidden their performance. This is known as vicarious liability. The same liability for the criminal acts of an employee is discussed in Chapter 19.

The injured person, of course, has a right of action against the offending employee and the question is asked: why should the employer also bear responsibility? Many reasons have been put forward to explain the doctrine of vicarious liability. The most practical explanation, however, is that the employer should be responsible because he has made it possible for the employee to do the injuring act and therefore he should bear the financial consequences as a part of the costs of running his business. A wise employer should be insured to cover such incidents.

What does matter is that it must be proved that the employee performed the injurious act whilst acting in the course of his employment, that is, he was employed to do that act even though he did it in a negligent or even an unauthorised manner.

Thus in *L.CC. v. Cattermoles Garages Ltd* (1953) a young garage attendant was employed to push cars to the side of the garage after they had been repaired. He was not licensed to drive motor vehicles and was instructed not to drive any car. However, he did drive a car on one occasion and steered it into the highway where it was involved in a collision with an L.C.C. vehicle. It was held that Cattermoles Garages Ltd were liable because he was doing what he was paid to do although in an unauthorised manner.

The act of the employee must be done for his employer's benefit and not for his own convenience. Even if the employer has given permission for the performance of the extraneous act which causes injury, the employee will bear full responsibility.

Where the injury is caused as a result of the commission of a criminal offence, whether or not the employer will be vicariously liable in a civil action for damages depends upon the degree of integration of the criminal act within the duty which the employee was performing.

Thus in *Warren v. Henlys Ltd* (1948) it was held that the employer was not liable when a garage attendant injured a customer by assaulting him during an argument about the price of petrol which had been supplied. The assault was not an integral part of his job to supply petrol.

However in *Lloyd v. Grace, Smith and Co.* (1912) the company, a firm of solicitors, was held to be vicariously liable when its managing clerk fraudulently induced Mrs Lloyd, a client, to sign papers which conveyed property to himself. This criminal action was an integral part of carrying out something which he was employed to do.

In both the above cases the actual offenders were liable to be convicted for their actions.

The case of *Stone v. Taffe* 1974 (p. 172) is also an illustration of vicarious liability arising even though the employee has acted against the orders of his employer and in circumstances which were contrary to the law.

A difficulty which can present itself in circumstances involving vicarious liability arises when the incident involves a 'loaned' employee, for example, the Castle Hotel, which is temporarily short of kitchen staff, borrows the services of a chef from the Gower Hotel. During that period of employment the chef, through negligence in his cooking, causes a guest to become ill. Which employer, the Castle Hotel or the Gower Hotel, is vicariously liable?

The question is resolved by an application of the control test described in Chapter 8. Has the Castle Hotel the ability, through its management, to control the manner in 'how' the chef performs his work? If so, it will be vicariously liable. If not, the vicarious liability will belong to the permanent employer, the Gower Hotel.

14
Food Regulations–
Protecting the Consumer

The greater part of this book is devoted to examining the law from the hotelier's point of view. However, in this chapter we examine the law from the consumer's point of view. In particular, we consider what legal action is possible by or on behalf of a consumer who has suffered after consuming contaminated food or drink. First of all, we look at the civil actions which the consumer himself may take against the guilty party, arising out of breach of contract or negligence, and then we examine the criminal prosecutions which may be instituted against the guilty party for breach of food regulations.

RIGHTS ARISING OUT OF A CONTRACT

The consumer who has purchased adulterated food may sue the seller for damages arising out of breach of the contract. Of particular importance in this respect is the Sale of Goods Act 1979 because this Act states the law regarding contracts for the sales of goods and supplements the rules of contract already set out in Chapter 7.

In order to succeed in his action the consumer must be a party to the contract. In other words he, himself, must have bought the goods from the shop-keeper, or the round of drinks from the licensee, or the meal from the restaurant owner. In *Buckley v. La Reserve* (1959) a woman guest who became ill after eating snails at a restaurant could not sue the owner for breach of contract as she herself did not pay for the meal. However, it is sufficient if the goods are bought for the consumer by somebody acting on his behalf as his agent. In *Chaproniere v. Mason* (1905) a solicitor who sent his clerk to the local baker's to purchase a bath-bun broke a tooth and developed an ulcer in his jaw after biting into the bun which contained a stone. His action against the baker was successful.

A claim for damages for breach of contract may even include a claim by a husband for loss of his wife's services. However, the special relationship of husband and wife must exist. In *Jackson v. Watson* (1909) a husband whose wife died from food poisoning after eating salmon purchased by the husband from the defendant obtained damages from him.

When the consumer sues the seller for breach of contract, he is alleging in effect that the seller has broken an implied term in the contract of sale relating to the merchantable quality or fitness of the goods. Section 14 of the Sale of Goods Act 1979 sets out these implied terms. Although the general rule states that in a contract of sale there is no implied promise about the quality or fitness of goods (*caveat emptor*—let the buyer beware), it is the following exceptions which are so important.

Merchantable quality

Section 14(2) states:

> 'Where a seller sells goods in the course of a business, there is an implied condition that the goods supplied.under the contract are of merchantable quality, except that there is no such condition—
> (a) as regards defects specifically drawn to the buyer's attention before the contract is made; or
> (b) if the buyer examines the goods before the contract is made, as regards defects which that examination ought to reveal'.

The rule applies to all goods 'supplied under the contract'. In *Geddling v. Marsh* (1929) a defective lemonade bottle, which was to be returned to the seller after use, was said to be within the rule.

Goods are said to be of merchantable quality 'if they are as fit for the purposes for which goods of that kind are commonly bought as it is reasonable to expect, having regard to any description applied to them, the price (if relevant) and all the circumstances'.

So, a business man selling a second-hand freezer may argue that it is 'merchantable' even though its condition is not perfect.

Notice must be taken of its age, its price and all other relevant circumstances.

Furthermore, as the packaging of goods is also covered by s.14 imperfect packaging may render them unmerchantable.

If the goods have to be treated by the buyer they must be merchantable after the treatment, though not necessarily before. A lady who became ill through inadequately cooking pork shops, could not claim that the sellers were liable under s.14 (*Heil v. Hedges* (1951)). Goods are expected to be of merchantable quality not only at the time when they are bought but for a reasonable time thereafter. Of course, much depends upon the type of goods: strawberries would be expected to last only a few days whilst potatoes would last several weeks.

If there is a defect in the goods which cannot be discovered on examination then the seller will be liable: it is no use the seller pleading that the buyer actually examined the goods. In *Wren v. Holt* (1903) the buyer who was taken ill after consuming beer which contained arsenic recovered damages from the seller for breach of merchantable quality, as no examination by the buyer would have revealed that defect.

Fitness

Section 14(3) states:

> 'Where the seller sells goods in the course of a business and the buyer, expressly or by implication, makes known to the seller any particular purpose for which the goods are being bought there is an implied condition that the goods supplied under the contract are reasonably fit for that purpose. . . .'

The words 'in the course of a business' in both sections includes sales from shops, restaurants and hotels; anywhere, in fact, where a business is conducted. However, it would not cover a sale by a private householder.

With regard to the purchase of food, the purpose for which the buyer needs the food is always understood 'by implication'. In *Chaproniere v. Mason* the solicitor's clerk had no need to state that he wanted the bun in order for his employer to eat it: that fact was presumed.

Exclusion clauses in contracts for the sale of goods

Section 55 of the Sale of Goods Act makes void any attempt by the seller to exclude from the contract these implied terms of merchantable quality and fitness when selling to a consumer (see Chapter 7).

THE SELLER'S NEGLIGENCE AGAINST THE CONSUMER

We have already seen how the sick lady in *Buckley v. La Reserve* could not sue the restaurant owner for breach of contract as she was not a party to the contract of purchasing the meal. However, such a person may have a good claim based upon the seller's or the manufacturer's negligence. Here we are moving into the realms of tort and of liability based on fault. The famous case of *Donoghue v. Stevenson* (1932) decided that manufacturers do owe a duty to the ultimate consumer to take care in manufacturing their goods where there is no likelihood of such goods being examined before they reach the eventual consumer. If they break this duty they are liable to pay damages for the injury caused to the consumer. What happened in *Donoghue v. Stevenson* was that two ladies went into a café, where one of them bought the other, Mrs Donoghue, a bottle of ginger-beer and an ice-cream. The ginger-beer bottle was opaque. After she had poured some of the ginger-beer into a glass and drunk it, Mrs Donoghue poured out the remainder. But it was not just ginger-beer which flowed from the bottle: the remains of a snail, in a decomposed state, also came out. Mrs Donoghue suffered both from shock and gastro-enteritis. She successfully claimed damages against Stevenson, the manufacturer.

The decision in this case was a landmark in the development of the law of tort. The case decided that all manufacturers who intend that their goods shall reach the consumer in the same condition in which they leave the factory have a duty to that consumer to take care and must compensate for any harm done. As so many goods these days are packeted by the manufacturer the rule is of vital importance. However, the rule is not confined just to manufacturers. It can apply to sellers of goods as well, in fact, any situation where a duty of care is owed by one person to another. Perhaps the lady in *Buckley v. La Reserve* might had succeeded had she claimed damages against the restaurant owner for negligence though the case would not have been easy to prove.

Lord Atkin explained what is meant by this duty of care:

'You must take reasonable care to avoid acts or omissions which you can reasonably foresee would be likely to injure your neighbour. Who, then, in law, is my neighbour? The answer seems to be persons who are so closely and directly affected by my act that I ought reasonably to have them in contemplation as being so affected when I am directing my mind to the acts or omissions which are called in question'.

The injured consumer does have a heavy responsibility of proving negligence by the seller. It is hardly surprising therefore, that he is reluctant to start legal proceedings himself, especially as they may be expensive and long drawn-out. A more suitable remedy may lie within the food regulations, which are discussed below.

PROTECTION UNDER THE FOOD REGULATIONS

We must now examine the standards set by Parliament concerning the quality of food and how it maintains those standards.

Protection for both the consumer and the honest trader against adulterated food can be traced back as far as the thirteenth century. Originally, it was the duty of the guilds to maintain the purity of their commodities with which their members dealt although it seems that they performed this duty more to protect themselves against dishonest traders than to protect the general public. For example, the Guild of Pepperers was responsible for maintaining the purity of pepper, which, as it has the effect of preserving meat and other food, has always been a very important commodity. The guild employed garblers, whose duty was to detect and remove impurities. The detection was done mainly by appearance, taste and smell rather than by any scientific means.

Other staple foods were bread and wine. An Act of 1202 aimed to control the price of bread whilst the Bakers' Company, founded in 1307, controlled its quality. The penalties for persistently making impure bread were harsh. Any baker whose bread contained sand was taken to the pillory, his load preceding him on a lance. It was a very common practice to water down the beer and then restore the froth and flavour by use of coperas, coriander seed and *cocculus indicus*. The brewer who was guilty of such an offence could expect a visit to the Tumbrel. The ale tasters who were under oath to taste the ale of any brewer, recorded the quality by making the casks X, XX or XXX.

At about the beginning of the nineteenth century two factors began to emerge which showed how ineffective was the control by the guilds, namely, the growth of scientific knowledge and the publication of literature, especially trade books and recipes, both of which disclosed evidence of adulteration of food. By the middle of the century public opinion was sufficiently aroused to urge Parliament to protect the public. We must realise that this was the era of the Industrial Revolution, the time when masses of people moved into towns and lived in close proximity to each other. Sanitation was deplorable, the fear of epidemic and disease was ever present and the problem of malnutrition very real. Against this background the Adulteration of Food and Drink Act was passed in 1860, the first in a series of Acts which set out a comprehensive system of controlling and testing food, and in 1878 the first Weights and Measures Act came into operation. By these Acts local authorities were empowered to appoint enforcement officers and this was sufficient to ensure that progress became a reality.

FOOD AND DRUGS ACT 1955

The aim of the Food and Drugs Act 1955, which consolidates all previous legislation, is to protect the public against adulterated food and to impose penalties against those persons who contravene its regulations.

Offences under Sections 1 and 2

By s.1 it is an offence to treat or add a substance to food intended for human consumption so as to render it injurious to health, or to sell such food or even to possess such food for sale. Mistake is no defence to a charge of adulterating food or selling it.

By s.2 it is an offence to sell food which is not 'of the nature or not of the substance or not of the quality demanded if the purchaser is prejudiced by the sale'. This section affords a general protection to purchasers of food.

What is meant by the phrase 'sell . . . food'? An offence is committed even though the substance sold is not classified as 'food' (or drink) and is, in fact, quite different. In *Knight v. Bowers* (1885) a customer who asked to purchase saffron (used at that time in the treatment for measles) was supplied with Savin (a drug improperly used for procuring an abortion). The retailer was found guilty of selling food not of the nature or quality demanded. Again, in *Meah v. Roberts* (1978) a restaurant owner and a third party were successfully prosecuted under sections 2 and 8 for serving caustic soda instead of lemonade to a customer's children. The mistake had arisen after the third party (an employee of a company servicing equipment at the restaurant) had put the chemical in an old lemonade bottle. In both cases the court felt that the Act was intended to protect customers from this type of situation.

How does the court decide whether a foodstuff is of 'the quality demanded?' The person who sells margarine for butter, or chicory for coffee is obviously guilty of an offence under s.2. However, it is not always as simple as this. So the Act gives power to the appropriate Minister to introduce regulations which set out the standards required for certain foods, and these regulations afford a guide. Listed below are some examples.

Foodstuff	Authority	Provision
Margarine	The Margarine Regulations 1967 S.I. 1967 No. 1867	Not less than 80% fat of which (*a*) not more than 1/10 is milk fat and (*b*) not more than 16% is water. Every ounce of margarine shall contain Vitamin A 760-940 i.u.'s, Vitamin D 80-100 i.u.'s.
Butter	The Butter Regulations 1966 S.I. 1966 No. 1074	Butter shall contain (*a*) not less than 80% milk fat (*b*) not more than 2% milk solids other than fat and (*c*) not more than 16% water. Butter may contain less than 80% but not less than 78% milk fat provided that: (*a*) the amount by which milk fat % falls below 80% does not exceed the amount by which % of salt in such butter exceeds 3% AND (*b*) the words 'SALTED BUTTER' are clearly legible on any container, label or ticket.

Not every item of food, however, is controlled by a food standard regulation. In the absence of such statutory standards, the court must fix its own standard based on the evidence presented before it, especially that presented by the public health inspector and the public analyst. Very often the court gains considerable help from a code of guidance. These codes, which do not have the force of law, were published from 1945 onwards by the Ministry of Food after consultation with representatives of the trade concerned. They set out what the traders consider to be minimum standard of quality in a particular food, but are purely voluntary. One example of a voluntary code in recent years is the code issued in 1970 by the Meat and Livestock Commission, which required meat to be labelled giving a description of it, including price and origin. However, the butchers were so afraid of contravening the Trade Descriptions Act 1968 that their campaign against making the code compulsory was successful.

Defences to Section 2 offences

The seller cannot plead that he made a mistake. However, by *s*.3 he does have a good defence:

1. If he can prove that he actually brought to the purchaser's notice the fact that the article was not of the nature, substance or quality demanded. In *Rodbourn v. Hudson* (1925) the licensee of a public house was convicted for selling spirits below the minimum strength required by law. He claimed that he did display a notice informing the purchaser of this fact, but his plea was dismissed by the court on the grounds that the notice was insufficient. The purchaser must be told in substance that the thing which he is getting is not the thing he asked for. Furthermore, in this case, the notice was ambiguous and misleading.
2. Or if he can prove that he did not act fraudulently and that the article carried a notice clearly stating the contents, or was sold in a wrapper clearly displaying such a notice. However, this defence is not available if the food has been rendered dangerous to health.
3. Or if he can prove that where the food contains some extraneous matter, it got into the food as an unavoidable consequence of the process of collection and preparation.

   Recently the House of Lords has placed a strict interpretation upon this defence under *s*.3 (3). In *Smedley's Ltd v. Breed* (1974), Smedley's Ltd were fined £25 for contravening *s*.2 of the Food and Drugs Act 1955 in respect of a sale to a housewife of a tin of peas containing a caterpillar. It was conceded that the caterpillar was harmless, having been cooked, and that not only would it have caused no injury to have been eaten, but might even have given benefit! There was no suggestion of negligence either on the part of the manufacturer or on the part of the seller. The court was told that in 1971 a total of three and a half million tins of peas had been manufactured by Smedley's and out of this number only four complaints had been received. Smedley's had a screening process which eliminated waste matter of a markedly higher or lower specific gravity than peas and a system of supervised visual inspection. Unfortunately, the caterpillar was of the same or similar density, diameter and weight as the peas and so had escaped the screening process, and, being of a green colour similar to the peas, it appeared to have been missed by the visual inspectors.

Smedley's were held liable for the following reason: whilst the presence of a caterpillar in a pea pod or in freshly cut cabbage might be an unavoidable consequence of the process of collecting the peas or the cabbage from the fields where they were grown, nevertheless, its presence in a tin of peas could not be said to be an unavoidable consequence of the preparation of the tins of peas, unless it could not be removed in the course of preparation. If any human agency in any way concerned in a proper process could avoid the consequences by the exercise of a high standard of reasonable care, the consequences were avoidable. Smedley's were found guilty because they could have avoided it.

In fairness to Smedley's, the court did comment that they could see little useful purpose in prosecuting the firm; no further suggestions were put forward as to how Smedley's could avoid such an event happening again, the chances of which are a million to one against. However, technically the firm was guilty of an offence under s.2 and therefore could not bring themselves within the defence set out in s.3.

4. If he can prove, if he is charged with selling diluted whisky, brandy, rum or gin, that the spirit had been diluted only with water and that its strength was still not lower than 35° under proof.

For further general defences under s.113 and s.115 see page 192.

Note: An employer can be charged under this section of the

Act with an offence which is committed by his employee, even if he had no knowledge of the employee's wrong-doing and even though he had taken steps to prevent a breach of the law.

Section 8 of the Food and Drugs Act

By *s*.8(*a*) it is an offence for a person to sell or offer for sale food which is unfit for human consumption. If the food has been sold to the offender by some other person, that other person is also guilty of an offence.

By *s*.8(*b*) it is an offence to deposit or consign food unfit for human consumption to any person for the purpose of selling it or preparing it for sale.

This section aims to protect a customer who has purchased contaminated food. It is a strict offence and difficult for the accused to evade liability. The accused cannot plead that he did not know the food was bad. In *Hobbs v. Winchester Corporation* (1910) a butcher sold unfit meat and was prosecuted under *s*.117 of the Public Health Act 1875 (a section with almost identical wording to *s*.8 of the Food and Drugs Act). He was found guilty of the offence even though the contamination could not have been discovered until it had been professionally analysed.

Unfit for human consumption. Whether or not the food is unfit for human consumption is always a question of fact. The following points should be noted:

1. Food which is putrid or decomposed is within the definition.
2. Where a wholesome article of food contains a single extraneous body, not itself toxic, although not fit to be eaten, then that food does not become unfit for human consumption. In *J. Miller Ltd v. Battersea Borough Council* (1955) a chocolate bun contained a small piece of metal, which a child, while eating the bun, got into its mouth. In *Turner and Sons Ltd v. Owen* (1955) a loaf of bread contained a piece of string. In neither case did the court find that the food was unfit for human consumption. (*Note:* In both these cases there would be an infringement of *s*.2 of the Act.)
3. But if a single extraneous article, which finds its way into food, is toxic, then the food will be unfit for human consumption. In *Chibnall's Bakeries v E. J. Cope-Brown* (1956) it was held that a loaf of bread containing part of a used and dirty bandage was unfit for human consumption.
4. Where an article of food is going mouldy, *prima facie* it is 'unfit for human consumption' and it matters not whether there

would be injury to health if it were eaten. It is a matter of degree in each case. In *David Greig v. Goldfinch* (1961) the appellants had sold, at 9.30 a.m. on a Saturday, a pork pie which had been baked on the previous Tuesday. At 5 p.m. on the day of the sale small particles of mould were found underneath the top crust. The mould was of the penicillin type which of itself is not harmful to human beings. The court accepted the evidence that at the time of the sale there was a small quantity of mould underneath the pie crust. The appellants were found guilty. Lord Parker, C. J., stated that he had no intention to say exactly what was meant by the expression 'unfit for human consumption'. Whilst agreeing that it meant something more than unsuitable—a stale loaf is unsuitable though not unfit for human consumption —he was not prepared to say that in every prosecution under this section the prosecutor must prove that if a person ate the food it would be injurious to his health and dangerous to him.

An employer can be charged for an offence under the Act committed by his employee, even if he had no knowledge of the employee's wrong-doing and even though he had taken steps to prevent a breach of the law, provided that the employee was acting in the normal course of his employment.

Defences under Section 8

1. An accused person can plead that, when he handed over the unfit food he informed the recipient that it was so unfit.
2. If charged under *s*.8(*b*) a consignor may plead that when he consigned the food either it was fit for human consumption or he did not know and could not with reasonable diligence have known of the condition of it. The consignor has a heavy responsibility. In *Jordan v. White* (1945), it was held that reliance by the consignor upon an inspection made on behalf of the public health inspector was not sufficient to show that the consignor had been reasonably diligent.

Section 6 of the Food and Drugs Act

By *s*.6 it is an offence to publish a false or misleading advertisement relating to food. It is a good defence to show that the advertiser did not know of the deception or that he received the advertisement in the ordinary course of his business.

Section 13 of the Food and Drugs Act

Power exists under *s*.13 of the Act for the appropriate Ministers to introduce food hygiene regulations. The most recent of these regulations were made in 1970 and a copy of them (Ref. 1970 No. 1172) is obtainable from any Stationery Office. Their purpose is to ensure that a minimum standard of cleanliness exists in premises where a 'food-business' is carried on, and where food is stored or transported. The regulations are made for the purpose of protecting public health so all catering establishments are covered whether they are run for profit or not.

The regulations deal with:

1. cleanliness of premises and equipment, including toilets and washing facilities;
2. personal cleanliness of the employee and his clothing;
3. preparing and packing food on domestic premises;
4. first-aid facilities;
5. lighting, ventilating and temperature of rooms.

Note: There is no specific regulation banning dogs from food premises, as it would involve too many technical difficulties. However, within the Food Hygiene Regulations it is stated: 'No person shall expose food to the risk of contamination'. The definition of contamination can be found within the Model Bye-Laws 1955, where it states that 'Contamination means contamination by water, dust, disease, insects and animals'. As these Model Bye-Laws are frequently adopted by local authorities many areas are covered by such a regulation.

Control of Food Premises Act 1976

Where there has been a conviction under the Hygiene Regulations then, under the above Act the court may order the closure of the food premises or stalls which it considers are dangerous to health. As such orders may take time before they can be obtained, power is also given to the court to grant an emergency order for closing food premises or stalls when there is an imminent risk of danger to health. Failure to obey such orders may result in fines not exceeding £400.

Section 7 of the Food and Drugs Act

Appropriate Ministers are empowered by *s*.7 of the Act to issue Labelling of Food Regulations. The most recent were issued in 1970 and amended in 1972 and 1976.

An offence is committed where food is sold or exposed for

sale within a label or in a container which falsely describes the articles or is calculated to mislead. It is a good defence if the seller can show that he did not know and could not with reasonable diligence have known of the deception.

Generally speaking, pre-packed foods must be labelled with the common or usual name of the food, or a description of the food which is clear enough to indicate its true nature. Unless the quantity or proportion of each ingredient is specified they must be listed in order of importance, according to weight, with the greatest first. With the main exceptions of bread, pastries and sweets, if goods are sold without being pre-packed then a ticket must be displayed near them, clearly visible to customers, stating the name or description of the food.

General defences: Sections 113 and 115

In addition to the specific defences already mentioned in relation to certain sections of the Food and Drugs Act, the following defences may be pleaded by a person charged with an offence either under the Act or under a Regulation.

1. *Default of another* (s.113). If the person charged alleges that the contravention was due to the default of another, he may ask that other person to be brought before the court. If the original person accused can prove that the other was in fact responsible, and that he himself used all diligence to observe the law, then he may be acquitted and the other convicted. Alternatively, the prosecution may proceed against the person actually responsible (s.115). In *Meah v. Roberts* (see page 186) the restaurant owner asked for the service company's employee to be joined as a co-defendant. Both were found guilty, the former because of his negligence, the latter because his actions caused the offence even though he had not actually sold the 'lemonade' to the injured parties.
2. *Warranty* (s.115). If the accused actually purchased the article in the name or description under which he sold it, and if he obtained from the vendor a written notice or warranty to that effect, e.g. on an invoice or even a label ('Pelican' Margarine), then he may plead this warranty as a defence. He must show:
   (a) that he had no reason to believe the goods were defective and
   (b) that the article was in the same state when he sold it as when he bought it. In *Tesco Stores Ltd v. Roberts* (1974) a

retailer who purchased 30 lbs of liver in bulk, cut it into pieces and sold it to customers in small packages was found guilty of selling food unfit for human consumption *s.*2). As a defence, he pleaded *s.*115 claiming that the liver was in the 'same state' when he sold it as when he had purchased it. But the court did not accept this defence, saying that since the liver had been cut up into separate pieces it was not in the same state. The court stressed that there must be some tampering with the article (cutting food with a knife) as opposed to separating articles bought in bulk (cases of oranges packaged by retailers in smaller numbers).

Note: It is important for the accused to treat the goods in the correct way in order to succeed in his 'warranty' defence, e.g. the vitamin content of margarine could be affected by strong sunlight, so exposing margarine in a shop window might allow the manufacturers to claim that the accused had not treated the product in the appropriate manner. Furthermore, he must inform the prosecutor and the person issuing the warranty at least three days before the date of the hearing that he intends to rely upon the warranty as a defence.

Penalties

A person found guilty of an offence under the Act, or of breaking a Regulation, is liable to a fine not exceeding £100, or to a term of imprisonment not exceeding three months, or to both, and, in the case of a continuing offence to a further fine not exceeding £5 for each day during which the offence continues after conviction.

WEIGHTS AND MEASURES ACTS 1963 AND 1976

Protection for the consumer is also to be found within the Weights and Measures Act 1963, which has three main purposes:

1. To allow the regular inspection and stamping of weighing and measuring devices by the Weights and Measures Inspectors. This provision is of particular importance to licensees, as it covers all weights and measures which are 'in use for trade'.
2. To enable penalties to be imposed for giving short weight and measure. It is an offence for any person selling goods by weight to sell short weight.

3. To inspect the labelling on packets where it concerns quantity. Most pre-packed foods, e.g. tins of fruit and packets of biscuits, must be marked with the weight and measures of the contents.

Defences

Similar defences are available to the seller charged with an offence under this Weights and Measures Act as are available under the Food and Drugs Act. For enforcement see page 196. The 1976 Weights and Measures Act covers the change-over to metric units. It is now an offence to use certain of the old units of measurement. Regulations can be issued to require persons to dual mark and issue conversion charts for explanatory purposes.

TRADE DESCRIPTIONS ACT 1968

Completing the protection of the consumer is the Trade Descriptions Act 1968. This Act prohibits the misdescription of goods, accommodation and facilities provided in the course of trade. It bridges some of the gaps which remain in the food legislation, e.g. it covers false description of price lists on menus or false description of food.

By *s.*1 of the Act, it is an offence for any person, in the course of a trade or business:
1. to apply a false trade description to goods or
2. to supply or to offer to supply any goods to which a false trade description is applied.

The term 'in the course of a trade or business' excludes Crown property so hospital kitchens are not caught by the Act. Doubt exists about supplies to Crown property.

The term 'trade description' relates to all manner of things including quality, composition and fitness for purpose. In the catering trade, for example, labels saying 'Cumberland Sausage', are now disappearing, and in their place are seen 'Cumberland-Style Sausage'.

By *s.*11 it is an offence to give any false or misleading statement concerning the price of any goods. This is why it is so important for hoteliers to set out their prices in full. Many prosecutions have been successful against hoteliers who impose a service charge upon their customers without prior warning.

Defences

A person may be found guilty of an offence under the Act without it being proved that he acted dishonestly. The only proof required is that the statement was false or misleading. However, by s.24, the accused may defend himself proving the following:

1. That he, himself, did not apply the false description and that he did not know and could not with reasonable diligence have found out either that the description was false or that it had been applied to the goods.

2. That the offence was due to a mistake, or to reliance on information supplied by someone else, or to the act or default of someone else, or to an accident or to some other cause beyond the control of the person accused, provided he shows that he took all reasonable precautions and exercised all due diligence to avoid the commission of the offence.

In *Beckett v. Kingston Bros.* (1970) it was decided that the act or default of 'some other person' under s.24 could include a person employed by the accused. In that case the defendant company had purchased from Denmark a consignment of turkeys in polythene bags wrongly labelled as 'Norfolk King Turkeys'. The defendants issued instructions to managers of their shops to replace these labels so as to correct the error. However, one manager failed to do so and a charge was laid against the defendants under s.1(*b*) of the Trade Descriptions Act 1968. The defendants were held not liable, the court accepting the defence that the commission of the offence was due to the default of 'another person'.

More recently in the leading case of *Tesco Supermarkets Ltd v. Nattrass* (1971) (a House of Lords decision) an advertisement was placed on the window of the Tesco Supermarket offering a special cut price on Radiant washing-powder. When the 'special offer' packets had been sold out, the shop went back to charging the regular price. A prosecution was instituted against the supermarket under s.11 of the Act. The supermarket successfully pleaded that the offence was committed through the 'default of another' namely, their manager. As the company proved that they had instituted an efficient system to try to prevent any offence being committed they themselves were relieved of criminal liability.

By s.23, where an offence under the Act is due to the fault of a third party, that third party may be charged with the offence.

Penalties

A person found guilty of an offence under the Act shall be liable to a fine not exceeding £400 or to imprisonment for a term not exceeding two years or both.

POWERS OF ENFORCEMENT

In April 1974 the restructured local authorities came into being (Local Authorities Act 1972). Public Health departments are now under the control of the District Councils or the London Borough Councils. Their inspectors are responsible for food, hygiene and safety, and their work includes investigating complaints under s.2 and s.8 of the Food and Drugs Act 1955 as well as over-seeing the Food Standard Regulations and the Food Hygiene Regulations.

The Weights and Measures departments are under the control of County Councils or the London Boroughs. The Chief Inspector now has the title either of County Trading Standards Officer of County Protection Officer. The Inspectors are responsible for enforcing regulations concerning the description of food found in sections 1 to 6 of the Food and Drugs Act 1955 as well as the regulations under the Weights and Measures Act 1963 and the Trade Descriptions Act 1968.

Powers of the officers

Both the Public Health Officers and the Weights and Measures Inspectors have power to make regular inspections and to take samples for examination. Also any consumer who purchases an article or goods may submit a sample of it to the appropriate authority for analysis.

The authorised officer has power to enter the following:
1. A dwelling house after giving notice.
2. Other premises at all reasonable times. If admission is refused, a magistrate may issue a warrant authorising the officer to enter, by force if necessary.

FAIR TRADING ACT 1973 PART III

The consumer may also be protected by the Director of Fair Trading implementing the powers given to him under Part III of the Fair Trading Act 1973 (see Chapter 7). When a trader persists in carrying on trade which is detrimental to the consumer's health or safety, then the Director may ask him, together with any employee who connives at such practice, to give a written assurance to stop such practices: if the trader (and employee) refuse to make such a promise, or, if they break such a promise, then the Director may bring proceedings against them both in the Restrictive Practices Court. In *Director General of Fair Trading v. Smith's Bakeries* (1978), the Director commenced proceedings against the Smith's Bakeries after they had been convicted of 46 offences under *s*.2 of the Food and Drugs Act 1955 *inter alia* of selling bread containing a rodent dropping, a metal bolt, a moth and a dead larvum: the necessary undertakings were obtained from the trader so the court took no further action in the matter.

THE CRIMINAL JUSTICE ACT 1972

At the beginning of the chapter we stated that we were examining the law from the point of view of the injured consumer. We have now seen that ample opportunities do exist for criminal prosecutions to be instituted against offenders. Of course, these prosecutions really do nothing to compensate the injured consumer as they only result in fines and imprisonment.

In fact, much of the food and drugs legislation does not even allow the injured party to claim compensation for breach of those rules. In *Square v. Model Farm Dairies (Bournemouth) Ltd* (1939), where the plaintiff's family became ill with typhoid fever after drinking infected milk, the court stated that although the sellers had contravened the Food and Drugs Act, that offence did not allow the plaintiff to claim compensation under the civil law as an additional right. The consumer is therefore left with the task of instituting his own civil action for breach of contract or negligence, and in many cases, either he is ignorant of his rights or he cannot be bothered to go to the trouble and possible expense of bringing his own action. Only two matters help him in his civil action; one is the rule of evidence which states that proof of the criminal conviction is *prima facie* proof of the facts on which it is based in a subsequent civil action, and the other is a new scheme introduced in 1973 which allows small claims under £75 to be referred to arbitration in the County Court with no legal costs being recoverable.

However, the Criminal Justice Act 1972 has brought about a tremendous improvement for the injured consumer. This Act allows a court which has convicted a person of an offence to make a compensation order against the offender in favour of the injured person. Compensation may be paid in respect of any personal injury, loss or damage caused by the offence. This now means, for example, that people who have suffered from eating contaminated food can be given compensation by the court. They do not have to make a special application.

15
Licensing

PURPOSE

The restrictions which exist on the sale of intoxicating liquors are entirely statutory in form. The Common Law provides no provisions in this area of law except that such sales should not constitute a nuisance. The beginning of control occurred in 1552 in the reign of Edward I. A system of licensing was introduced which brought ale houses or tippling houses under the supervision of the justices of the peace. The purpose of this move was to reduce drunkenness by limiting the number of ale houses. Since then other controls developed culminating in the requirement that the granting of a magistrate's certificate is the sole authority for the retail sale or exposure for sale of intoxicating liquor. Therefore, the jurisdiction of justices of the peace exercising their local knowledge, in conjunction with the law, forms the foundation of the control of the retail sale of intoxicating liquor in the United Kingdom.

An excise licence is required for the manufacture and wholesale dealing in intoxicating liquor. However, this control is not complete; for historical reasons certain exemptions exist. In *R. v. Graham Campbell ex parte A. P. Herbert* (1935) a summons was sought against the kitchen committee of the House of Commons for the unlawful sale of intoxicating liquor within the precincts of the House. It was held that the majority of the provisions of the Licensing Acts could not apply to the House of Commons and that the privilege of Parliament excluded any jurisdiction by the courts. Similar exemptions exist in respect of freemen of the Vintners Company in the City of London to whom a charter was granted in 1611; and the chancellors, masters and scholars of the University of Cambridge.

These are special cases; general exemptions to the need for the approval of licensing justices are as follows:

1. Theatres for the performance of theatrical works can sell intoxicating liquor provided they are licensed by the local authority under the Theatres Act 1968 and the clerk to the licensing justices has been informed in writing of the intention to sell.

2. Intoxicating liquor can be sold to passengers travelling on an aircraft, vessel or railway train provided facilities are available for the supply of food during the journey. These conveyances are not classed as licensed premises and need not observe any limitation as to the time of sale.

3. Naval and military canteens can sell intoxicating liquor provided the sales are normally confined to service personnel.

4. A registered club can supply intoxicating liquor to its members.

Control of the manufacture, sale and transportation of beverage, alcohol or intoxicating liquor takes on different forms in different civilised countries. The system in the United Kingdom exemplifies a single homogeneous system evolved after long experience, especially since the middle of the nineteenth century, during which period rapid urbanisation, industrialisation, mechanisation and transportation have caused a need for sobriety in the interests of public order and personal efficiency.

THE LICENSING JUSTICES

The control of licensing is vested in justices numbering not less than five and not exceeding fifteen who are appointed in each licensing district during the last quarter of each year. Those appointed form the Licensing Committee for its district for the next year as from the first of January.

Such committees must be appointed in the districts of the City of London, in each borough which has a separate commission of the peace, in each petty sessional division or in the absence of the latter, in the county district. The most important meeting of the committee is the annual licensing 'brewster sessions' which must take place in the first two weeks of February on a date of which at least twenty-one days' notice is given and which is advertised in the local Press. Between four and eight transfer sessions at equally spaced intervals must also be held during any one year. Most of the licensing control over the granting, removal and transfer of justices' licences for the appropriate district is exercised in the transfer sessions, but the renewal of licences and the determination of permitted hours can only be decided upon at the annual meeting.

A register of licences has to be maintained by the clerk to the licensing justices and must contain a comprehensive list of all the licences issued for premises in the district for which the committee was appointed, together with other relevant details such as convictions of licensees, forfeitures and disqualifications. The register is open to inspection by any individual upon the payment of a small fee.

THE JUSTICES' LICENCE

The relevant statutory authority for the granting of a justices' licence is contained in the Licensing Act 1964 as amended by the Licensing Act 1967 and the Finance Act 1967. The licence, when granted, authorises the holder, the licensee, to sell by retail specified intoxicating liquor in the premises approved by the justices. In the case of a registered club, authority is given to supply intoxicating liquor to members of the approved club; the supply is not recognised as a sale and consequently a justices' licence is not required (see Chapter 17). The licence, therefore, is granted by the justices when they are satisfied with the following:

1. The need for the sale of the stated intoxicating liquor in the area.
2. The suitability of the applicant to hold a licence, and
3. That the premises named are in good condition and adequately constructed for the purpose of the licence.

Intoxicating liquor

Intoxicating liquor includes spirits, wines, beer, cider and any other fermented, distilled or spiritous liquor but except for cider, does not include liquor, the sale of which by wholesale does not require an excise licence. By way of interpretation it must be noted that the term 'wine' includes British wine, home-made wine, mead and metheglin (i.e. a fermented drink made from water and honey); 'beer' includes stout and porter and 'cider' includes perry. A preparation containing beer, such as shandy, may in the form in which it is consumed fall outside the definition of beer, but in *Hall v. Hyder* (1966) it was decided that the provisions relating to intoxicating liquor will apply to the beer if the mixture takes place at the time of the sale.

The exclusions provided for in the definition include liquor under the specified gravity or under 2 per cent proof, perfumes, flavouring essences not used as or with intoxicants, spirits and wines prepared to be medicines and not beverages, spruce of black beer, liqueur chocolates and similar confectionery of limited alcohol content and in separate pieces not exceeding 1½ oz each in weight or designed to be broken up into such pieces for consumption.

Section 167 of the Licensing Act 1967 provides that it is an offence to sell such confectionery to a person under 16 years.

The applicant

The applicant must be over 21 years, a suitable person to hold a licence and not disqualified. That the applicant is under 21 years does not, *per se*, disqualify him or her from holding a licence. In *Rose v. Frogley* (1893) Pollock, B., said:

> 'There may be cases where it may be difficult to say what would be the best course to take in the case of a child of tender age. But here the appellant was of such an age (he was twenty) that apparently the justices might have in their discretion granted him a licence if he required one'.

That an applicant is a woman is not a legal bar to the grant of a licence. The justices must consider, in each case, her suitability.

Disqualification from holding a justices' licence is based upon the following grounds:

1. Holding office such as a Sheriff's officer, any officer executing the process of any court including a police constable, or a licensed pilot.
2. Having been convicted of certain offences, i.e. forgery of a justices' licence or knowingly using such a forged licence, permitting licensed premises to be used as a brothel; for retailing or exposing for retail intoxicating liquor without a licence or at premises not so licensed. In the two last cases, the court can order a disqualification for up to five years on a second conviction and for a period up to life on a third or subsequent conviction.
3. Disqualification of the premises in that within two years two licensees have forfeited their licences for the same

premises. The consequence which follows is that the premises are disqualified for twelve months.

The premises

Sections 4(2) and 5(4) of the Licensing Act 1964 provide that on the grant of a new on-licence or on the removal of an existing on-licence, the licensing justices must be satisfied that the premises are structurally suitable for the class of licence for which the application is made. Section 113 of the same Act allows an exception in the case of temporary premises in new towns.

Even where an on-licence is in existence, the licensing justices have a measure of control over alterations to premises to which that licence relates. Sections 19 and 20 of the 1964 Act provide that:

1. They can order structural alterations to the premises which, in their opinion, are required for the proper conduct of the business, and,
2. Their consent is required for any alterations intended to be made which would increase facilities for drinking on the premises, which would have the effect of concealing a public or common part of the premises used for drinking from observation, or which would interfere with communication between a public part of the premises used for the sale of intoxicating liquor and other parts of the premises or the public highway.

An appeal against any order of the justices relating to structural alterations can be heard in the Crown Court.

Special provisions exist for premises which are used as restaurants and residential hotels. Section 94 (1–3) of the 1964 Act provides that a restaurant licence can be granted for premises suitably structured for the purpose of supplying main meals. Section 96(1), in relation to residential licences, and residential and restaurant licences, requires that the licence holder must normally provide a sitting-room for the use of residents where meals and intoxicating liquor are not served.

Sections 70 and 77 make provision for structural suitability in the granting of:

(*a*) a 'supper hour' licence, and,
(*b*) a special hours certificate where the premises are to be used for music and other entertainment in addition to providing refreshment and an extension in permitted hours

for one or the other is requested.

TYPES OF JUSTICES' LICENCES

Full on-licence

The holder of a full on-licence is authorised to sell intoxicating liquor to anyone who is not prohibited by law from consuming it, for consumption on or off the premises. The licence can either allow the sale of all intoxicating liquor or can be restricted to the sale of specified types, for example:

1. beer, cider and wine only,
2. beer and cider only,
3. cider only, or,
4. wine only, when it would not be regarded as a full on-licence.

Whether or not the licence should be restricted is within the discretion of the justices after they have taken relevant factors into consideration, the most important being the extent to which that particular district is already catered for by full on-licenced premises and whether or not the application before them would satisfy a public requirement.

Restrictions as to the operational time of the licence may also be imposed at the request of the applicant limiting the sale of liquor to week days only, i.e. a six-day licence, s.65(4); to a certain period of the year, i.e. a seasonal licence, obviously most commonly operative in seaside resorts, s.64; and to a reduced period of hours during the day terminating one hour before the end of normal permitted hours, s.65(1).

The licensee can apply for the removal of these restrictions at any subsequent application for the removal, transfer or renewal of the licence.

Off-licence

An off-licence restricts the holder to the sale of intoxicating liquor for consumption off the premises. It authorises the sale of either intoxicants of all types or of beer, cider and wine only. The number of premises subject to off-licences have increased considerably during recent years, it now being common practice to grant such licences to general grocery stores whether they be supermarkets or small local shops.

Section 164 of the Act provides that the licensee commits an offence if he sells any spirits or wine in an open vessel and also if he permits or has knowledge that liquor sold by him on his premises is consumed on those premises or on nearby premises under his control or on the adjoining highway.

Residential licence

The conditions that have to be observed in the granting of a residential licence are contained in *ss*.93 and 94 of Part 4 of the 1964 Act. These conditions also apply to a restaurant licence or a combination licence, i.e. a residential and restaurant licence. Such licences are commonly called Part 4 licences.

A residential licence permits the sale or supply of intoxicating liquor to residents of that licensed hotel at any time. To qualify for such a licence the premises must be *bona fide* used or intended to be used for habitually

(*a*) providing bed and breakfast for payment, and,

(*b*) providing at least one other main meal for payment.

Therefore an establishment which supplies bed and breakfast only cannot qualify for such a licence.

The Act qualifies the grant of the licence with the following conditions:

1. Intoxicating liquor can be sold or supplied only to residents or their private friends entertained by them at their own expense on the premises or where it is to accompany a meal, such as a packed lunch, to be consumed off the premises.
2. Beverages (including drinking water) other than alcoholic liquor must be made available for consumption with meals.
3. The licence, unless there are special circumstances for not doing so, must state a condition that a sitting-room or rooms must be provided for the use of residents and guests including children, which are not used for the service of food or the supply or consumption of liquor.

Restaurant licence

A restaurant licence permits the sale of intoxicating liquor for consumption in a restaurant, that is, a structurally suitable premises *bona fide* used or intended to be used for the habitual provision of the main mid-day or evening meal, or both.

The sale is restricted to persons consuming a table meal although this may be interpreted as applying to persons seated at a counter which is not used for service other than to those people. Therefore the liquor must be consumed with a meal and cannot be purchased even by a diner for consumption by a friend not taking a meal. However, it is recognised that the

consumption of aperitifs before the meal and liqueurs afterwards is common practice and the licence permits such sales
even in another room, provided it is recognised that this is associated with a meal, and they are consumed by the customer
whilst seated.

As in the case respecting a residential licence, other drinks,
(including water) must also be made available for consumption
with or ancillary to the meal.

As the purpose of the licence is directly connected with the
supply of meals there is, of course, a limitation on the hours (the
permitted hours) during which intoxicating liquor can be sold
or supplied. The permitted hours limit such sales to the times
during which table meals are served. In some cases, however,
the time for sale might exceed the permitted hours allowed generally for the district, that is, after a 3.00 p.m. or 10.30 p.m. 'stop
tap' which prevails for the normal full on-licence.

Residential and restaurant licence

This licence is obviously a combination of the two already described, but is only granted for premises which qualify for both
residential and restaurant uses, e.g. a private hotel which has
also a public restaurant. It permits the sale of intoxicating
liquor to residents and friends being *bona fide* entertained by
them at their own expense at any time and to persons who are
not residents but who are consuming table meals. The larger
and strategically situated residential hotels provide the facility
of public bars which of course necessitates the obtaining of full
on-licences.

Occasional licence

An occasional licence permits a person who already holds a
justices' on-licence to sell intoxicating liquor within the limits
specified in the original licence at some other premises which
are not the subject of a licence. An application for an occasional
licence is normally made when it is desired to sell intoxicating
liquor at special events such as fetes, dances, sporting events,
etc.

The holder of a restaurant licence can apply for an occasional
licence but only to supply liquor with a substantial meal. The
holder of a residential licence cannot apply for an occasional
licence.

Certain conditions attach to the issue of the licence which is entirely within the discretion of the Magistrates' Court which has authority to grant this type of licence:

1. The period for which the licence will apply must be stated; there is a statutory maximum of three weeks.
2. The permitted hours for sale of intoxicating liquor must be stated on the licence.
3. An occasional licence cannot be issued for Christmas Day, Good Friday, or any day of public thanksgiving or mourning, nor for a Sunday in those parts of Wales where Sunday opening is not authorised.

Obviously, the premises concerned assume all the characteristics of a permanent licensed premises especially respecting drunkenness, employment of persons under 18 years and the sale of liquor to them, offences relating to the supply of liquor to constables and the right of entry by the police.

Refreshment-house licence

A refreshment-house licence is necessary when refreshments are served for consumption on a premises between the hours of 10 p.m. and 5 a.m. and that premises is not licensed for the sale of beer, cider, wines or spirits.

What is a refreshment-house is dependent upon the facts of each case. The Refreshment Houses Act 1860 refers to 'all houses, rooms, shops or buildings open for public refreshment, resort and entertainment'. Case law has qualified the Act's definition in many circumstances. In the following cases it was held that the premises concerned qualified as a refreshment house for the purpose of licensing. In *Howes v. Inland Revenue* (1876) a shop contained no seating facilities, but a table and counter were provided at which customers could stand for a few minutes whilst they consumed lemonade or ginger beer. In *Muir v. Keay* (1875) the shop provided only coffee, cigars and ginger beer for on-consumption; and in *Cooper v. Dickenson* (1877) the shop sold tripe on plates but did not provide knives or forks or have seating facilities. In *Kellaway v. MacDougal* (1881) the premises was a temperance hotel which provided ordinary refreshments.

However, in *Taylor v. Oram* (1862) it was held that a premises in which refreshments were supplied to residents after acquisition from outside at their request was not a refreshment house.

Therefore a refreshment-house licence is not required when the premises concerned is licensed for the sale of beer, cider, wines or spirits; is not open between 10 p.m. and 5 a.m.; is only open for consumption of its wares away from the premises or the refreshment consumed is acquired from outside the premises.

A refreshment-house licence is granted and renewed annually by a county or district council and since the Refreshment Houses Act 1967 a register of licence holders must be kept by the licensing authority of the council. The same Act provides that the council has powers to impose conditions when granting or renewing licences, but not to affect the holder and premises before 11 p.m., to guard against the possibility of disturbance to neighbouring residents.

The failure to obtain a licence and breach of any of its conditions are offences punishable by a fine. The police have powers of entry and refusal by the holder of a refreshment-house licence or his employee to allow such entry incurs liability.

In the London area these powers are provided by the Greater London Council (General Powers) Act 1968. Part VIII of the Act requires the registration of premises used as night cafes, and requires that their fire precautions and management are suitable in the same manner as does the Refreshment Houses Act 1967 for premises in other parts of the country. In *Sudders and Others v. Barking London Borough Council* (1974) the Court of Appeal decided that the supplying of fish and chips for consumption only off the premises does not constitute those premises as a night cafe for the purposes of Part VIII of the Act.

Section 47(1) of the Act defines a 'night cafe' in the context of the above case as any premises in a borough which are kept open for public refreshment at any time between the hours of 11 p.m. and 5 p.m. In the case considered, 'no fish and chips were sold after 11 p.m. for consumption on the premises. No sitting down was allowed; the customer bought the food and then went out and consumed it elsewhere', (*per* Lord Justice Russell).

Finally, the Refreshment Houses Act 1964 provides that it is unlawful for the holder of a licence to make an additional charge for any supply, service or entertainment in the premises except for cloakroom and toilet facilities unless a tariff of charges is displayed in a position which can be observed by customers or it is directly specified to the customer.

16
Applications for Licences

The procedure for the application of licences is provided in Schedule 2 of the Licensing Act 1964.

The granting of new licences and the renewal or transfer of licences can be authorised by any of the licensing sessions held within the relevant district.

Each application to the court must conform with the procedure detailed in Schedule 2 of the Act.

APPLICATION FOR A NEW JUSTICES' LICENCE

The procedure to be followed with regard to new licences is as follows:

Written notice

The applicant (usually through his solicitor) is required to give written notice of the application to the justices' clerk, the chief of police, the fire authority and the proper local authority at least twenty-one days before the date on which the licensing sessions will be held. Which is the proper local authority in each case is important. That authority is the one in which the premises to be licensed is situated and paragraph 5 of the Schedule provides that the appropriate authority is as follows:

1. The clerk to the rating authority in an urban parish.
2. The town clerk (as well as the clerk to the rating authority) in a borough included in a rural district.
3. The clerk of the parish council in a rural parish, or, where there is no parish council, the chairman of the parish meeting.

Display notice

The applicant must display a notice of the application for a period of seven days in a place where it can be conveniently read by the public on or near the premises to be licensed. The period of seven days must not commence more than twenty-eight days before the date of the licensing sessions.

Newspaper advertisement

The applicant must advertise notice of the application in a newspaper circulated in the place where the premises to be licensed are situated. It is not necessary that the newspaper be a local one (*R. v. Westminster Betting Licensing Committee* (1963)). This only applies to an application for a new licence and must be published not more than twenty-eight days nor less than fourteen days before the date of the licensing sessions and at the command of the licensing justices on a day or days or specified day or days outside that period to be determined by them.

Deposit of plans

A deposit of plans also applies only to an application for a new on-licence or for an ordinary removal of a justices' on-licence and must be submitted with the application to the clerk of the licensing justices. The plans, with copies if necessary, must conform to standards of quality, scale and accuracy and should show the proximity of the premises in question to other nearby buildings and roads and bear clear references to the entrances to the proposed licensed premises. The name and address of the architect, the draughtsman responsible for the plans, the premises address and the name and address of the owner must also be shown.

Attendance at court

The applicant must be prepared to attend the appropriate licensing sessions if required to do so.

TRANSFER OF A JUSTICES' LICENCE

The definition of a justices' licence clearly requires its grant in respect of a specified premises to a specified person. It often becomes necessary, before the date of renewal, to substitute another person for the one named in a licence. This can become necessary in the following circumstances:

1. Upon the death, incapacity through sickness, the bankruptcy

of the licence holder or his retirement from that business or transfer to another licensed premises.

2. When there has been a wilful omission or neglect to apply for a renewal of the licence on the determined date.

3. When there has been a suspension of the licence or a disqualification of the former licence holder for a recognised reason.

The application for a transfer must be made as if an application were being made for a new licence, copies being sent to the clerk to the justices, the local authority and the police. An additional copy must be served upon the present holder of the licence if that is possible. There is, however, no need to fulfil the obligations of displaying copies on the premises or in the Press, neither is it necessary, as in an application for a new licence, to submit plans with the application to the clerk to the licensing justices.

The important factor that has to be considered by the justices in this type of application is the suitability of the applicant to hold a licence. Evidence is considered of his previous experience in that particular trade, his occupation during the previous six months, whether or not the police have any objection to his holding a licence and his good character verified by references; this might not be necessary if he has satisfactorily held a licence for local premises before. That the applicant has been previously convicted might affect the justices' decision but it is not a legal bar. His conviction or last conviction might have been some time ago and he might be able to adduce evidence that he has behaved himself as a good citizen should since that time. The applicant and the former licensee together with any other witnesses can be compelled to attend the hearing and give evidence on oath or to produce any relevant documents. Persons who object to the transfer can attend to voice their objections without having given notice of their intention to appear.

The applicant has a right of appeal to the Crown Court if the justices refuse his application.

In order that the continuity of the licensed character of the premises should not be broken, a transfer should be applied for and granted before the date of the installation of the new licensee and it may be post-dated for this purpose. There must of course be an application for renewal at the next annual 'brewster sessions' even though the transferred licence might have been granted only two or three months before.

PROTECTION ORDER

Circumstances can on occasion necessitate the control of licensed premises being taken over by someone before a transfer licence can be obtained at the official transfer sessions.

In such a case, that person can apply for a 'protection order' which has the effect of giving temporary permission for the premises to continue to be licensed in that person's name until a proper transfer can be effected at the next transfer sessions or at the latest the second transfer sessions after the decision.

Application for a protection order must be made to the appropriate Magistrates' Court, not the licensing justices, by serving the necessary form on the clerk to the magistrates at least seven days before the date set for the hearing. The magistrates, however, have a discretion to accept a shorter period of notice in an emergency.

Here again, the important factor to be determined is the suitability of the applicant and this is judged as though a full transfer was being considered and the same procedure as to witnesses and objections is followed.

The protection order is also used by the owner of premises to bridge the period between the unexpected termination of the licence held by his manager and the time when he is able to employ a suitable replacement.

RENEWAL OF A JUSTICES' LICENCE

A justices' licence is the holder's licence when it is granted and he is responsible for the observance of all conditions contained in that licence. He is particularly responsible for ensuring that his licence is renewed at the appropriate time under the provisions of *s.*7 of the 1964 Act. Although in most cases a renewal is arranged by the solicitors representing the brewery, hotel groups or the Licensed Victuallers' Association with which he is associated, a failure to renew is, in law, held to be the fault of the licensee.

Liquor licences have to be renewed annually; they expire on the 4th April each year. The renewal is effected by the annual licensing meeting of brewster sessions, held by law during the first two weeks of February, after an application has been made to the local licensing justices through the justices' clerk.

As soon as the justices have decided upon the date of the brewster sessions, the clerk must publicise this information in a local newspaper and also send notice to each licensee through the post. The form of application for renewal is not laid down but in most licensing areas the notice to the licensee is accompanied by a renewal application form which must be completed and returned to the clerk. Nevertheless, the application in whatever form is recognised must be in the possession of the clerk on or before the date of the hearing. When a late application can be explained by extenuating circumstances the notice can be dealt with at the next transfer sessions, but then the justices can treat it as an application for a new licence as far as the preliminary procedure is concerned. If, however, there has been a failure to renew before the date of the next brewster sessions, the application must be treated in all respects as if it were for a new licence.

Whether or not the applicant should attend the hearing depends upon the local licensing authority. In the case of a routine renewal this is not normally required but if an objection to the renewal is raised the licensee must be present with his witnesses to contest the objection.

Objections

A person who wishes to object to the renewal of a licence must submit to both the licensee and the clerk to the justices a written notice stating the reasons for his objection at least seven days before the date of the hearing at the brewster sessions. If this time limit is not observed the justices can order an adjournment to allow the licensee at least seven clear days to prepare his evidence to contest the objection. All evidence relating to the objection must be given on oath and the justices can only decide upon the issue arising out of the objection.

Although it is unusual, objections to the renewal of the licence can be raised by the police principally on the grounds that the licensee has been convicted of a serious criminal offence, or on the grounds that the particular licensed premises has been conducted in a disorderly manner, etc. The local fire authority also has the right to object on the grounds that recommended safety measures have not been observed. If the renewal is refused, the licensee has the right to appeal to the Crown Court. An objector who fails in his objection has no similar right.

Where the objection is based upon the need for structural alterations or for safety measures and are recognised by the justices as necessary, the licence can be renewed subject to a condition requiring the necessary alterations, etc., to be carried out in a specified period. A failure to obey the implied order will make the licensee liable to conviction and a fine. Again, the licensee has a right to appeal against the condition or the time limit.

The law and procedure governing renewal of licences as outlined above relates to premises which acquired new licences since 1904. Premises which are subject to:

1. an 'old on-licence', i.e. one acquired according to the law existing prior to the Licensing Act 1904, and,

2. an 'old beer house licence', i.e. one which permitted the sale of beer and cider only, acquired before the Wine and Beer-houses Act 1869,

are subject to different criteria with regard to renewal and if this is refused can be the subject of compensation which will be paid to the licensee or the owner of the premises if the renewal is refused without good cause.

The circumstances which come within the interpretation of 'good cause' in respect of an 'old on-licence' are limited and can be summarised as follows:

(*a*) That there is evidence that the business has been badly conducted or that the premises are structurally inadequate or otherwise unsuitable.

(*b*) The applicant can be shown to be unfit or not a proper person for the purpose of holding a licence.

(*c*) The renewal in any case would be void in that for example, the applicant is already disqualified.

(*d*) There is a record in the register maintained by the clerk to the licensing justices that the applicant has been convicted of bribery in connection with elections.

'Good cause' with regard to an 'old beer house' licence comprises the following:

(*a*) There is unsatisfactory evidence adduced by the applicant to establish his good character.

(*b*) The premises to be re-licensed, or adjoining premises are conducted in a disorderly manner or are allowed to be frequented by thieves and prostitutes, etc.

(*c*) The applicant has previously been denied a licence in that

(*i*) it has been forfeited, or

(*ii*) he has been disqualified from holding a licence.

(*d*) There is a record of his being convicted of bribery at elections.

If the justices refuse the renewal on the grounds mentioned in both types of licence an explanation in writing must be supplied by them. In both cases the normal right of appeal to the Crown Court is available to the rejected licensee.

Where a renewal is refused based upon grounds other than those within the meaning of 'good cause' the justices must refer the matter to the local compensation authority with a report; but they must grant a provisional licence to cover the period until the date of the meeting of the compensation authority.

THE COMPENSATION AUTHORITY

The compensation authority is responsible for the administration of the compensation fund which is subscribed to by all holders of an 'old' licence through an annual levy. The levy is not imposed if the fund is of sufficient proportions to meet the demands anticipated upon it but the Home Office must be informed.

A person who holds his licence as a tenant of the premises for a stated number of years can have the compensation levy taken into consideration in the rent which he has to pay to the owner of the premises. That is, his rent can be reduced by a percentage of the compensation levy in inverse proportion to the unexpired term of his tenancy ranging from 100 per cent for one year remaining to 1 per cent for sixty years remaining, but the reduction cannot exceed 50 per cent of the total rental.

The fund exists to provide compensation to the holder of an 'old licence' when the licence he holds is refused renewal for other than 'good cause'.

The compensation authority which comprises between nine and fifteen appointed justices has to decide whether to renew the old licence or grant compensation and also the amount and the person or persons to whom it should be paid, e.g. the licensee, tenant or an owner, etc.

The authority normally holds three meetings to decide upon the distribution of the compensation.

The preliminary meeting

Frequently the justices meet in private at this stage of the proceedings to examine the cases which have been submitted to them by the licensing justices. The primary object here is to decide whether or not there is sufficient evidence available to substantiate the withdrawal of the licence. If there is not, the interested parties must be informed and this amounts to a renewal of the licence.

This does not, however, prevent the licensing justices from adducing additional evidence the following year in another reference to the compensation authority.

The principal meeting

This meeting is equivalent to a trial on the question as to whether or not the decision of the licensing justices should be supported. The licensee, objectors and all witnesses must be made aware of the date of the hearing and there must be an appropriate advertisement in the local newspaper. Evidence is heard from all persons who have an interest and the meeting will then decide whether or not the licence should be renewed or compensation granted in lieu.

If the decision is not to renew, the clerk to the authority must publish a notice in two local newspapers stating the name and address of the premises concerned together with an invitation to interested persons to make a written claim for compensation. Claims for compensation should be received by the authority within twenty-one days of the publication; the acceptance of late claims is subject to the discretion of the authority. The clerk must then give at least seven days' written notice of the supplemental meeting at which details of the compensation to be paid to the licensee, the owner of the premises and other claimants will be decided.

The supplemental meeting

The determination of the compensation to be paid has to take into consideration the loss incurred by refusing to renew the licensed character of the premises including a sum to cover the depreciation in value of fixtures which must result from such refusal. This meeting must also decide upon the apportionment of the decided compensation amongst the persons who have a right because of some loss incurred.

The meeting can adjourn until a solution is finally resolved but ultimate failure will result in the question of total compensation being referred to the Commissioners of Inland Revenue for assessment with reference back to the authority for apportionment.

On matters of detail, particularly apportionment, the claimants have a limited right of appeal to the High Court, or the authority can refer the matter to a County Court judge from whence an unsatisfied claimant might be able to appeal to the Court of Appeal (Civil Division).

If the dispute is not resolved before the date of the next brewster sessions, a provisional licence must again be granted. Of course, when the question of compensation is resolved that licence will terminate by law within seven days of the settlement.

REMOVAL OF A JUSTICES' LICENCE

The removal of a justices' licence, as it implies, involves the transference of an existing licence from one premises to another.

Ordinary removal

In the case of an ordinary removal the application can be made even if the new premises are situated in another licensing district, but of course, that application must be made to the licensing authority of the district which will have jurisdiction over the new premises.

The form of application is the same as for a new licence, notices being sent to the same officials, but the applicant need not state his occupation or the type of licence required. It is, however, necessary that the owner of the existing premises should be informed by serving a copy of the notices upon him. The clerk to the justices must also be supplied with adequate plans of the new premises.

The decision by the justices whether or not to effect the renewal is discretionary. As with the grant of a new licence, they must be satisfied that there are no objections from persons who have the right to object, especially from the owner of the present licensed premises.

The renewal of a licence is confined to on-licence, off-licence and even possibly to an old on-licence and old beer house licence when the obligations of the compensation fund will continue. A residential, restaurant or a combined licence cannot be removed from one premises to another; an application for a new licence is necessary for the second premises.

Very often the new premises will not have been completed. In such cases the application should be for a provisional removal which will be made into a full ordinary removal upon the completion of the premises, but only if the justices are satisfied that the completed premises conform with the plans already agreed to by them.

The same right of appeal exists as with other forms of application.

Special removal

The application here relates to the removal of a licence from premises which are about to be demolished as a result of some public planning and which are the subject of an old on-licence or an old beer house licence. The need to retain the licence for use with other premises could also arise when the original premises are destroyed or damaged by accident so as to be made unsafe structurally for further use.

The removal in these circumstances can only be effected for another premises situated in the district of the same licensing authority, and these premises must already exist and be suitable for use as licensed premises when the application is made.

Again the procedure is the same as that required in an application for a new licence although it is not legally necessary to submit plans of the second premises. If the new premises are approved the justices can refuse the removal on two grounds only

1. That the old premises were not properly conducted or,
2. That the applicant is not a fit and proper person to hold a licence.

The reasons for a refusal must be given in written form and if for any cause other than the two mentioned, the application must be transferred to the compensation authority, but in this case a provisional removal cannot be granted.

If the payment of compensation is agreed upon it is assessed in relation to the value of the premises before its demolition or destruction.

STRUCTURAL ALTERATIONS TO LICENSED PREMISES

All justices' licences are granted subject to the premises for which the licence is granted being approved by the justices as structurally suitable for the type of business to be carried on. Therefore certain major structural alterations cannot be made without the consent of the local fire authority, the local authority and the licensing justices.

The consent of the licensing justices is certainly required in the following cases:

1. Where the drinking facilities in the public part of the premises will be increased, or in the case of a residential licence, where the drinking facilities of guests staying in the hotel will be increased.
2. Where the alterations will reduce the licensee's supervision over public parts of the premises or in the case of a residential licence, over those parts of the hotel which are accessible to its guests.
3. Where communication between public parts where intoxicating liquor is sold and the remainder of the premises is affected or there is interference with the access to the street or public way.

Alterations which are ordered by the local authority, such as those which would improve the sanitary facilities, do not require the sanctioning of the licensing justices.

The procedure for application for alterations varies from one licensing district to another, but in all cases copies of a plan showing the proposed alterations should be forwarded to the clerk to the justices with a letter indicating that an application for approval of the plan will be made at the next licensing sessions. A copy of the plan should also be sent to the police with an explanation that an application for approval of certain alterations will be made and that the hearing of the application will be on a stated date.

One copy of the plan will be returned to the applicant, with a suitable endorsement signed by the chairman of the licensing sessions if the approval is granted. A refusal to approve can be contested, on appeal, to the Crown Court.

If alterations are effected without the prior consent of the justices, the licensee is liable to be prosecuted and fined by a Magistrates' Court which has the power, following such a conviction, to order that the premises be restored to their former structural condition within a stated period. The court can also order a forfeiture of the licence.

17
Registered Clubs

Reference has been made above to the exemption of registered clubs from the necessity of obtaining a justices' licence in order to sell intoxicating liquor (see page 200). A registered club is not recognised as a commercial venture by English law. It is regarded as a combination of people who meet together for social and recreational purposes, e.g. workmen's clubs and sports clubs.

What is important in law is that the club and all its property, including all consumable goods, is owned by the members in equal shares and that its profits are diverted to purposes other than private gain, e.g. club funds, charitable organisations and the provision of sports facilities.

Theoretically, therefore, as the members own the intoxicating liquor served to them, there is a supply rather than a sale. However, this facility can only exist if the club is registered.

In *Graff v. Evans* (1884) it was decided that in a charge involving the supply of intoxicating liquor to a member of a registered club outside permitted hours, the wording of the charge should refer to 'supplying' and not 'selling' because a sale could not be made to a person who was himself a joint owner of the commodity involved. Also in *Stevens v. Wood* (1890) it was held that a member of a registered club who supplied a non-member with liquor and accepted money from him could be convicted for selling intoxicating liquor without a licence.

A registered club is different from a proprietary club which is totally owned by an individual, a limited group of individuals or a company who control its activities simply as a commercial venture with a view to individual profit. Such a club requires a justices' licence to enable it to sell intoxicating liquor and *s.*55 of the 1964 Act makes provision for the issue of such a licence limiting the sale of liquor to members and their guests or even to members only.

REGISTRATION OF A CLUB

Section 40 of the 1964 Licensing Act provides that a club can become registered upon application to the magistrates on a form signed by the chairman or secretary of the club. The application requires that considerable information should be furnished, principally, the description of the club, details of its committee members (names and addresses), a copy of the rules of the club and the relationship of the club, that is, owner or tenant, etc. to the property which will contain it.

From the information supplied the magistrates will decide whether or not the club is entitled to be registered.

Section 41 of the 1964 Act provides that the Magistrates' Court must grant or renew a registration certificate, if, there being no objections to the application, the club has shown in the information supplied that it possesses the following qualifications:

1. No person will be admitted to membership until an interval of at least two clear days has elapsed between nomination and admission.
2. The club has shown that it has been established and will be conducted in good faith and that it has not less than twenty-five members. When assessing the former the court has to consider and be satisfied:

   (*a*) that the club has complete freedom to purchase its liquor from any source, i.e. there must be no agreement that the purchase shall be from a particular brewery or any other source so that any person directly or indirectly gains a financial advantage from the transaction or from the supply of liquor in the club;

   (*b*) that the club applies or intends to apply its profits to the advantage of the club. It is not necessary that the whole profits should be ploughed back into the club or the recreational facilities it offers. The club rules can provide, and be acceptable to the court, that a proportion of the profits can be donated to charitable, benevolent or political purposes;

(c) that the means of communication to inform members of the financial state of the club are adequate;

(d) that the premises occupied by the club are satisfactory for the club's purposes.

3. The club is solely responsible for the supply of liquor by the club and that this and its purchase is controlled by the members or an appointed committee of members.

4. Copies of the application for registration must be forwarded to the local authority, the fire authority and the police who within fourteen days have the right to inspect the premises. The police, however, can only inspect for special reasons. Such inspections must be preceded by a minimum of forty-eight hours' notice and arranged for a reasonable time of the day.

The three authorities together with other interested persons can object to the registration. Other than the authorities, obvious potential objectors would be the occupiers of nearby premises and licensees within the immediate location of the club. Any objections must be in the possession of the clerk of the court within twenty-eight days of the application stating the substance of the objection. The applicant must be supplied with a copy of the objection by the clerk.

GROUNDS FOR OBJECTION TO REGISTRATION

It has become recognised that the following are the only grounds for objection.

1. That the application is lacking in some legal requirement or the information required is incomplete or inaccurate.
2. That the premises are not suitable or conveniently situated.
3. That the club does not satisfy the legal requirements authorised above.
4. That the premises have already been disqualified by a court from being 'registered'.
5. That a person who will be concerned in the management of the club has been convicted of an offence which makes him or her an unsuitable person for such responsibility.
6. That a licence in respect of the premises has been forfeited within the last twelve months.
7. That other premises belonging to the club have different permitted hours and the new registration could lead to an abuse in connection with permitted hours.

8. That the club rules are regularly not observed or that the club is known to be mismanaged in that disorderly conduct is not prevented.
9. That the premises are allowed by the management to be used for unlawful purposes, indecent exhibitions, a resort for criminals and prostitutes and that drunkenness is frequent.
10. That there have been illegal sales of intoxicating liquor or that non-members have frequently been admitted without observance of the rules.

The hearing upon the issue of registration is dealt with at a normal meeting of the magistrates. The applicant, i.e. the club chairman or secretary, need not be present if no objection has been lodged but otherwise attendance is required and all persons interested have the right to give evidence.

If the magistrates decide to grant a registration certificate it will, as a first certificate, be valid for twelve months, obviously regarded as a probationary period at the end of which an application must be made for renewal. A renewal can maintain the registered character of the club for any period up to ten years according to the discretion of the magistrates. The procedure for renewal is the same as that which is required for a new registration. There is a right of appeal to a Crown Court following a Magistrates' Court's decision with regard to original registration and renewal of registration.

The Magistrates' Court maintains a register of all registered clubs within its area which is open to any person to inspect upon the payment of a small fee.

Registered clubs are mainly conducted according to their rules although overriding these they must in the main observe the same statutory rules which apply to premises operating under a justices' licence (see Chapter 16).

For example, sales within permitted hours must be observed and they have the same obligation to control drunkenness, unlawful gaming, disorderly conduct, etc. There are one or two exceptions, e.g. in a licensed premises a person under eighteen generally must not be sold intoxicating liquor; this does not apply to registered clubs.

The rules are all important. If any alteration is made, that alteration must be communicated to the clerk of the local authority and the police within twenty-eight days.

Another difference between registered clubs and licensed

premises is that the police have no right of entry into the former as they have to licensed premises. Clubs are regarded as private premises and the police can only enter under the authority of a warrant issued by the magistrates. The grounds for the issue of a warrant are:

1. the police have reason to believe that liquor is being sold illegally or
2. that the club is being conducted in such a manner as would allow a magistrate to cancel the club's registration certificate.

Under the authority of a warrant, the police are entitled to seize all material evidence such as documents which relate to the management of the club.

If the raid upon the club is made for good reasons the evidence seized could result in a summons upon which the Court could cancel the club's registration certificate; this would automatically cause the name of the club to be removed from the register.

18
Permitted Hours

'It is certainly not the intention of these proposals that licensees should be forced to do anything they do not want to do. We are not suggesting, for example, that licensees should be compelled to open from 10 a.m. to midnight . . . irrespective of the suitability of the premises or the wishes of their regular customers.

The proposed framework of permitted hours is one which we suggest licensees should operate as they themselves think fit'.

This extract from the Erroll Committee's *Report on a Review of the Licensing Laws of England and Wales*, published in January 1973, qualifies the *Report's* suggestion that there should be an extension of opening hours, relating to licensed premises, to fourteen instead of the present nine or nine and a half. The suggestion does not restore the position which existed in the pre-First World War period when opening hours were completely at the discretion of the licensee.

Immediately following the outbreak of the First World War, Parliament decided that it was in the national interest to control certain aspects of public life and behaviour. This concerned the control of factories, railways, lights, information, shop hours and the sale of food and intoxicating liquor. This area of law was established by the Defence of the Realm Act (D.O.R.A.) on 8th August 1914 and was subsequently consolidated and amended in 1915. When the Act lapsed at the end of the war, an Emergency Powers Act 1920 enabled the government departments concerned to keep many of the provisions in force, especially those concerned with the sale of food and drink. The time limitations on the sale of alcoholic liquor have been maintained in various Licensing Acts since that time.

THE PRESENT POSITION

For consumption on premises

The present position is provided by s.60(1) of the Licensing Act 1964, which authorises the local licensing justices, subject to the limitations provided in the Act, to decide on the permitted laws for drinking in its area. The opening hours which are basic to all premises licensed for 'on' consumption during each weekday are the following:

1. Nine and a half hours from 11 a.m. to 3 p.m. and 5.30 p.m. to 11 p.m. in the Metropolis.
2. Nine hours from 11 a.m. to 3 p.m. and 5.30 p.m. to 10.30 p.m. in the Provinces.

Where it appears to the licensing justices and the brewster sessions that the character and inhabitants of a particular district show that it would benefit by an extension to the above limited periods it can, by s.60(4),

1. allow a provincial area to adapt the Metropolis periods, i.e. nine and a half hours finishing at 11 p.m. or alternatively or additionally,
2. allow opening before 11.30 a.m. but not earlier than 10 a.m. provided that:
   (a) the total opening hours do not exceed nine and a half and,
   (b) the afternoon break must be of at least two hours duration.

In *R. v. Wisbech Justices* (1937) it was held that a need for an extension as in (1) above was required when it was shown that most of the inhabitants of the district were occupied in fruit growing during the summer months and worked until the limit of the permitted hours.

In this case, however, such extensions as were granted could be limited to the relevant period of the year. This also applies to different days during a week, the normal practice being an extension to 11 p.m. on Fridays and Saturdays.

Section 60(1) of the Act provides that the permitted hours on Sunday, Christmas Day and Good Friday shall be five and a half in periods of noon to 2 p.m., and, 7 p.m. to 10.30 p.m.

This subsection applies to Wales with respect to 'Sunday Opening' only in that each county district in the Principality can decide for or against its adoption by a poll of its local government electors held every seven years if requisitioned by not less than 500 electors.

The periods detailed above, which relate to the consumption of alcoholic liquor 'on the premises' are referred to as the 'general licensing hours' and apply to 'on-licenses', 'licensed clubs' and 'restaurant licences'.

Registered clubs

The limits of the periods allocated for consumption on the premises in a registered club is decided by the authority delegated by the club members to decide this matter. It might be laid down in a club rule or be pronounced by a committee elected for that purpose in accordance with the club rules. Notification of the decision must be forwarded by the clerk to the local licensing justices. The decision must, however, conform with the 'general licensing hours' which operate within that area in that:

1. it must not, on weekdays, relate to a longer daily period nor commence earlier nor end later than the particular 'general licensing hours' and there must be an afternoon break of at least two hours;
2. the period on Sundays, Christmas Day and Good Friday must be five and a half hours with a break between 3 p.m. and 5 p.m. and a limit of three and a half hours after 5 p.m.

Drinking-up time

Section 63 of the 1964 Act provides that,

1. there is no restriction, during the first ten minutes, after the end of any licensing hour period, upon the consumption of liquor on the premises or the taking of liquor from the premises (unless it was supplied and taken away in an open vessel) provided that it was supplied during the licensing hour period;
2. where liquor is supplied as an ancillary to a meal, it can be consumed during the first half hour, after the end of the period.

Off-licence sales

The permitted hours for the sale of liquor for consumption off the premises falls into two categories:

1. An 'on-licensed' premises can supply for this purpose but the 'general licensing hours' must be observed.
2. A premises specifically licensed as an 'off-licensed' premises can supply liquor to be taken from the premises between 8.30

a.m. and the termination of the general licensing hours for the area. There is no need for an afternoon break. In the case of an off-sales department attached to a public house or a hotel, however, two conditions must be observed.

(a) The department must be suitably constructed for the purpose and the licensing justices must be satisfied that there is no customer communication between it and the on-licence part of the premises.

(b) The licensing justices when satisfied as to the suitability of the premises must qualify the licence with a condition allowing the off-sales department to be open all day on weekdays.

On Sundays, Christmas Day and Good Friday the permitted hours for any 'off-licensed' premises are nationally as defined by statute the same as the general licensing hours, i.e. 12 noon to 2 p.m. and 7 p.m. to 10.30 p.m. in maximum. A substantial number of such premises open during the first period only.

EXTENSION OF PERMITTED HOURS

Long-term extensions

The provisions of s.60(4) of the Licensing Act 1964, which allow a provincial licensing area to extend its general licensing hours to conform to those in the Metropolis, have already been outlined. Such extensions apply to the district and all premises with it.

In addition to these provisions, various extensions can be applied for in respect of individual public houses, hotels and restaurants.

General extension. The reasons for an application under this heading are similar to those provided in s.60(4).

Section 74 of the 1964 Act provides that the holder of an on-licence or the secretary of a registered club whose premises are situated in the immediate neighbourhood of a public market or a place where people follow a lawful trade or calling (e.g. Billingsgate) can apply for a general order of exemption adding, generally or for certain days, such hours to the permitted hours to enable people concerned in the market, etc., to obtain alcoholic liquor.

The application is made to the local Magistrates' Court and if granted, attaches to the premises so that it continues until revoked, even if the licensee changes.

In the different circumstances which can exist it must be appreciated that the extension could operate for one or two days or perhaps for the whole of a working week.

The licensee must show a notice in a prominent position indicating the extension granted by the order and must be ready to produce the licence when demanded by the police or H.M. Customs and Excise.

In the metropolis of London the application is not made to the magistrates but to the Commissioners of the City of London Police and the Metropolitan Police each acting with the approval of the Lord Mayor and the Home Secretary respectively.

The police can apply to have the licence revoked on the grounds that the special circumstances no longer exist.

In *R. v. Bungay J. J.* (1959) the police made such an application. The exemption existed because over twenty years before a cattle market had been held on Thursdays in the town and business was conducted by farmers in the public houses during the extension period. In 1959, and for several years previously, the cattle market as such had not existed. It was held that it was not sufficient to show that it had been the custom to meet in the public house during the extension time; this did not constitute a market day. The original order was quashed.

Supper hour certificate. Even though a restaurant, a hotel or a registered club which serves meals is allowed half an hour drinking-up time after the normal expiration of general licensing hours, any such premises may, through its licensee or secretary, as the case may be, apply for an order allowing liquor to be served up to 3 p.m. if the licensing hours for the district terminate earlier, and up to one hour, served with a meal, longer than the permitted hours during an evening. If the application is granted, the half an hour drinking-up time operates in addition to the one-hour extension.

The application is made to the licensing justices in the case of a 'licensed premises' and to a Magistrates' Court in the case of a registered club and cannot by law be refused if the evidence adduced shows that the premises are suitable and that the establishment provides meals in a proper manner in a dining-room.

A meal means substantial refreshments served at a table or counter in a recognised dining-room.

In *Soloman v. Green* (1955) in a licensed restaurant where the supper hour extension was until 11.30 p.m., at 10.30 p.m. a waitress asked customers if they intended staying and then supplied sandwiches and sausages to these customers and continued to serve liquor until 11.30 p.m. It was held that no offence had been committed.

A supper hour certificate is not subject to annual review but can be varied or revoked by the licensing justices.

The application for a supper hour certificate must be presented to the appropriate granting authority at least seven days before the meeting of that authority.

As the exemption cannot be operated until the applicant has served fourteen days' notice on the local police, it is usual to submit the application in duplicate fourteen days before the hearing, one copy to the licensing authority and the second copy to the police.

Revocation of the certificate can be applied for by the police or any interested person at the appropriate court or sessions. In such case the holder of the certificate must be given at least seven days' notice of the application so that he can appear or be represented at the hearing to give combatting evidence.

Special hours certificate. The granting of this certificate is authorised by *ss.* 77 and 78 of the 1964 Act. The sole purpose of the provision is to allow premises which:

1. are licensed for music and dancing,
2. are in whole or in part structurally adapted and *bona fide* used or intended to be used for that purpose,
3. provide substantial refreshments, and,
4. sell intoxicating liquor as an ancillary to the other purposes, to operate within specially extended permitted hours, i.e. generally the extension for drinking with a meal can be to 3 p.m. in the afternoon and to a limit of 2 a.m. in the morning or weekdays. In central London the later extension can be up to 3 a.m. The extension cannot affect the Sunday licensing hours but it is possible to extend the licensing hours to allow drinking with a meal in the early hours of Sunday.

Other limitations which are imposed upon a special hours certificate are:

(*a*) it cannot extend beyond midnight on Maundy Thursday and so into Good Friday; the same applies to Easter Saturday, and,

(*b*) it cannot operate on Good Friday or the early morning following Good Friday.

It is important to appreciate that the special hours certificate is entirely dependent upon the existence and use of a music and dancing licence. Therefore, if on any occasion music and dancing ceases after midnight in a premises subject to a special hours certificate, the supply of alcoholic liquor must cease, even though the permitted time has not expired. Also, if the music and dancing licence for any reason becomes a nullity, the special hours certificate is automatically revoked.

The form of application for a special hours certificate is the same as for a supper hour certificate, and for the reasons stated in that case, it is usual to give fourteen days' notice of the application to the appropriate authority and the police.

Extended hours certificate

This certificate has the effect, when authorised, of extending the permitted hours of a public house or restaurant to 1 a.m. but three conditions must exist as a prerequisite to its being granted:

1. In the case of a public house it must have a recognised dining-room.
2. In the case of a public house or restaurant it must provide live entertainment as opposed to television, radio or film shows; and
3. In both cases there must exist a supper hour certificate adding an extra hour to the normal permitted hours.

An extended hours certificate is granted at a meeting of the licensing sessions after an application has been submitted to the clerk of that court at least twenty-one days before the date of the hearing. Copies of the application must also be served upon the local authority, the police and the fire service at the same time.

The applicant is also required to exhibit a notice in or near the premises concerned informing the members of the public of the details of the application. The notice must be displayed for at least seven days in the period of twenty-eight days prior to the relevant licensing sessions. A similar notification must be published in a local newspaper in the period between fourteen and twenty-eight days before the hearing.

The magistrates have a complete discretion as to the granting of the certificate and if they are in favour of the extension can impose conditions with regard to its operation, for example, they can limit it to any time up to 1 a.m. or specify the season or days of the week during which it will apply. Details of such conditions must be recorded in the certificate. A copy of the magistrates' authorisation must be served upon the police within fourteen days of its receipt; failure to do so is an offence. Also, the licensee must post in his premises in a prominent position a notice informing interested parties of the purpose of the magistrates' order.

An extended hours certificate is of limited duration in that:

(a) it must be renewed annually at the brewster sessions held in February each year. The authority actually lapses on the 14th April. The renewal is subject to the same procedure as applies to the renewal of an ordinary on-licence;

(b) the authorisation is personal to the applicant and if he ceases to be the licensee of the premises concerned, the incoming licensee must apply to have the certificate renewed in his name when he applies for the transfer of the basic licence.

The usual opportunities exist for an application to be made by the police or any person for the cancellation of an extended hours licence. The police must, as in other cases, serve a written notice on the holder of the certificate and the clerk to the licensing justices at least seven days before the relevant sessions.

Statutory limitations upon an extended hours certificate

1. The order cannot operate on Good Friday or after midnight on Maundy Thursday or Easter Saturday. However, the authority of a supper hour certificate can be implemented on Good Friday.

2. The facility of an extended hours certificate is automatically cancelled if no entertainment is being performed even though refreshment is being provided.

3. Intoxicating liquor must not be sold or supplied to a person who enters the relevant part of the premises after midnight or less than thirty minutes before the anticipated termination of the entertainment unless the time of arrival is within the time permitted by the supper hour certificate.

4. When the supply of refreshment or entertainment stops, the sale or supply of intoxicating liquor must also stop; but then, of course, thirty minutes 'drinking-up' time is allowed.

Short-term extensions

Licensed premises which are limited by the general licensing hours cater on occasions for functions which require the sale of intoxicating liquor at a later time than that permitted. In such cases a licensee can apply for a Special Order of Exemption.

In most provincial areas the application has to be made to the local Magistrates' Court but in the Metropolitan Police Area and the City of London the application is made to the Commissioners of Police.

The application is made in writing, either by letter or on a standard form, and forwarded to the relevant magistrates' clerk and the local police. It must state the date of the hearing at which the applicant intends to apply, the extension of hours which is being sought, the body or person whose function will benefit, the date of the function and the name of the licensee and premises involved.

It is usual for the licensee to attend the hearing at which the police can state objections to the grant of the order. The magistrates have an absolute discretion with regard to their decision and when granting the Special Order must be satisfied that the occasion is a special one.

A licensee must produce the Special Order of Exemption within a reasonable time upon the request of a police or customs and excise officer.

Postal applications

In the majority of licensing areas outside the metropolis facilities exist for applications to be made by post and without the requirement of the licensee's attendance at court.

At least one month before the function, the licensee must post two copies of the application to the magistrates' clerk who will then forward one to the police. The police, if they object to the application, must submit their reasons in duplicate to the magistrates' clerk who will then forward one copy to the applicant informing him of the date arranged for the court hearing.

If there are no objections and the magistrates agree to the extension the licensee will receive his order of extension by post.

THE ERROLL REPORT

If the recommendations of the *Erroll Report* (see page 251) are implemented they will have the effect, amongst other things, of allowing a licensee, holder of a club registration, etc., to sell or supply intoxicating liquor, at his discretion, from 10 a.m. to 12 midnight. This will have the effect of making the majority of extension applications unnecessary. However, as the general licensing hours will then terminate at 12 midnight, there will still be a need for extensions beyond that time and it would appear that the Special Hours Certificate, the Extended-Hours Certificate and on occasions the Special Order of Exemption will survive.

19
The Responsibilities of the Licence Holder

The person named as the holder of a justices' licence and also the representative of a club in a registration certificate carry responsibilities to ensure that the many conditions and provisions of the Licensing Act 1964 and other relevant Acts are observed. Contravention of these numerous statutory provisions can result in a conviction and punishment by a Magistrates' Court and possibly disqualification from the future holding of a justices' licence or participation in the management of a registered club.

The offences provided by the various Acts are too numerous to detail. It is possible only to survey generally those which seem to be most common. For the purpose of simplicity in the following explanation, liability will be assumed to belong to the licensee, etc., as he is the person, through his licence, who has the authority to do what the licence allows. The varying ways in which this strict or vicarious liability can be interpreted will be discussed and explained later. It appears that responsibility can be classified under three broad headings:
1. The sale of intoxicating liquor.
2. The control of the premises.
3. Ancillary use of the premises.

SALE OF INTOXICATING LIQUOR

1. Despite common belief to the contrary, a licensee is not under any legal obligation to sell liquor to anyone who demands service unless his establishment can be interpreted as being an inn and the person demanding service is a *bona fide*

traveller. Although the normal licensee may refuse to serve for no stated reason, he must be sure that the refusal is not governed by racial prejudice in which case he could incur liability under the Race Relations Act 1968.

2. Where he does sell, he must not supply liquor outside the limits of sale stated in his justices' licence. Therefore, a licensee who sells, attempts to sell or exhibits for sale any liquor which is not included within the terms of his licence commits an offence under *s*.160 of the 1964 Act. The licensee will also be liable if the actual sale is made by an employee who also can be convicted for aiding and abetting. There are in certain circumstances defences available to this liability which will be discussed later. A first conviction is punishable with imprisonment and/or a fine. Subsequent convictions can result in a forfeiture of the licence and a disqualification of the holder from holding a licence.

3. Section 161 of the Act provides that liquor can only be sold to persons in circumstances allowed by the licence. Therefore, it is an offence for the holder of a restaurant licence to sell liquor to a person who is not partaking of a meal. Section 169 provides a general rule prohibiting the sale of intoxicating liquor to or for persons under eighteen years of age whether for consumption on or off the premises. Contravention of this rule will incur liability as will also permitting such a person to consume liquor on the premises. There is an exception to the latter, however. A person over sixteen but under eighteen can be supplied with beer, porter, cider or perry to be consumed with a table meal in a room set apart from a bar or in a bar which is customarily used for the service of table meals. The court has to interpret what is a table meal. In *Soloman v. Green* (1955) it was held that a sandwich was a table meal. This exception does not include the consumption of liquor as an aperitif before the meal. The general rule concerning sales to persons under eighteen does not apply to registered clubs.

4. Section 166 provides that intoxicating liquor should not be sold on credit, although, of course, a restaurant-licence holder can accept payment for liquor consumed at the end of a meal and a residential licence holder can charge for liquor consumed by a guest during his stay in the final bill when the guest is about to leave.

5. Section 172 creates liability when a licensee sells liquor to a drunken person or when the liquor is supplied by one of his

staff. That he or his employee did not know that the person was drunk is not a defence. Under the same section, it is also an offence for any person to buy or attempt to buy intoxicating liquor for consumption by a drunken person or to assist such a person to obtain it or consume it.

6. Section 178 provides that it is an offence to supply a police constable with intoxicating liquor whilst he is on duty without the authority of a superior officer. It is immaterial whether the supply is by sale or as a gift.

CONTROL OF THE PREMISES

1. The holding of a licence makes the holder responsible for the proper conduct of his premises. Observance of the many provisions of the Licensing Act 1964, the Gaming Act 1968, the Prevention of Crimes Act 1871 etc., define the context of 'proper conduct'.

2. Section 168 of the Licensing Act 1964 gives guidance regarding the minimum age at which persons may be allowed in a bar of licensed premises during permitted hours. The general rule is that persons under fourteen years should not be allowed admittance. This does not, however, include parts of the premises which are normally set apart for the supply of table meals although intoxicating liquor is available for service with the meal. Again, the licensee is solely responsible for the offence which results. He can, however, plead two defences:

   (a) The offence was committed despite his use of diligence to prevent it.

   (b) The person allowed in the bar appeared to be over fourteen years. The case of *Wallworth v. Balmer* (1965) is no doubt an authority on this question.

   However, a person under fourteen years can be allowed to be present in a bar during permitted hours if:

   (i) that person is the licensee's child, or

   (ii) he or she is resident on the premises, or

   (iii) he or she is just commuting from one part of the premises to another by the only convenient route.

   (c) The restriction as to age also applies to persons employed in the bar. Section 170 provides that no person under the age of eighteen can be employed in a bar which is open for the sale and consumption of liquor. The term employment is not dependent upon whether or not there is a payment of wages. But the rule does not apply where a person under eighteen is employed in the bar which is a part of the premises normally used for the supply of meals and his or her function is to deliver or receive messages in relation to communication between the bar and the dining-room or to pass through the bar because it is the only convenient way of communication.

(*d*) The licensee is responsible for ensuring that at all times his premises is free of drunkenness, or violent or disorderly conduct. He will be liable if he cannot show that he took reasonable steps to prevent any of the above types of conduct occurring on his premises and this will include liability for lack of reasonable care on behalf of his staff in this connection.

Section 174 gives the licensee authority to refuse to admit a drunken person to his premises and also to eject such a person. A refusal to vacate the premises will make the person concerned liable for committing an offence and the licensee can request the police to use whatever force is necessary to effect that person's removal.

(*e*) The same principle applies with regard to persons whose continued presence is not desired because they are known thieves or prostitutes.

Another way of dealing with the problem of prostitutes is to seek a perpetual injunction in the High Court barring the prostitutes from entering or loitering outside the premises. This method has been successfully pursued by one large hotelier and is likely to be used again as a means of stamping out soliciting by prostitutes.

3. The Prevention of Crimes Act 1871 provides that it is an offence for a licensee to harbour thieves or to allow frequent meetings of thieves on his premises or permit them to deposit goods there having good reason to believe that they are stolen goods. The latter activity would also now involve the licensee in liability for handling stolen property under *s*.22 of the Theft Act 1968, the penalty for which, on conviction on indictment, could be imprisonment for a term not exceeding fourteen years.

4. Section 175 of the 1964 Act deals with the presence of reputed or known prostitutes on licensed premises. Although they may remain on the premises for as long as is reasonable for

them to take refreshment, the licensee must not allow them to use his premises as an habitual resort.
5. Section 176 forbids the use of licensed premises as a brothel. Contravention of s.176 results in an automatic forfeiture of the licence whilst other offences concerning thieves and prostitutes could lead to disqualification and possible forfeiture if the offence is repeated, besides the obvious penalty of a fine.

ANCILLARY USE OF THE PREMISES

Gaming

Section 177 of the 1964 Act provides that a licensee must not allow his premises to be used for the purpose of unlawful gaming. The word gaming as it appears in this section is not clearly defined and resort must be made to the Gaming Act 1968 to establish the precise law on this point concerning licensed premises. Again, it is found that the law which applies to public houses and hotels differs from that concerning clubs.

The 1968 Act defines gaming as 'the playing of a game of chance for money or money's worth whether any person playing the game is at risk of losing any money or money's worth or not'.

Games which come within the definition are, for example, poker, chemin de fer, roulette and games involving the use of dice. These are forbidden. Games of pure skill or a sport are not 'gaming'. Therefore darts, billiards and snooker, chess and draughts, etc., do not come within the definition. However, some games can be said to be a mixture of skill and chance, e.g. dominoes, pontoon, cribbage, and these are within the control of the 1968 Act.

The general mood of the Act is that there must be severe limits upon gaming in places to which the public have access whether upon payment or not unless it is authorised by the grant of a gaming licence or a gaming certificate. Public houses, hotels and restaurants are caught in the net of this general provision.

However, s.6 makes a special provision for public houses. The playing of dominoes and cribbage for money is allowed, together with any other game authorised by the licensing justices following an application by the licensee.

The justices can impose conditions to the authorisation, for example:

1. The stakes must not be too high.
2. The gaming is merely ancillary to the business of the premises and not its main attraction.

Persons under eighteen are prohibited from taking part and the authorised games must not include a bank or be one in which the players' chances are not equal. Finally, the licensee must not profit monetarily for allowing the games to be played.

Section 41, which applies to all premises, licensed or not, allows the organisation of gaming where the end point is not for private gain but is to benefit an established charity.

Again, the game must be one in which all participants have an equal chance and must not be one in which they are playing against a bank.

The second requires certain conditions to be observed:

1. A player can make only one payment or stake which must not exceed 50p.
2. The prizes offered must not exceed £50 in value.
3. The residue of the proceeds after deduction of the value of the prizes and expenses must be donated to purposes other than private gain.

Any gaming may be allowed in the residents' lounge of a hotel to which other members of the public are refused access as long as all players have an equal chance and a bank is not involved. Again, the proprietor must not profit by allowing the gaming to take place.

Gaming machines

Section 26 of the 1968 Act defines a gaming machine as 'any machine which is constructed or adapted for playing a game of chance and which has a slot or aperture for the insertion of money or money's worth in the form of cash or tokens'.

Section 34 of the 1968 Act provides the conditions with which a gaming machine must comply if it is to be installed for use in any premises other than a registered club.

Firstly, the licensee must obtain from the licensing justices a 'justices' permit' before a machine or machines can be installed. A limit upon the number of machines in one premises can be stipulated by the justices and the permit can operate for any period not less than three years in duration.

Secondly, each machine must then be adapted to fulfil the following requirements:

1. The playing of one game must not exceed a total value of 10p represented by the insertion of one or more coins or tokens into the machine.
2. The playing of that game can result in a prize, reward benefit or advantage, if at all, which conforms with one of the following:

   (*a*) A money prize of not more than £1 or tokens which can be exchanged for that amount in money.

   (*b*) A prize other than money of not more than £2 in value or tokens which can be exchanged for such a prize.

   (*c*) A combination of (*a*) and (*b*) as long as the money prize does not exceed £1 and the total £2.

   (*d*) The prize can take the form of tokens which can be used for playing further games, or which can be exchanged for prizes other than money at the appropriate rate.

   (*e*) The automatic action of the machine can as a result of one game give an opportunity to the player to play one or more games without a further charge so long as, in respect of all these games, he does not receive a prize which exceeds the 20p in money or value and any other benefit other than an opportunity to play further games.

A licence duty is payable on each machine installed and used. It varies according to the charge required for playing one game and is considerably greater for a second or further machines. The duty payable is determined by the appropriate Minister from time to time.

Music and dancing

The law regarding the licensing of music and dancing is not consistent throughout the country. In some parts a licence can be granted by the local authority, in others the responsibility is that of the licensing justices, whilst occasionally the matter is covered by a local Act of Parliament. Greater London has its own particular set of rules.

What is important is that a licence is necessary when premises are habitually used for public music. A licence is therefore not required for such occasions as a wedding reception or a private party or if a restaurant only provides music by some mechanical means or if the music and dancing is provided by one or two performers. However, the use of performers in excess of this does require a special licence.

The application for the appropriate licence must be made to the authority which has jurisdiction in the district concerned. When granting the licence, the authority can attach to it conditions which seem to it to be appropriate in the circumstances, e.g. the hours during which it will be operative and a limit upon the number of persons who may be admitted at any one time. The licence usually lasts for one year and can be transferred to a new licensee upon application. The licensee is usually required to exhibit a notice at the entrance to the premises to indicate whether the premises is authorised for music only or for both music and dancing.

When the licence becomes due for renewal at the expiration of twelve months, the court will be prepared to hear objections to the renewal. Any objection in this context is usually based upon excessive noise and annoyance to the occupiers of nearby premises.

When the applicant for a music and dancing licence intends that the premises is to be used frequently for the holding of public dances and alterations to or reconstruction of his premises are required to accommodate a large number of people, he must serve notices upon the police and fire authorities before any alterations or reconstruction can be affected. These authorities will ensure that if there is a fire outbreak quick egress from the premises is possible by the provision of an adequate number of doors opening outwards.

AN ANALYSIS OF THE LICENSEE'S LIABILITY

Earlier in the discussion it was assumed that the holding of a licence made the licensee responsible for the strict observance of all conditions and statutory provisions relevant to that licence. Theoretically this is so, but his liability under the law for breaches of those conditions and statutory provisions is not now absolute. When the system of licensing began it was assumed that in order to ensure the maximum control of licensed premises it was necessary that, through the doctrines of strict and vicarious liability, the holder of the licence should be responsible for offences that occurred by failure to observe the laws governing the licensing system.

It is unfortunate that all these offences are regarded as criminal in character, but, as the sanction behind them is punishment in the form of a fine and sometimes imprisonment, they conform to the definition of a criminal offence and are therefore triable by a criminal court, usually the Magistrates' Court.

In the main a finding of guilt in respect of a criminal offence involves proof of (*a*) the act causing the offence and (*b*) an intention or appreciation that the result prohibited by law would be accomplished.

The doctrines of strict and vicarious liability dispense with the second requirement. A licensee is therefore strictly liable when he performs an act even though he has no appreciation of the surrounding circumstances that make it one prohibited by the law. For example, *Cundy v. Lecocq* (1884) a publican was convicted of selling intoxicating liquor to a drunken person. The prohibiting section (*s*.13 of the Licensing Act 1872) was constructed in such a way as to create liability as a result of the performance of the act only. The court believed the accused person's assertion that he had not known that the customer was drunk but, even so, he was found guilty of the offence.

Vicarious liability means the projection of liability on to one person for the acts of another. Therefore, a licensee can be liable for the delinquencies of his employees who are working within the terms of their employment even though he has no knowledge of the offending act and they have or have not an intention to commit the wrong prescribed by the relevant statute. Thus in *Police Commissioners v. Cartman* (1896) the licensee was held to be liable when intoxicating liquor was sold to a drunken person by a barman whilst he, the licensee, was in another bar, and again in *Mullins v. Collins* (1874) when drink was supplied to a constable on duty in the absence of the licensee. It is argued that these decisions could not have been otherwise decided as the statutory provisions concerned made no mention of the requirement of an intention or knowledge of the circumstances, i.e. that the person was drunk or that the police constable was on duty. It was really intended that licensees should bear responsibility for the ordinary acts of their employees.

Even when an element of intention is required decisions as recent as *Allen v. Whitehead* (1930) and *Linnett v. Metropolitan Police Commissioners* (1946) have held that even though unaware of the offending act, an employer or licensee must have the required intention or knowledge imputed to him. In the latter case the secretary of a company was joint holder of a licence in respect of licensed premises owned by his company. He took no part in the running of the premises but he was, nevertheless, found to be liable for the misconduct of the manager to whom he had delegated the responsibility.

However, whether or not a licensee is absolutely liable either by reason of strict or vicarious liability depends upon the exact wording of the prohibiting statutory provision and the court's interpretation of that wording and, more liberally, the surrounding circumstances. To indicate that knowledge of the relevant surrounding circumstances is required the words 'did knowingly . . .' do the offending act are generally included in the statute.

In *Sherras v. De Rutzen* (1895) a publican was charged with supplying intoxicating drink to a police constable who was on duty. The constable was in uniform but had removed the arm band which would indicate that he was off duty. Whilst the relevant section (*s.*16(2) of the Licensing Act 1872) was not qualified by the words 'did knowingly', *s.*16(1) of the same Act used it in creating the offence 'did knowingly harbour or suffer to remain on his premises any constable on duty'. The court inferred that this indicated that for the purposes of *s.*16(1) the onus of establishing knowledge rested on the prosecution, whilst for *s.*16(2) the burden of proving lack of knowledge that the police constable was in fact on duty lay upon the defendant. This the publican had achieved and he was found not guilty. This decision, however, depended upon the court interpreting that it must have been the intention of the legislature that the words 'did knowingly' included in subsection 1 should automatically apply to subsection 2. The result would not have been the same if the subsection could not be qualified through interpretation against a constituent subsection, e.g. *Cundy v. Lecocq* above.

Fortunately, numerous prohibiting provisions are so qualified, for example, *s.*169 of the Licensing Act 1964 which relates to the sale of intoxicating liquor to persons under eighteen years. Here the words 'did knowingly sell' refers to knowledge of the true age of the customer (*Emary v. Nolloth* (1903)) and in a prosecution dependent upon these circumstances it would rest upon the prosecution to prove that the licensee or his employee knew that the young person was less than eighteen years.

The liability of the licensee based upon the acts of his employees is established according to the arguments outlined above; where the substantive offence committed by his employee is one which does not require proof of knowledge or intention, he will be liable as well as the employee.

Again, if he knows of the circumstances of an offence requiring knowledge committed by his employee he will be liable. However, when the offence is committed in his absence, knowledge and thus liability will be imputed to him only if it can be shown that he had delegated the responsibilities of controlling the premises to the person who committed the offence.

In *Vane v. Yianappoulas* (1964) the defendant Yianappoulas was the licensee of a restaurant. He had given instructions to a waitress that she should not sell intoxicating liquor unless it was supplied with a table meal as was required by *s*.22 of the Licensing Act 1961 (now *s*.161(1) of the Licensing Act 1964). The waitress, however, was seen to serve drinks in disobedience of her employer's orders whilst he was in the basement of the premises. He was charged with the offence and was found not guilty by the Magistrates' Court. The case went to the Queen's Bench Divisional Court by way of case stated where the decision of the Magistrates' Court was upheld. The prosecution then appealed to the House of Lords which agreed with the former decisions. The offence provided by the relevant section used the words 'did knowingly . . .'. The grounds for the House of Lords decision were that 'knowledge' could not be imputed to the licensee unless he had specifically delegated control of the restaurant to his employee. This he had not done. He was in the premises at the time of the incident, retained control and had to be shown to have had specific knowledge of the circumstances if he were to be held liable.

In *Ross v. Moss* (1965) a licensee who was absent on holiday was held liable for the acts of the manager to whom he had delegated control. The knowledge necessary for guilt of the offence was imputed to him. In *R. v. Winson* (1968) the principle of imputed knowledge resulting from delegation was again affirmed.

The more recent case of *Taylor v. Speed* (1978) shows that liability simply based upon the possession of a licence is not to be entertained. In this case, the defendant held a licence for the sale of intoxicating liquor in a restaurant owned by a company. A transfer of the licence to permit the company to sell intoxicating liquor had not been arranged. On at least two occasions intoxicating liquor was supplied outside permitted hours by the employees of the owner of the restaurant. The defendant was charged with relevant offences under the Licensing Act 1964 and convicted at the magistrate's court even though the magistrate recognised that he had no connection with the company and was not present at the times of the offences.

He appealed by way of case stated to the Divisional Court of the Queen's Bench. The conviction was quashed. The Appeal Court ruled that as the licensee was unconnected with the company owning the restaurant, he might be liable for the offences only if he had delegated to it his authority under the licence.

20
Powers to Inspect Licensed Premises

LICENSING JUSTICES

When an application is made for a new licence or for the removal of a licence to different premises the licensing justices have to be satisfied with the structural suitability of the premises concerned. Very often this can only be achieved by a visit to the premises by the justices and whilst no statutory provision exists which supplies authority for this, Common Law precedent, in the form of High Court decisions, has approved this form of inspection.

The inspection may reveal that certain repairs or renovations are necessary and in such cases the clerk of the justices should write to the licensee, brewery, hotel or restaurant owner informing him of the required alterations or additions. Failure to implement the recommendations can lead to a refusal to renew the licence at the next brewster sessions, or perhaps, a renewal with a condition that the recommended repairs or renovations be carried out by a certain date.

A right of appeal to the Crown Court is available to a licensee who believes that the condition is unreasonable.

The inspection, of course, applies only to the business part of the premises. It does not include the living quarters of the licensee, but can include staff accommodation.

Factors which will concern the visiting magistrates include the following:
1. The cleanliness of the premises.
2. The condition of decoration.
3. The facilities for washing glasses, crockery and cutlery.

4. The adequacy and condition of the toilets.
5. Cellar, pantry and other storage facilities.
6. In the case of a restaurant, the condition of the kitchens and other factors concerning the supply of food.

THE POLICE

The powers of entry by the police into licensed premises are set out in *s.*186 of the 1964 Act. A constable may at any time, for the purpose of preventing or detecting any offence against the 1964 Act, enter any licensed premises or premises for which a special hours certificate is in force. This can include a registered club.

Refusal by a licensee or an employee to allow a constable admission in the circumstances covered by the section is an offence which on conviction can affect the licensing justices' decision to renew the relevant licence at the brewster sessions.

The following decisions illustrate interpretations of similar provisions in earlier licensing legislation.

In *R. v. Dobbins* (1899) it was held that a constable was entitled to enter licensed premises even though he did not suspect that an offence was being committed but was only making a routine visit to check upon the conduct in the premises.

Alexander v. Rankin (1899) established that when a constable knocks on the door of licensed premises to gain admission, he must identify himself and state the authority under which he claims powers of entry.

In *Duncan v. Dowding* (1897), it was decided that a constable was properly refused admission by the licensee when he demanded entry, without giving a reason, to a room let for the evening to lodge members of the R.A.O.B.

CUSTOMS AND EXCISE OFFICERS

Section 248 of the Customs and Excise Act 1952 provides authority to an officer of H.M. Customs and Excise to enter the premises of an excise trader. Although a person who sells and supplies intoxicating liquor does not require an excise licence he is still an excise trader for the purposes of this section. The holder of a registered certificate is also included within this meaning.

It is an offence to refuse entry to a customs and excise officer who may enter at any time. However, at night he must be accompanied by a police officer. Entry can be gained by force if necessary. The provision also includes any form of transport, e.g. train, ship, aircraft or hovercraft, from which intoxicating liquor is sold by retail. The purpose of the inspection is to examine any machinery, vessels, goods or materials connected with the licensing trade.

THE PUBLIC HEALTH AUTHORITY

Section 100 of the Food and Drugs Act 1955 makes provision similar to the above for an authorised officer of a local authority. The Act and the regulations made with its authority are concerned with the storage, preparation, handling and serving of food and drink and, consequently, its provisions apply to all licensed premises.

The entry by the appointed officer should be made at a reasonable hour but can only concern the operational part of the premises. Admission to a part used as a private dwelling house cannot be achieved as of right; the occupier must be given twenty-four hours' notice of the intended entry unless it is reasonable to believe that the giving of such notice would defeat the object of the entry. Then a magistrate's warrant can authorise immediate entry using force if necessary. Such a warrant cannot be executed on a Sunday.

THE FIRE AUTHORITY

The rights of entry into licensed premises derive from three sources:
1. The fire authority must be informed of and has a right to inspect premises which are the subject of an application for a new house or for the removal to it of a licence from other premises. The purpose of the inspection is, of course, to ascertain any fire risk and make recommendations to be presented to the licensing justices at the hearing of the application.
2. The Offices, Shops and Railway Premises Act 1963 and the Health and Safety at Work Act 1974 lay down a minimum standard of welfare, safety and health to be observed by the owners and occupiers of the premises catered for in the Acts. Public houses and the bars and dining rooms of hotels used

mainly by the public are recognised as 'shops' within the meaning of the Acts.

3. Although several statutes exist which make obligatory the provision of safety precautions in respect of certain premises, the coverage supplied was by no means complete, e.g. residential rooms in a hotel were exempt from the provision of the Offices, Shops and Railway Premises Act 1963.

The Fire Precautions Act 1971 was passed to cover this statutory inadequacy (see page 173).

This Act provides complete control over public houses, hotels (whether licensed or not), restaurants and clubs with regard to the efficiency of their fire precautions.

Again, to maintain satisfactory control, authority to inspect the premises within the above definitions is required. This is provided for by *ss*.18 and 19 of the 1971 Act in that inspectors can be appointed to have power to enter the premises at any reasonable time for the purposes of inspection. A person who intentionally obstructs an inspector in the exercise or performance of this duty is guilty of an offence.

2 I

The Erroll Report

The Erroll Committee's Report (published in January 1973 by H.M.S.O.) reviewing the licensing laws of England and Wales made a number of recommendations which, if made statutory, will change considerably the pattern of liquor supply and the facilities necessary to it. The *Erroll Report* is the first government review of licensing in forty years.

The changes suggested are recognised by most sectors of society as tending towards progress. Lord Erroll, commenting upon the *Report* just before its publication, said 'I prefer to say that the Report will recommend changes which are evolutionary not revolutionary'; he felt that the *Report* catered for 'What the British people wanted'.

Before submitting its *Report* the Erroll Committee had to consider the case submitted to it for complete and unrestricted *laissez-faire* with regard to the sale and supply of liquor.

It came to the conclusion that:

'The case for total freedom is fairly easy to destroy. The arguments in favour of control vary in emphasis according to the type of outlet with which we are concerned. However, in the case of on-licences, there are a number of considerations which apply generally.

First, the sale of liquor is not like that of any other commodity. It is not necessary to delve into history in order to establish that alcohol has effects on human behaviour which may be socially undesirable. They embrace a whole range of actions from minor brawls, to violent crimes committed under the influence of drink. It would be difficult, therefore, to contemplate the establishment of a retail outlet, particularly for on-consumption, without regard to the ability or will of the operator to maintain adequate standards of conduct without any consideration of the possible effect on neighbourhood amenities or policing.

Drinking, moreover, implies a convivial social activity. It frequently involves large gatherings of people in one premises which raises a number of consequential issues. These include considerations of hygiene, safety and, as stated above, the problems of conduct and policing. It is well established that in this country public assemblies for the purpose of entertainment or recreation are usually capable of some regulation either by Act of Parliament or local bye law'.

The Committee formed the opinion that it would be difficult to exempt the sale of liquor from this general pattern.

With regard to off-sales, the Committee conceded that the argument for relaxation of control was more forceful. The nature of the business is akin to an ordinary shop and there is no need to control public gatherings.

However, the peculiar nature of the trade justified special provision. If the present control based upon sales from premises licensed for the purpose were abolished, a situation could arise in which sales would be possible in conditions which would make the distinction between on and off-sales impossible to maintain. The Committee foresaw the impossibility of prohibiting the sale of intoxicating liquor from street barrows. The Committee therefore conclude that:

'Some form of control is still necessary for off-sales, even though the case for special treatment is not nearly as strong as for on-sales'.

The most important areas of the licensing laws reviewed by the *Report* are:
1. The permitted hours for the sale of intoxicating liquor.
2. The age at which drinking should be permitted.
3. Parity between public houses and clubs.
4. An encouragement of public house cafés.
5. Provision of facilities to allow children on licensed premises.
6. An improved status for licensees.

PERMITTED HOURS

On-Sales

The suggested extension of hours has already been mentioned in Chapter 18. Whilst the *Report* suggests that permitted hours should extend from 10 a.m. to 12 midnight, Lord Erroll has emphasised that licensees must be allowed to use their discretion with regard to the way in which they operated their opening hours within these limits and also that his committee has been given an assurance by the Brewers' Society that tenancy contracts would not contain a condition that the tenant should open during all permitted hours.

It appears that the Licensed Victuallers' Association, having regard to the economics of extended hours for the 10 a.m. to 12 midnight limits with which they agree, would appreciate an understanding that, generally, whatever hours are appropriate for a particular premises, they should not exceed nine and a half hours in total. But, of course, this will entirely be within the discretion of the licensee, especially if there is a demand and he has the staff facilities available to cope with any hours in excess of the accepted nine and a half.

The *Report* deals specifically with the permitted hours which should operate on Sundays, Good Friday and Christmas Day.

> 'We see no reason in principle why the permitted hours on these days should differ from those on ordinary weekdays. We have considered the argument that the special character of Sundays, in particular, should be preserved, but we do not think that this is endangered by allowing licensed premises to open on these days at the same time as on other days of the week.
>
> The fact remains that for increasing numbers of people, Sunday has become a day of leisure on which they expect the same facilities as are available on other days. We do not see why licensees, if they so wish, should not be enabled to open in order to meet public demand on Sundays. This freedom, however, ought to be subject to safeguards against disturbance in areas where public worship takes place. We accordingly recommend:
>
> (*i*) That the permitted hours on Sundays, Good Friday and Christmas Day should not differ from those on any other day of the week, but:
>
> (*ii*) That the circumstances in which local justices should be empowered to impose restrictions on the permitted hours of individual public houses should include disturbances to places of public worship'.

No mention is made in the *Report* about 'drinking-up time'. Lord Erroll's comment on this is, 'That is up to the licensee, if say, he is closing at 11.30 at night there is nothing to stop him ending serving at 11.15 p.m.'

The *Report* appears to recommend that licensees be given complete freedom to use the additional facilities if they required them. They could not be dictated to by brewers nor licensing justices as to what their hours should be.

Off-Sales

The *Report* recommends that off-licence premises should be able to extend the terminal limit of their permitted hours to bring them in line with on-licence premises. The effect will be that the permitted hours of these premises will be between 8.30 a.m. and 12 midnight instead of the present 8.30 a.m. and 10.30 p.m. However, it is recommended that the licensing justices should have a measure of control to enable them to restrict the opening hours for off-sales in the same way as that proposed for on-licence premises, i.e. in relation to Sundays, Good Friday and Christmas Day so that there should not be any disturbance to places of public worship.

Implementation of the suggested hours will allow public houses licensed for both 'on' and 'off' sales to apply the same opening hours to both its departments. The *Report* anticipates that its suggestion will not lead to longer trading hours in respect of most off-sales premises, especially in cases where the licence is ancillary to another commercial business, e.g. supermarkets and multiple stores, because such businesses will only remain open as long as it is economic to do so having regard to the demand upon its trade.

THE AGE FOR DRINKING

The *Report* recommends that the present age, eighteen years, under which it is an offence to buy alcoholic liquor in a licensed premises or to consume it in a bar, should be reduced to seventeen years.

This recommendation should not prohibit the sale to or purchase by someone of sixteen years of age of beer, porter, cider, perry or wine as at present provided for by s.169(4) of the 1964 Act, provided that anyone taking advantage of this provision should not be able to purchase such drinks for consumption by anyone other than himself.

The Committee had to decide whether to leave the age at eighteen or to reduce it to seventeen or perhaps sixteen. In reaching a decision between the latter alternatives the Committee had two main considerations before them. The first was whether young people of sixteen or seventeen were sufficiently physically and emotionally mature to be allowed to buy liquor and, secondly, the difficulties attached to the enforcement of any age limit.

The *Report* states: 'We think that most 16 year-olds are too young to cope successfully with alcoholic liquor. We think it highly undesirable, for instance, that 16 year-olds still at school should be able to visit a public house during school hours, particularly during the lunchtime break'.

Different considerations apply to seventeen year-olds, most of whom have left school, are working, and might even be married. 'We find it difficult to support the proposition that young people who are over school-leaving age and might well be married with children should be subject to an age limit for the purchase of liquor which in present social circumstances appears to be increasingly arbitrary. . . . In some cases, an age limit of 17 might make it slightly easier for licensees to challenge a person on grounds of age', declares the *Report*.

PARITY BETWEEN PUBLIC HOUSES AND CLUBS

The Erroll Committee could see no reason why members' clubs should be treated differently from public houses. That clubs should have special privileges because it is claimed they were in effect an extension of the home, 'seemed to them a nonsense'. During their visits to clubs and public houses, they found, particularly in the bars, that the sort of social activity provided in each type of premises was fundamentally the same.

It was, therefore, the Committee's opinion 'that any premises whose main activity at any time, amounts to some form of entertainment for large numbers of people, accompanied by drinking requires to be run at at least as high a standard as any premises open to members of the public'.

The Committee could not accept that clubs sell liquor simply as an ancillary to the convenience of their members. In fact, the sale of alcoholic liquor was fundamental to their finances and an essential feature of their activities. It had also observed that in some areas of the country the registered club had largely ousted the public house as the main centre of drinking and other social activities and in these circumstances did not think '. . . it enough to rely solely on the good intentions of management committees of clubs, nor is the fact of restricted membership any guarantee against abuse or neglect of standards of safety, structural suitability or hygiene'.

Therefore, the *Report* suggests that in the public interest clubs should be subjected to supervision which will entail giving the police the right to enter a club without first obtaining a warrant from a magistrate; this to apply to all types ranging from the working man's club to the most exclusive London club.

Finally, the *Report* recommended that as the facilities of public houses became equivalent to these enjoyed by clubs, the separate registration procedure which applied to the latter would no longer have any practical purpose.

PUBLIC HOUSE CAFÉS

The *Erroll Report* suggests that within a future restructuring of the licensing laws provision should be made for the establishment of 'continental cafés'. The form that these premises should take is somewhat vague, but the *Report* states that: 'What people seem to have in mind is an establishment which sells light refreshment (tea, snacks, etc.) as well as liquor, and which allows access to people of all ages'.

It is anticipated that this type of premises will be distinct from the ordinary public house, in that, besides the additional refreshment facilities, it will be structurally adapted to provide more seating accommodation, freedom of movement and easy accessibility. The majority concept of such premises is more in the nature of a 'café-pub' than the traditional 'continental café' and should be treated as such because the latter would not conveniently fit in with the climatic conditions and social habits of England and Wales. Neither would there be a demand for such a facility in large areas of the two countries. However, premises of this nature could operate viably in most holiday areas and tourist resorts or where a demand does exist. The known support for this concept envisages licensed premises where a whole family could sit down together—somewhere where one could purchase alcoholic drinks, soft drinks and other beverages such as tea or coffee.

CHILDREN ON LICENSED PREMISES

Even though some premises already operate in the style of café-pubs care has to be taken to ensure that they do not come within the definition of a bar. It is difficult at the present time to absolutely ensure that s.168 of the 1964 Act, which relates to the prohibition of the presence of children under the age of fourteen years in a public bar is not contravened.

The Committee considered how the difficulties regarding access by children could best be circumvented; to convince café-pub operators firstly that they would not be breaking the law by admitting children, and secondly, that there would not be any abuse of this facility.

The *Report* of the Committee states:

> 'It is equally important . . . that any measures to allow for relaxation of the prohibition on access by children should apply with equal force to all types of licensed premises, not simply to specific types such as café-pubs. We think it right, therefore, to find some way of allowing all licensees, where they so wish, to admit children to any part of their premises which are thought to be suitable, including parts used mainly or exclusively for the sale and consumption of alcoholic liquor (i.e. bars). Children under 14 should be allowed in bars at the licensee's discretion, provided that the justices think the premises are suitable'.

It would be necessary for the licensee to obtain a certificate from the justices who would grant the required authority if they are satisfied that:
1. the request is not contrary to the public interest and
2. the premises or part of the premises concerned is suitable for this purpose.

The certificate could be qualified by conditions, e.g. the hours of access could be restricted.

The ideal implementation of this facility therefore rests with the licensee who should be able to assess whether or not his premises is suitable and the acceptability of such a change by his customers and the justices who would themselves have to be satisfied with the licensee's judgment.

The *Report* states:

> 'There are clearly large numbers of premises into which, for a variety of reasons, it would be quite wrong to bring young children. They include premises which are crowded and noisy (without necessarily being disorderly); premises notorious for disorder or drunkenness or simply premises with a regular clientele who prefer an adult atmosphere'.

IMPROVED STATUS FOR THE LICENSEE

At the present time a licence is granted by the licensing justices subject to their being satisfied with:
1. the suitability of the applicant and
2. the structural adequacy of the premises and the conduct of its customers.

The Erroll Committee proposes that there should be a radical departure from the present system. The *Report* states:

'This situation seems to us to have a number of disadvantages. It appears to confuse two essentially different issues and, in the process, to allow at least the possiblity of some hardship or injustice'.

It goes on to explain that most licensees have no responsibility for the siting of their premises, their structural suitability or for the provision of obvious facilities such as toilets, etc. Usually these matters are the responsibility of the brewers in the case of a public house or, of a firm owning a restaurant or an hotel, etc. In the latter case the licensing justices ensure some degree of liability with regard to structural requirements by requiring that a director of the firm be associated as a joint licensee of the premises. Licensees and tenants of public houses, however, are in practice the sole holders of the licence and this can result in either losing the licence through the fault of an employee or manager respectively in not maintaining the premises to an acceptable standard.

The converse can also apply in that the licence can be jeopardised by the conduct of the licensee and tenant.

The *Report* comments that:

'The Committee can see some positive advantage in a licensing procedure which deals with each of these two sets of considerations separately. It has, therefore, concluded that, in respect of each licensed premises, two licences should have to be in force' viz:

(*a*) The person responsible for the day-to-day conduct of the premises should hold a licence, personal to himself, certifying his suitability for this function and should be called a 'personal licence'.

(*b*) A 'premises licence' should be issued to the owner of the premises or the person having the principal interest in the business.

It is emphasised that these two licences would have an entirely separate existence and a refusal to grant or renew one would not have an adverse effect upon the other. However, it would be an offence:

(*a*) for any person or organisation to use premises for the sale of intoxicating liquor without a premises licence applicable to those premises; and

(*b*) for any person to sell or supply intoxicating liquor on any premises without a personal licence certifying his suitability.

The personal licence would entitle the holder to operate or manage an establishment with an appropriate premises licence anywhere in England and Wales. The continuing existence of a personal licence would be independent of any licence applying to particular premises except that, to avoid frivolous applications, an initial grant should be made with particular premises in mind.

The various licensee's organisations envisage that implementation of the *Report's* recommendation in this respect will give the licensee a true professional status and that only suitable persons vetted by their own organisations will be able to become holders of personal licences which will enable them to take charge of any liquor sale or supply after following a well-planned scheme of training.

When considering an application for a premises licence the licensing justices would have to take into account matters such as location, structure, potential for nuisance and suitability of premises.

Index